SECOND EDITION

INTEGRATING THE ARTS IN MATHEMATICS

30 Strategies to Create Dynamic Lessons

Linda Dacey, Ed.D.
Lisa Donovan, Ph.D.

Contributing Authors

Jennifer Bogard, Ph.D., Adjunct Faculty, Lesley University Integrated Teaching Through the Arts Program

Karen Gartland, K-8 Mathematics Supervisor, Groton Dunstable Public Schools, Massachusetts

Katina McClain, Doctoral Student, Lesley University

Celeste Miller, M.F.A., Choreographer, Associate Professor of Dance, Grinnell College

Louise Pascale, Ph.D., Professor Emerita, Creative Arts in Learning, Lesley University

Dana Schildkraut, Arts Integration Specialist, Berkshire Regional Arts Integration Network

Consultants

Devin Feirrera, M.Ed., Music Director, Charlestown Boys and Girls Club

Susan Griss, M.A., Adjunct Faculty, Lesley University Creative Arts in Learning Division

Francine Jennings, Ed.D., Adjunct Faculty, Lesley University Creative Arts in Learning Division

Jennifer Roosa, Mathematics Teacher, Lee Public Schools, Massachusetts

Carrie St. John, Teacher, Lee Public Schools, Massachusetts

Publishing Credits

Corinne Burton, M.A.Ed., *Publisher*
Aubrie Nielsen, M.S.Ed., *EVP of Content Development*
Véronique Bos, *Creative Director*
Cathy Hernandez, *Senior Content Manager*
Laureen Gleason, *Editor*
David Slayton, *Assistant Editor*

Special thanks for the love and support of Rick, Alex, and Jack Donovan, and John Dacey.

Image Credits: pp. 200, 209, and 215 Lisa Donovan; all other images from iStock and/or Shutterstock

Standards

A Division of Teacher Created Materials
5482 Argosy Avenue
Huntington Beach, CA 92649-1039
www.tcmpub.com/shell-education
ISBN 978-0-7439-7025-9
© 2022 Shell Educational Publishing, Inc.
Printed by: **51307**
Printed In: **USA**
PO#: **14837**

Table of Contents

Preface

Welcome to the second edition of the Integrating the Arts series! Now more than ever educators are experiencing what the arts have always accomplished: instructional approaches for social-emotional learning and culturally responsive teaching that value students' funds of knowledge and lived experiences.

This series of books was launched initially to share more widely the success of arts integration in transforming classrooms and to foreground effective and easy-to-implement ideas. Since the first editions were published, educators have reached out telling us their stories and experiences using these strategies with their students.

We're so grateful for the feedback we received from educators about the first edition of this series. We loved hearing how you could flip through the books with your colleagues at planning time and choose a lesson to implement that afternoon or the next day. The practical aspect of the books was a highlight of the feedback. We learned that the lessons were versatile and worked with a wide variety of topics and learning targets. You'll find this continues to be a focus in our latest work, where we offer even more learning experiences for your classroom.

> "The arts help children develop creative problem-solving skills, motor skills, language skills, social skills, decision-making skills, risk-taking skills, and inventiveness."
> —Sharuna Segaren
> (2019, para. 20)

Here's what you'll find new and different in the second edition:

- inclusion of diverse perspectives and culturally responsive strategies that invite students to tap into their individual ideas and lived experiences

- a variety of student examples

- carefully selected ideas for mentor texts of multiple genres and modalities

- suggestions for the inclusion of primary sources

- several new strategies to bring to your classroom

- call-out boxes to highlight key insights and ideas

- resources for finding texts that bring diverse voices to your classroom

- a new structure in the movement chapter that provides additional details for classroom implementation

- a focus on the elements and key vocabulary of each art form

- updated standards

Dig in and enjoy! Let the power and novelty of the arts bolster deep engagement with your content areas. We hope you create, experiment, and explore the artistic strategies alongside students, curating your own portfolio of creative work.

The Importance of Arts Integration

Study after study points to compelling evidence of the significant outcomes linked to arts integration. According to the President's Committee on the Arts and the Humanities, "Studies have now documented significant links between arts integration models and academic and social outcomes for students, efficacy for teachers, and school-wide improvements in culture and climate. Arts integration is efficient, addressing a number of outcomes at the same time. Most important, the greatest gains in schools with arts integration are often seen school-wide and also with the most hard-to-reach and economically disadvantaged students" (2011, 19). According to the *New Jersey Arts Integration Think and Do Workbook*, "The key benefits of arts integration primarily fall into four categories: Improving student academic achievement, student social emotional development, teacher practice, and classroom culture" (Bruce et al. 2020, 21). Now more than ever, integrating the arts into our teaching creates opportunities for deep engagement and connection and an opportunity for our students to find relevance in course content to their lives.

A study funded by the Ford Foundation and led by researchers from Lesley University's Creative Arts in Learning Division and an external advisory team conducted research with over 200 Lesley alumni teaching across the country who had been trained in arts-integration strategies. The findings suggest that arts-integrated teaching provides a variety of strategies for accessing content and expressing understanding of learning that is culturally responsive and relevant in students' lives. This leads to deep learning, increased student ownership, and engagement with academic content. Not only does arts integration engage students in creativity, innovation, and imagination, it renews teachers' commitment to teaching (Bellisario and Donovan with Prendergast 2012).

> "The key benefits of arts integration primarily fall into four categories: improving student academic achievement, student social emotional development, teacher practice, and classroom culture."
> —Eloise Bruce et al. (2020, 21)

Really then, the question becomes this: *How can teachers provide students with access to the arts as an engaging way to learn and express ideas across the curriculum?*

Arts integration is the investigation of curricular content through artistic explorations, where the arts provide an avenue for rigorous investigation, representation, expression, and reflection of both curricular content and the art form itself (Diaz, Donovan, and Pascale 2006). This book provides teachers with concrete strategies to integrate the arts across the curriculum. Arts-integration strategies are introduced with contextual information about the art form (storytelling, drama, poetry, music, visual arts, and creative movement).

The Importance of Arts Integration *(cont.)*

Each art form provides you with innovative strategies to help students fully engage with and connect to the content area under consideration. Storytelling connects us with our roots in the oral tradition and can heighten students' awareness of the role of story in their lives. Drama challenges students to explore multiple perspectives of characters, historical figures, and scientists. Poetry invites students to build a more playful, fresh relationship with written and spoken language. Music develops students' ability to listen, to generate a sense of community, and communicate and connect aurally. Visual art taps into students' ability to observe critically, envision, think through metaphor, and build visual literacy in a world where images are pervasive. Creative movement encourages students to embody ideas and work conceptually.

Providing students with the opportunity to investigate curriculum and express their understanding with the powerful languages of the arts will deepen their understanding, heighten their curiosity, and bring forward their voices as they interact more fully with content and translate their ideas into new forms. This book is a beginning, a "way in."

We invite you to see for yourself by bringing the strategies shared in this book to your classroom and watching what happens. We hope this resource leaves you looking for deeper experiences with the arts for both you and students.

> "Early career teachers attribute much of their differentiation ability to the arts integration class. They also report the joy it brings to both teaching and learning, even within a crowded instructional day."
> —Jamie Hipp and Margaret-Mary Sulentic Dowell (2021, para. 8).

What Does It Mean to Integrate the Arts?

When am I ever going to use this? No doubt, nearly all math teachers have heard these words and perhaps even uttered them. For the majority of students, the idea that what they are learning will be useful later—whether for college, work, or life—is simply not enough. Samuel Otten (2011) suggests that a better approach to teaching mathematics is to establish a learning environment in which "students are happily engaged in learning mathematics and unlikely to challenge its purpose (e.g., students are finding intrinsic value in mathematical discovery and sense making)" (24). We believe that a vital element necessary in establishing such a learning environment can be found in the integration of math and the arts, because active involvement in the arts can help students explore different perspectives and internalize new ideas and ways of thinking.

Mathematics is too often taught in a rote manner, ignoring its beauty. "Instead of teaching mathematics as the mere manipulations of numbers, lines, and algorithms, it is both important and possible to bring the beauty of mathematics into the classroom" (Nascimento and Barco 2007, 69). When we integrate mathematics into the arts, learning activities become multisensory, gain relevance, and add joy to the learning experience. The arts

The Importance of Arts Integration *(cont.)*

provide a vivid and dynamic context within which students can wrestle with mathematical ideas, test conjectures, and hone their mathematical reasoning.

Interestingly, arts integration is most likely to happen in subjects other than mathematics (Catterall and Waldorf 1999). This happens, in part, because of how our society too often attributes an aura of mystique to these two bodies of knowledge. Many of us conclude that both of these areas belong to the few who have been given special gifts, who have rare expertise. But you don't need to be an artist or a mathematician to add this teaching approach to your repertoire. We cannot emphasize this point enough. No special abilities or talents are needed, except for the willingness to try.

Most of us recognize that there are many connections between the arts and mathematics, particularly in the visual arts and music. For example, architects, sculptors, and musicians rely on mathematical knowledge every day. And there are times in the mathematics classroom when the arts are used to introduce or culminate the study of a mathematical topic. Many teachers may have favorite lessons in which quilts, tessellations, or the golden rectangle are explored. What we are aiming for here, though, is a seamless blending of the two areas in a sustained manner, where experience and knowledge in both disciplines are enhanced. We will make it possible for you to teach lessons in which the arts provide a context in which mathematical ideas take shape and deepen, while the arts inform and enrich the lives of students. We don't want you to do this in a tangential manner or on an enrichment basis. Rather, we want you to use arts integration as an approach to teaching the most prevalent standards in your mathematics curriculum and to do so frequently. In teaching mathematical ideas through artistic explorations, students will develop skills and knowledge in both disciplines. So we will share strategies with you that are flexible enough to be used across content strands and grade levels.

> "The arts can lead to 'deep learning' in which students are more engaged with academic content, spend more time on task, and take ownership of their learning."
> —Kerrie Bellisario and Lisa Donovan with Monica Prendergast (2012)

Why Should I Integrate the Arts?

As educators, we want to teach the whole child. Students need both the arts and academic disciplines. Research suggests that academic achievement may be linked to the arts (Kennedy 2006). As noted by Douglas Reeves (2007), "The challenge for school leaders is to offer every student a rich experience with the arts without sacrificing the academic opportunities students need" (80). By integrating the arts with mathematics, we are able to place mathematical ideas within rich settings *and* provide students with access to the arts. In fact, the arts can lead to "deep learning" (Bellisario and Donovan with Prendergast 2012), where students are more engaged with academic content, spend more time on task, and take ownership of their learning while deepening their imaginative and creative skills.

Mathematics and science are frequently linked together in schools, with STEM (Science, Technology, Engineering, and Mathematics) initiatives formalizing this association. While we applaud STEM efforts, we seek to expand the potential for other interdisciplinary connections. The arts also offer particular advantages for learning that should not be ignored. In a briefing on changing STEM to STEAM with the inclusion of the arts, John Maeda, former president of the Rhode Island School of Design, noted that STEM would benefit by adding the arts and design to trigger more innovation (Rhode Island School

The Importance of Arts Integration *(cont.)*

of Design 2011). Beth Baker (2012) states that "innovation happens through science, technology, engineering and mathematics. Could it be missing something that is actually quite important? It's missing the arts—the right-brain innovation that has propelled our country, made us competitive" (253).

> "Some of the most basic art principles like balance, proportion, and variety, and concepts like line, space, and shape can be found in math equations and story problems. Students use art skills when finding math solutions, and math concepts when creating art…Instead of separating these skills and concepts, the similarities between the two are used to reinforce both subjects."
> —Schoolyard (2019)

Rinne et al. (2011) identify several ways in which arts integration improves long-term retention through elaboration, enactment, and rehearsal. Specifically, when students create and add details to their own visual models, dramatize a concept or skill, sing a song repeatedly, or rehearse for a performance, they are increasing the likelihood

that they will remember what they have learned. This retention lasts over time, not just during the span of the unit. Through arts integration, students eagerly revisit, review, rehearse, edit, and work through ideas repeatedly and in authentic ways as they translate ideas into new forms.

As brain research deepens our understanding of how learning takes place, educators have come to better appreciate the importance of the arts. The arts support communication, emotional connections, community, and higher-order thinking. They also are linked to increased academic achievement, especially among at-risk students. Eric Jensen (2001) argues that "the arts enhance the process of learning. The systems they nourish, which include our integrated sensory, attentional, cognitive, emotional, and motor capabilities, are, in fact, the driving forces behind all other learning." Lessons and activities that integrate math and the arts provide a rich environment for the exploration of mathematical ideas for all students, particularly those who need new ways to access curriculum and express themselves. Integrated math and arts lessons also can motivate students.

Teaching through the arts provides authentic differentiated learning for every student in the classroom. As neurologist Todd Rose (2012) notes, all learners learn in variable ways. The Center for Applied Special Technology (n.d.) suggests that in meeting the needs of variable learners, educators should expand their teaching to provide universal design. That is, teachers should include strategies that "are flexible and responsive to the needs of all learners" by providing "multiple means of engagement, methods of presentation of content and multiple avenues for expression of understanding." The integration of the arts provides opportunities to address all three universal design principles.

The Importance of Arts Integration *(cont.)*

For example, the process of enacting a scene provides a meaningful opportunity for metacognition, or "what a child knows about [their] own thinking and how the child is able to monitor that thinking" (Yellin, Jones, and DeVries 2007). Imagine students who, as they prepare to enact a word problem, determine what parts are unclear, go back through the text and reread, visualize the events, and visualize themselves performing the scene. Arts integration benefits students not only by deepening their connection to content and fostering interdisciplinary learning in the arts and mathematics but also by promoting what the Partnership for 21st Century Learning (2019) researchers note as the 4 Cs: creativity, critical thinking, communication, and collaboration. Arts integration brings these significant benefits to learning and also engages teachers and students in curiosity, imagination, and passion for learning.

Arts and the Standards

Connections to the Standards for Mathematical Practice

Within the 2010 College and Career Readiness Standards are the eight Standards for Mathematical Practices:

1. Make sense of problems and persevere in solving them
2. Reason abstractly and quantitatively
3. Construct viable arguments and critique the reasoning of others
4. Model with mathematics
5. Use appropriate tools strategically
6. Attend to precision
7. Look for and make use of structure
8. Look for and express regularity in repeated reasoning

These practices are intended to be interwoven with the content standards and can be thought of as the mathematical habits of mind that students need to develop. Sense making, communication, perseverance, and representation are prominent in these standards. As students represent mathematical ideas in artistic forms, they are involved in interpreting or making sense of ideas. The creation of related artistic products also engages students' interest, provides contexts for math, and encourages perseverance as students translate ideas into new forms. Thus, these lessons strengthen students' expertise in these standards and help them actively engage in making mathematical ideas meaningful.

Artistic Habits of Mind

In addition to developing the essential qualities of mathematics programs, students will also develop these artistic habits of mind (Hetland et al. 2007). With these habits of mind, students are able to:

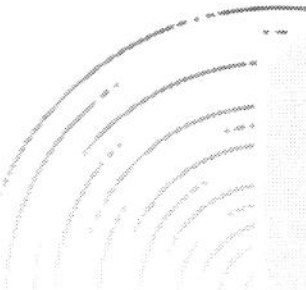

1. Develop craft
2. Engage and persist
3. Envision
4. Express
5. Observe
6. Reflect
7. Stretch and explore
8. Understand the art world

Although these habits were identified in an investigation of visual art practices, they are relevant for the practice of all the arts.

The skills that the arts develop are valued in every field. The arts develop these skills naturally as students explore and translate ideas into artistic forms. Researcher Lois Hetland (2009) notes that "it is these qualities—intrinsic to the arts—that are valued in every domain but not necessarily taught in those subjects in school. That's what makes the arts such potent resources for teaching valued dispositions—what the arts teach well is not used uniquely in the arts but is valuable across a wide spectrum of contexts" (37).

Arts and the Standards *(cont.)*

Classroom Environment

Whether you are in a virtual learning space or face-to-face, a safe classroom environment is needed for mathematical ideas and artistic expressions to flourish. Learners must feel comfortable to make mistakes, critique the work of others, and celebrate success. Think back to groups to which you have presented new ideas or creative works. How did you feel as you waited for their reactions? What was it about their behavior that made you feel more or less comfortable? What was it about your thinking that made you feel more or less safe? Such reflections will lead you to ways you can talk about these ideas with students. As teachers, we must be role models for students as we model our willingness to take risks and engage in new ways of learning. You will find that the arts by their nature invite risk taking, experimentation, and self-discipline as well as encourage the development of a supportive learning community.

Developing a learning community in which learners support and respect one another takes time, but there are things you can do to help support its development:

- **Establish clear expectations for respect.** Respect is nonnegotiable. As students engage in creative explorations, it is crucial that they honor one another's ideas, invite all voices to the table, and discuss the work in ways that value each contribution. Self-discipline and appreciation for fellow students' creative work is often a beneficial outcome of arts integration (Bellisario and Donovan with Prendergast 2012). Take time for students to brainstorm ways in which they can show one another respect and what they can do when they feel that they have not been respected. Work with students to create guidelines for supporting the creative ideas of others and agree to uphold them as a group.

- **Explore several icebreakers** during the first weeks of school that give students the opportunity to get to know one another informally and begin to discover interests they have in common. As students learn more about one another, they develop a sense of themselves as individuals and as a classroom unit and are more apt to want to support one another. Using fun, dynamic warm-ups not only helps students get their brains working but also builds a sense of community and support for risk taking.

- **Tell students about ways in which you are engaged in learning new ideas.** Talk about your realizations and challenges along the way, and demonstrate your own willingness to take risks and persevere.

- **Find ways to support the idea that we can all act, draw, sing, rhyme, and so forth.** Avoid saying negative things about your own art or math skills, and emphasize your continuous growth.

- **Learn to ask open-ended questions rather than give answers.** By asking a question such as, "What does this symbol represent to you?," students are able to articulate, refocus, or clarify their own thinking.

- **Avoid judgment.** Students who are trying to earn your praise for their artistic products will not take the risks necessary for creative work. Encourage students to reflect on their own goals and whether they think they have met them.

- **Emphasize process over product.** Enormous learning and discovery take place during the creative process. This is as significant as the final product that is produced and in some cases even more so.

How This Book Is Organized

Strategies

The strategies and model lessons in this book are organized within six art modalities:

1. Storytelling
2. Drama
3. Poetry
4. Music
5. Visual Arts
6. Creative Movement

Within each modality, five strategies are presented that integrate that art form with the teaching of mathematics. The strategies are not intended to be an exhaustive list but rather exemplary ways to integrate the arts into mathematics.

Although we have provided a model lesson for each strategy, these strategies are flexible and can be used in a variety of ways across a variety of content areas. These models will allow you to try out the ideas with students and envision many other ways to adapt these strategies for use in your teaching. For example, we emphasize shapes in our drama strategy of monologues, but you may prefer to integrate the arts into other areas of mathematics, such as the four basic operations or specific classifications of numbers (fractions, decimals, negatives). Also note that strategies can be implemented across the art forms. For example, the strategy of songwriting could be associated with any of the arts, as we can write songs about stories, dramatic scenes, a character's perspective, images, movement, or poems. Furthermore, as you become more familiar and comfortable with the strategies, you can combine a variety of them across the art modalities within one lesson. For example, you might have students begin with creative movement to explore shapes, then dramatize experts in the field finding examples of shapes and listing the terms and characteristics they associate with those shapes, and finally use those words as a resource of "found words" to write a poem. The goal is to make the choices that best fit you and the students.

How This Book Is Organized *(cont.)*

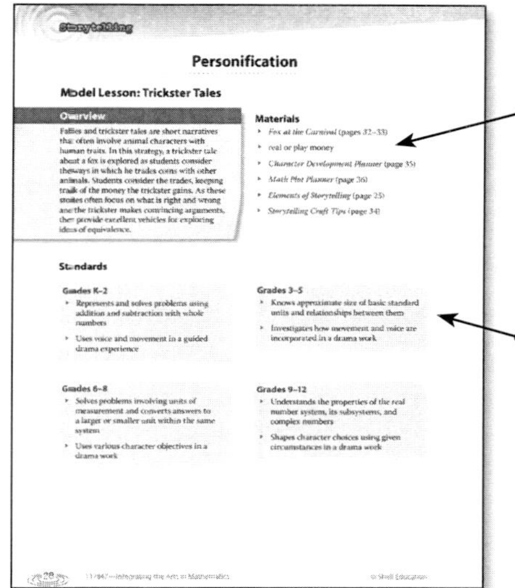

Organization of the Lessons

• Each model lesson begins with an **overview** and a list of **materials** you will need.

• A list of **standards** addressed is provided. Note that the standards involve equal rigor in both mathematics and the arts.

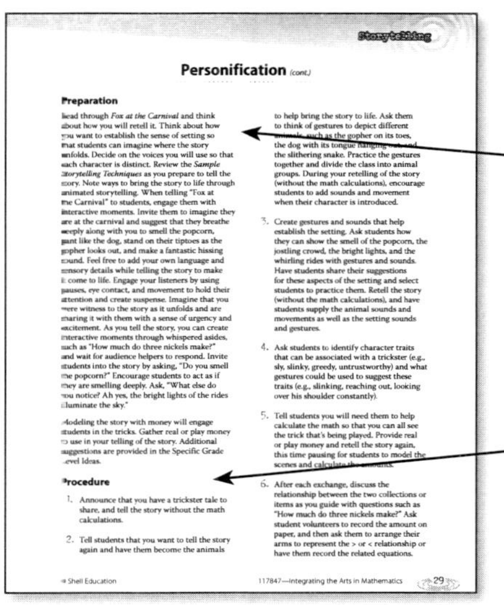

Next, a **preparation** section describes ways you can help ensure a successful learning investigation. Ideas may relate to grouping students, using props to engage learners, or practicing readings with dramatic flair.

The **procedure** section provides step-by-step directions on how to implement the model lesson.

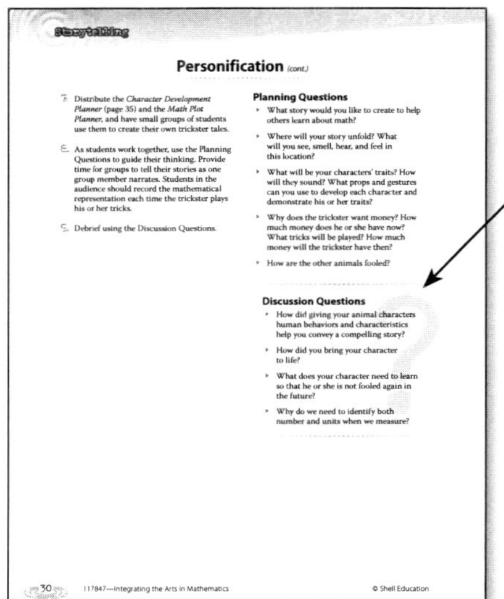

Each model lesson includes **questions** that you can ask as students work. The questions serve to highlight students' reasoning in mathematics, stimulate their artistic thinking, or debrief their experience.

How This Book Is Organized *(cont.)*

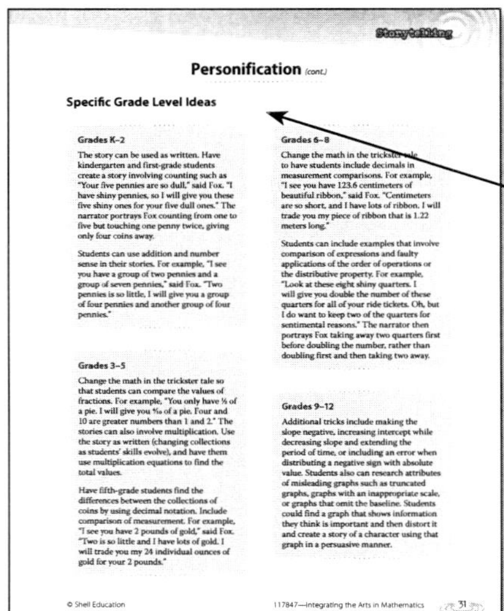

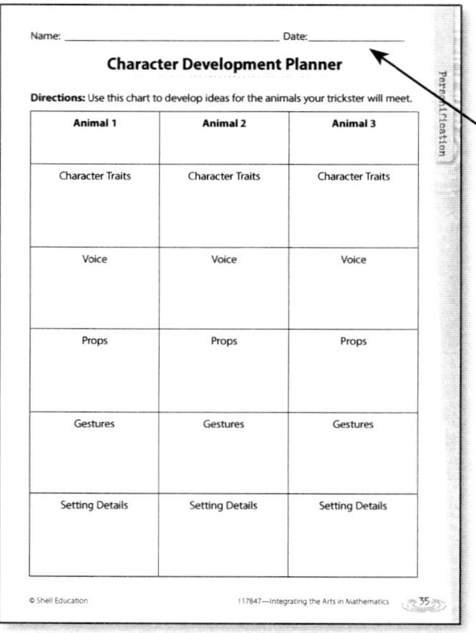

Organization of the Lessons

Specific grade-level ideas follow with suggestions on how to better meet the needs of students within the K–2, 3–5, 6–8, and 9–12 grade levels. They also may suggest others ways to explore or extend the ideas in the model lesson at these levels. Read all the sections, as an idea written for a different grade span may suggest something you want to do with students.

Reproducibles are provided for all applicable model lessons. Often in the form of graphic organizers, the reproducibles are designed to help students brainstorm ideas, organize and record their thinking, or reflect on their learning. Reproducibles also are available as digital downloads in PDF form (see page 283).

How This Book Is Organized *(cont.)*

How to Use the Lessons

These strategies can be used to teach mathematics in any K–12 classroom with any mathematics curriculum. A strategy lesson can be implemented as a lesson for a day or, if you have the flexibility, expanded to several days or a week. You may choose to use the strategy lesson within your mathematics lesson or in combination with time assigned to the arts or, when considering storytelling or poetry, perhaps in conjunction with language arts periods.

You may wish to focus on one art form at a time to help yourself become familiar with using that art modality to teach mathematics. Or you may want to look through the content index and explore models that relate to what you are teaching now or are about to teach. Over time you will become familiar with the strategies and find that you choose to integrate them on a regular basis. If integrating arts and mathematics is new to you, consider working with another teacher to explore the ideas together. Think about collaborating with art, dance, drama, or music teachers in your school system to draw from their expertise in deepening the artistic work.

How This Book Is Organized *(cont.)*

Recommended Resources

1. *The Classroom Bookshelf: A School Library Journal* **Blog**

www.theclassroombookshelf.com

This site is an absolute treasure trove of current book reviews for children's and young adult literature. Every review features teaching ideas and related grade-level resources, focusing on "literacy in diverse contexts" to help students learn about the world around them. Co-creators Dr. Mary Ann Cappiello, Dr. Erika Thulin Dawes, and Dr. Grace Enriquez, along with Dr. Katie Cunningham and Dr. Denise Dávila, reveal the many ways that teachers can use "multigenre, multimodal print and digital texts" as they plan their lessons and units together to inspire learning in and out of the classroom.

2. **Math+Arts (part of PBS Learning Media for Teachers)**

pbslearningmedia.org/collection/matharts/

This valuable website offers lesson plans for teaching math through the integration of dance, drama, music, and the visual arts. Most lessons focus at the elementary or middle-school levels. The website provides significant support materials for teachers for each of the 25 lessons provided. Support materials include lesson plans, background information, handouts, assessments, and videos. Mathematics teachers will find the background information related to the arts particularly helpful.

3. **National Council of Teachers of Mathematics**

www.nctm.org

According to its website, "the National Council of Teachers of Mathematics (NCTM) is the world's largest mathematics education organization." As such, its website is extremely valuable, especially for arts educators who want to learn more about the teaching of math. It provides numerous resources that support high-quality teaching and equity for all learners. While comprehensive, a search for math and art will provide you with more specific resources for integrating the teaching of the arts and math.

4. **Academy of American Poets**

www.poets.org

This incredible website features a wide variety of poems and poets; poem-a-day; National Poetry Month; *American Poets* magazine; and many resources geared specifically toward teachers, including Teach This Poem and Materials for Teachers. Be sure to watch the video "A Teacher's Guide to Poets.org," in which Richard Blanco—poet and education ambassador for the Academy of American Poets—shares an inspiring talk to welcome you into the world of resources on this website.

5. **Brainworks**

brainworks.mcla.edu

Created by arts integration practitioners through a federally funded grant, Brainworks offers curated resources for educators of all grade levels. The website includes videos that demonstrate arts-based strategies in action such as creative movement and movement strings, drama and tableau, music and soundscapes, and more. Model curriculum and teachers' learning stories are also available on this website.

How This Book Is Organized (cont.)

6. Youcubed

www.youcubed.org/?s=art+and+math

Founded at Stanford University by Dr. Jo Boaler, youcubed is a comprehensive resource. This collection of ideas provides teachers with cognitive research that indicates the importance of teaching math differently, along with ways for doing so. As stated on the website, its purpose is to, "inspire all students with open, creative mindset mathematics." We especially appreciate the portion of the website devoted to lessons that integrate math and the arts. Explore lessons for investigating neighborhood art, drawings on sidewalks, and art from diverse cultures. Learn about the connections between poetry and math and the importance of visualizing mathematical ideas.

7. Artful Math

www.artfulmaths.com/mathematical-art-lessons.html

Created by teacher Clarissa Grandi, this website focuses on geometric connections to the visual arts with the stated purpose of bringing, "bold, bright, and beautiful ideas for mathematics teaching." Lessons, puzzles, and resources are featured as well as a blog written by the founder. Wonderful art displays are shown, including a great mural of bugs to depict symmetry.

8. Math Munch

mathmunch.org/math-art-tools/

This website offers rich and ever-changing resources for teachers and students. Geared at the middle and high school levels, upper-elementary folks may also find it useful. As stated on the website, each week a post is created that, "curates some of the great mathematical resources of the internet." The focus is on videos websites, articles, games and applets, all available online. We think teachers will appreciate the many archived materials as well as the constant inclusion of new materials to the site.

9. Google Arts and Culture

artsandculture.google.com/

This global resource brings art from more than two thousand museums to your classroom. The site includes virtual tours of museums, exhibitions, and artist collections. We especially appreciate the quick access to diverse artists and traditions that can fuel student research, provide rich artistic work to enhance any curriculum, and enhance a variety of teaching resources.

10. Jacob's Pillow Archives: Dance Interactive and Online Database

www.jacobspillow.org/archives

This robust offering of online archives, videos, essays, and podcasts documents the history of dance at Jacob's Pillow. This resource provides access to "documentation of the ongoing activities of Jacob's Pillow and Audience Engagement programming," including exhibitions and talks that explore various aspects of dance history. We especially appreciate access to footage of dance through the Jacob's Pillow Dance Interactive. This resource documents "hundreds of artists who have appeared at the Pillow from the 1930s to the present day, . . . and offers carefully-chosen excerpts from the Archives' extensive video collection accompanied by contextual information, plus an extensive section of multimedia essays that include talks, photos, and other exclusive content organized into various themes."

How This Book Is Organized *(cont.)*

Assessment

Data-driven decision-making, documentation of learning, and meeting benchmarks are all phrases that refer to assessment practices that are embedded in our schools. Assessment has become a time-consuming activity for all involved in education, and yet the time and effort spent does not always yield what is needed to improve learning. As you think about how to assess lessons and activities that integrate mathematics and the arts, it is important to stop and consider how to best use assessment to increase learning for students. In addressing that goal, you also will be documenting learning in ways that can be shared with students, families, administrators, and other interested stakeholders.

We encourage you to focus on formative assessment—that is, assessment that is incorporated throughout the learning process. This assessment will inform your instructional decisions during the process of teaching. The purpose of this assessment is to provide feedback for students and teachers along the way in addition to assessment of learning at the end. As such, we are most equally as interested in the data collected during the learning process as we are after learning is completed. The goals are to make the learning process visible, determine the depth of understanding, and note the process students undergo as they translate their mathematical knowledge into an art form or explore mathematical ideas through artistic exploration.

You can use a variety of tools to gather data to support your instructional decision-making:

- **Ask questions to draw out, clarify, and probe students' thinking.** The questions in each strategy section will provide you with ideas on which you can elaborate. Use questioning to make on-the-spot adjustments to your plans as well as to identify learning moments as they unfold. This can be as simple as posing a new question or as complex as bringing a few students together for a mini-lesson.

- **Walk around with a clipboard or notebook to capture students' comments and your own observations.** Too often, we think we will remember students' words only to find ourselves unable to reproduce them at a later time. These annotations will allow you to note patterns within a student's remarks or among students' comments. They can suggest misconceptions that provide you with an entry to the next day's work through a comment such as "Yesterday, I heard a few of you say that you drew a square instead of a rectangle. Let's talk about what that means."

- **Use the graphic organizers in the model lessons** as support for the creative process. Have students use these forms to brainstorm ideas for their artistic process and mathematical connections. These organizers provide a snapshot of students' thinking at various points in the creative process and create opportunities for you to collect evidence of their learning from various perspectives (student planning, reflection and synthesis, peer review, and teacher observation). They also serve as to document different stages of the learning process (planning, implementation of ideas, review of work, revision, and so on).

- **Use a camera to document student learning.** Each strategy leads to a creative product but not necessarily one that provides a tangible artifact or fits on a standard size sheet of paper. Use a digital camera to take numerous pictures that can capture, for example, a piece of visual art at various stages of development or the gestures actors and storytellers use in their dramatic presentations. Similarly, use video to capture

How This Book Is Organized (cont.)

planning sessions, group discussions, and final presentations. In addition to documenting learning, collecting such evidence helps students reflect back on their learning. Consider developing a learning portfolio that students can review and add to over time.

- **Recognize that each strategy not only leads to a final creative product, but the creative processes leading to final work are laden with evidence of learning.** You and students can make comparisons across products to note student growth.

- **Invite students to become an integral part of the assessment process.** Provide them with opportunities to reflect on their work. For example, have students choose artifacts to include in their portfolio and explain the reasons for their choices. Have students reflect on their work as a class. Encourage discussion of artistic work to not only draw out what students have learned in their own creative process but also how and what they learned from the work of their peers. In this way, students teach and learn from one another.

- **Design rubrics that help you organize your assessment data.** A well-crafted rubric can help you gather data more quickly as well as increase the likelihood that you are equitable in your evaluation of assessment data. Select criteria to assess learning in math as well as in the art form, because arts integration supports equal rigor both in content and in the arts.

As an example of how you might combine these methods, consider the Exaggeration strategy in the Storytelling section. In the model lesson for this strategy, the teacher tells students a trickster tale in which a sly fox tricks other animals out of their money by suggesting, for example, that two quarters would be better than a dollar bill that can easily rip and burn. In the first part of the lesson, students engage with the story by using gestures that model the behavior of the other characters in the story. A photograph of the students can document them in their roles. Next, students create their own stories. The graphic organizers they use provide a record of their initial thinking. Students then create their own trickster tales, which are recorded for documentation purposes.

In Carrie St. John's classroom at Lee Elementary School in Lee, Massachusetts, students wanted to write their stories in addition to recording them. The variation in their stories demonstrates the wide range of learners in this second-grade classroom, which is made more apparent by the open-ended nature of the task. Some students provided one scenario in their stories, while others included several "tricks." Some of the stories replicated the exchanges in the original story, while others created quite different exchanges. The variation in the amount of mathematical detail included in the stories is quite notable. In their telling of the stories, students demonstrated their different abilities to capture the characters through voice, gestures, and stance. Students' use of language varied greatly as well. Also, it is interesting to note how some students were stronger in their storytelling than in their development of mathematical ideas, or vice versa. Noting such differences can inform your planning for instructional focus and grouping decisions. Most important is their teacher's reflection that the students were excited to create and tell their stories and that their use of language was more creative and descriptive than they had demonstrated previously. Consider the following excerpts from those students' stories.

Dylan provided an interesting introduction to his story, establishing the setting, character, and plot. He set himself apart by choosing a trickster that was not an animal.

How This Book Is Organized *(cont.)*

Once upon a time, in fact it was just a couple of hours ago, there was a tiny green leprechaun named Lucky. He lived in Ireland and was known far and wide for being a trickster! Lucky was enthusiastic when it came to his pranks, but he had a big problem. Lucky lived on a magic rainbow that could only be unlocked if you paid the mystery amount. Lucky only had 3 nickels, and he was sick of being broke. "What's a leprechaun to do with only 3 nickels?" he asked himself. "Hmmmm, I need a good trick to play!"

The actual tricks in the story involved trading a big nickel for a small dime, an exchange that was repeated three times.

Hayden and Maya provided four different exchanges in their story and gave detailed mathematical information about each trade:

Fish said, "Thanks!" Now pig had 10 cents. It costs 1 dollar to get into the game. He needs 90 more cents. Next, he saw octopus. Octopus had 15 pennies. Pig said to him, "I'll give you this one, light dime for all those heavy pennies. This will be much easier for you to carry to the game."

Pig then tricks a seahorse, an octopus, and a stingray before meeting up with a whale. Note the vivid imagery and humor at the end of this story:

She [whale] sneezed and the water wooshed and splashed like a tidal wave. Pig's dollar flew out of his hand and right back to whale. And then whale said, "Hey, aren't you a pig? You shouldn't be underwater anyways!"

Madison did not have his trickster lose the money at the end, but he did capture the motivation for learning mathematics. Note this section at the end of his story:

So snake got to go to the beach, and dog couldn't go. When dog tried to get in, he found out that he had less money than before. He was sad that snake tricked him. He didn't want to get tricked again, so now he's going to learn to count money.

As there are so many aspects of this task to capture, a rubric can be quite helpful. A suggested rubric is provided in the Digital Resources (see page 283). Observation protocols help teachers document evidence of student learning, something all teachers must do. A variety of forms could be used, and it is not possible to include all areas that you might attend to in an interdisciplinary lesson. Two suggested forms are included in the Digital Resources (see page 283). For more guidance on assessment, see *Integrating the Arts Across the Curriculum, Second Edition*, by Lisa Donovan and Louise Pascale (2022).

Correlation to the Standards

Shell Education is committed to producing educational materials that are research and standards based. To support this effort, this resource is correlated to the academic standards of all 50 United States, the District of Columbia, the Department of Defense Dependent Schools, and the Canadian provinces. A correlation is also provided for key professional development organizations.

How to Find Standards Correlations

To print a customized correlation report for your state, visit our website at **www.tcmpub.com /administrators/correlations** and follow the online directions. If you require assistance in printing correlation reports, please contact the Customer Service Department at 1-800-858-7339.

Purpose and Intent of Standards

The Every Student Succeeds Act (ESSA) mandates that all states adopt challenging academic standards that help students meet the goal of college and career readiness. While many states already adopted academic standards prior to ESSA, the act continues to hold states accountable for detailed and comprehensive standards. Standards are designed to focus instruction and guide adoption of curricula. They define the knowledge, skills, and content students should acquire at each level. Standards also are used to develop standardized tests to evaluate students' academic progress. State standards are used in the development of our resources, so educators can be assured they meet state academic requirements.

College and Career Readiness

Today's college and career readiness (CCR) standards offer guidelines for preparing K–12 students with the knowledge and skills necessary to succeed in postsecondary job training and education. CCR standards include the Common Core State Standards as well as other state-adopted standards, such as the Texas Essential Knowledge and Skills. The standards listed on the lessons describe the content presented throughout the lessons.

Storytelling

Storytelling

Understanding Storytelling

Storytelling has been part of every culture since the beginning of time (Norfolk, Stenson, and Williams 2006). Stories have been used to educate, inspire, and entertain. There is the story itself, and there is the telling of the tale by a skilled teller. Storytellers use language, gesture, eye contact, tone, and inflection as they share a story with an audience. A good storyteller can create a sense of instant community among listeners as well as a deep connection with the material (Hamilton and Weiss 2005). Because storytellers interact with the audience as they tell a story, listeners often feel part of the story world. If you've ever heard a good storyteller tell a compelling story, you know it can transport you to another time and place.

In the following strategies, students benefit from both listening to stories and becoming storytellers themselves. As listeners, students are supported in their visualization of the story, which makes a narrative easier to imagine and remember (Donovan and Pascale 2022). As storytellers, students develop additional skills, including use of voice, improved verbal and nonverbal communication, and sense of pacing. Once stories are developed, you also can ask students to write them down, further enhancing their literacy skills.

When students become storytellers, they fine-tune their communication skills. Oral fluency is developed as students explore vocal tone and inflection, pacing, sound effects, and the addition of rich sensory details. Listeners feel invited on a journey. Also, participating in the creation and telling of stories brings forth students' voices and ideas.

Storytelling is not often part of the mathematics classroom (Zazkis and Liljedahl 2009), yet mathematical ideas are easily embedded in or teased out of stories. Students find that stories provide vivid contexts for showing the relevance and use of mathematical thinking. Well-placed mathematical problems easily can be connected to characters' dilemmas, requiring solutions in order for the story to advance. Such dilemmas can provide additional points of interaction for students and heighten the dramatic tension of the story.

As students create, tell, and retell stories, they gain fluency in their communication skills, use of descriptive language, and persuasive abilities. They also expand their willingness to revisit, revise, and polish their work. By placing mathematics in story settings, we provide a context that gives further meaning to mathematical ideas and adds interest to the stories.

Elements of Storytelling

There are five key elements to storytelling (National Storytelling Network, n.d.). To learn more about these elements, visit **storynet.org/what-is-storytelling/**.

- **Interaction:** The storyteller actively engages the audience and adapts in response to the energy and response of the audience. As a result, every time the story is told, it changes.

- **Words:** The storyteller uses words (spoken, signed, or manual) to create connections and invite listeners into the story world through sensory details.

- **Actions:** The story is activated through vocalization, physical movement, and small and large gestures.

- **Story:** The storyteller shares a narrative with characters and action.

- **Imagination:** Storytellers encourage the active imagination of the listeners.

Storytelling *(cont.)*

Strategies for Storytelling

Personification

Some people describe assigning human qualities to inanimate objects or ideas as *personification* and assigning human qualities to animals as *anthropomorphism*. Other folks use these terms interchangeably (Literary Devices, n.d.). We will use *personification* to refer to all such assignment of human characteristics, as it is most familiar to teachers and students, but feel free to use what best fits your curriculum.

Personification is an ancient storytelling tool that continues today; think of both Aesop and the *Toy Story* movies (Cahill 2006). Stories that give animals and objects human traits allow listeners to think about their shortcomings in a safe way and invite us to think about moral or ethical values. These tales engage learners and allow them to consider different perspectives. Because animals and objects take on human characteristics, the strategy also lends itself to figurative language. Creating stories that present interesting characters and perspectives makes for engaging mathematical explorations that have interesting contexts, where math feels relevant and critical to understanding the story.

Scenarios

Students are invited to become storytellers as they brainstorm, develop, and perform stories from a given prompt. In this strategy, we use prompts as story starters. Students are given both a scenario and a visual cue to be woven into their stories. Students are charged with finding a way for the story to unfold and are in control of its progression. This strategy works to develop many skills—understanding of beginning, middle, and end; character development; and the significance of circumstance, setting, and mood in creating compelling stories that are performed and engage the listener.

In language arts, students might be given a story starter such as "It was cold and damp and the wind was fierce, but I had to go out to save my friend." Students then continue the story, using their imaginations to build the tale. In mathematics, we usually provide students with a word problem without allowing them to add details that would make the story more interesting. Occasionally, we present an equation and ask students to create a word problem to match it. The result is usually standard stories that mimic those found in textbooks. According to Gadanidis, Gadanidis, and Huang, a good mathematics story offers students the incentive to give their attention and the opportunity to gain mathematical insight (as cited in Toor and Mgombelo 2015).

Story Box Tales

In this strategy, math stories are developed based on objects pulled out of a "story box," a box containing a variety of items that spark mathematical connections and provide inspiration for the storyteller. "Using a piece of fabric, or 'story map,' each storyteller then places their chosen object onto the cloth and adds their own piece of the narrative to the emerging plot based on their object" (Light 2021, para. 3). Reed and Railsback (2003) note that realia "give students the opportunity to use all of their senses to learn about a given subject, and are appropriate for any grade or skill level" (29). Having tangible items to spark a story can "create a bridge between something tangible and the newly introduced concepts or words as the students begin to explore a story and its vocabulary. The items also provide a means for making the experiences in the story concrete" (R. Collins, 2009, 18). As in other storytelling techniques, embedding math concepts in a story allows students to experience a context in which math knowledge is useful.

Storytelling *(cont.)*

The Untold Story

In this strategy, students are asked to consider the fact that every story is told from a particular perspective. In foregrounding one vantage point, the viewpoints of others are minimized, marginalized, or even left out. Perspective taking is critical to students' social development, and "understanding the perspective of others is an important skill that benefits children in their complex reasoning abilities that are important in math problems, such as story problems" (Heagle and Rehfeldt 2006, 32). This strategy asks students to consider whose perspective is prominent in a story and what voices or concepts are missing. Inviting students to begin looking for missing voices or ideas can develop critical thinking skills and empathy.

"We tell stories in the mathematics classroom to achieve an environment of imagination, emotion, and thinking. We tell stories in the mathematics classroom to make mathematics more enjoyable and more memorable. We tell stories in the mathematics classroom to engage students in a mathematical activity, to make them think and explore, and to help them understand concepts and ideas."
—Kalpana Modi (2012)

Points of Entry

Entering at different points of the story can provide different structures for building a narrative. We have prequels that start before stories, we can add a new segment to the middle of a story, and in daily life, we sometimes work backward to figure out where we need to begin. These different points of entry provide a frame that can support students' abilities to create a story as well as gain a deeper understanding of cause-and-effect relationships. In creating such stories, students analyze, evaluate, and create, the three highest-order thinking skills in Benjamin Bloom's revised taxonomy (Anderson et al. 2000).

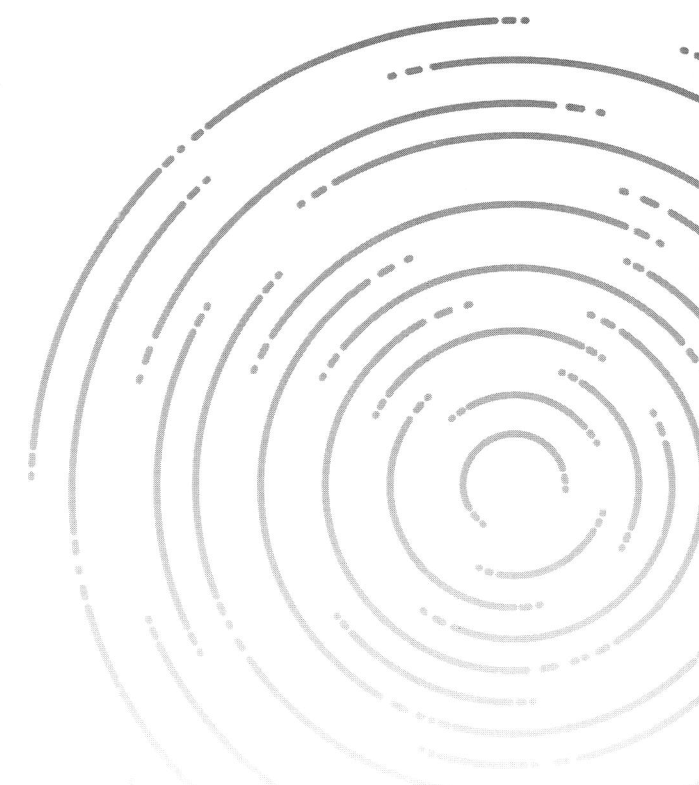

Personification

Model Lesson: Trickster Tales

Overview

Fables and trickster tales are short narratives that often involve animal characters with human traits. In this strategy, a trickster tale about a fox is explored as students consider the ways in which he trades coins with other animals. Students consider the trades, keeping track of the money the trickster gains. As these stories often focus on what is right and wrong and the trickster makes convincing arguments, they provide excellent vehicles for exploring ideas of equivalence.

Materials

- *Fox at the Carnival* (pages 32–33)
- real or play money
- *Character Development Planner* (page 35)
- *Math Plot Planner* (page 36)
- *Elements of Storytelling* (page 25)
- *Storytelling Craft Tips* (page 34)

Standards

Grades K–2

- Represents and solves problems using addition and subtraction with whole numbers
- Uses voice and movement in a guided drama experience

Grades 3–5

- Knows approximate size of basic standard units and relationships between them
- Investigates how movement and voice are incorporated in a drama work

Grades 6–8

- Solves problems involving units of measurement and converts answers to a larger or smaller unit within the same system
- Uses various character objectives in a drama work

Grades 9–12

- Understands the properties of the real number system, its subsystems, and complex numbers
- Shapes character choices using given circumstances in a drama work

Personification *(cont.)*

Preparation

Read through *Fox at the Carnival* and think about how you will retell it. Think about how you want to establish the sense of setting so that students can imagine where the story unfolds. Decide on the voices you will use so that each character is distinct. Review the *Storytelling Craft Tips* as you prepare to tell the story. Note ways to bring the story to life through animated storytelling. When telling "Fox at the Carnival" to students, engage them with interactive moments. Invite them to imagine they are at the carnival and suggest that they breathe deeply along with you to smell the popcorn, pant like the dog, stand on their tiptoes as the gopher looks out, and make a fantastic hissing sound. Feel free to add your own language and sensory details while telling the story to make it come to life.

Engage your listeners by using pauses, eye contact, and movement to hold their attention and create suspense. Imagine that you were witness to the story as it unfolds and are sharing it with them with a sense of urgency and excitement. As you tell the story, you can create interactive moments through whispered asides, such as "How much do three nickels make?" and wait for audience helpers to respond. Invite students into the story by asking, "Do you smell the popcorn?" Encourage students to act as if they are smelling deeply. Ask, "What else do you notice? Ah yes, the bright lights of the rides illuminate the sky."

Modeling the story with money will engage students in the tricks. Gather real or play money to use in your telling of the story. Additional suggestions are provided in the Specific Grade-Level Ideas.

Procedure

1. Announce that you have a trickster tale to share, and tell the story without the math calculations.

2. Tell students that you want to tell the story again and have them become the animals to help bring the story to life. Ask them to think of gestures to depict different animals, such as the gopher on its toes, the dog with its tongue hanging out, and the slithering snake. Practice the gestures together and divide the class into animal groups. During your retelling of the story (without the math calculations), encourage students to add sounds and movement when their character is introduced.

3. Create gestures and sounds that help establish the setting. Ask students how they can show the smell of the popcorn, the jostling crowd, the bright lights, and the whirling rides with gestures and sounds. Have students share their suggestions for these aspects of the setting and select students to practice them. Retell the story (without the math calculations), and have students supply the animal sounds and movements as well as the setting sounds and gestures.

4. Ask students to identify character traits that can be associated with a trickster (e.g., sly, slinky, greedy, untrustworthy) and what gestures could be used to suggest these traits (e.g., slinking, reaching out, looking over their shoulder constantly).

5. Tell students you will need them to help calculate the math so that you can all see the trick that's being played. Provide real or play money and retell the story again, this time pausing for students to model the scenes and calculate the amounts.

Personification (cont.)

6. After each exchange, discuss the relationship between the two collections or items as you guide with questions such as "How much do three nickels make?" Ask student volunteers to record the amount on paper, and then ask them to arrange their arms to represent the > or < relationship or have them record the related equations.

7. Distribute the *Character Development Planner* (page 35) and the *Math Plot Planner*, and have small groups of students use them to create their own trickster tales.

8. As students work together, use the Planning Questions to guide their thinking. Provide time for groups to tell their stories as one group member narrates. Students in the audience should record the mathematical representation each time the trickster plays their tricks.

9. Debrief using the Discussion Questions.

Planning Questions

- What story would you like to create to help others learn about math?

- Where will your story unfold? What will you see, smell, hear, and feel in this location?

- What will be your characters' traits? How will they sound? What props and gestures can you use to develop each character and demonstrate their traits?

- Why does the trickster want money? How much money do they have now? What tricks will be played? How much money will the trickster have then?

- How are the other animals fooled?

Discussion Questions

- How did giving your animal characters human behaviors and characteristics help you convey a compelling story?

- How did you bring your character to life?

- What does your character need to learn so that they are not fooled again in the future?

- Why do we need to identify both number and units when we measure?

Personification *(cont.)*

Specific Grade-Level Ideas

Grades K–2

The story can be used as written. Have kindergarten and first-grade students create a story involving counting such as "Your five pennies are so dull," said Fox. "I have shiny pennies, so I will give you these five shiny ones for your five dull ones." The narrator portrays Fox counting from one to five but touching one penny twice, giving only four coins away.

Students can use addition and number sense in their stories. For example, "I see you have a group of two pennies and a group of seven pennies," said Fox. "Two pennies is so little, I will give you a group of four pennies and another group of four pennies."

Grades 3–5

Change the math in the trickster tale so that students can compare the values of fractions. For example, "You only have ½ of a pie. I will give you 4/10 of a pie. Four and 10 are greater numbers than 1 and 2." The stories can also involve multiplication. Use the story as written (changing collections as students' skills evolve), and have them use multiplication equations to find the total values.

Have fifth-grade students find the differences between the collections of coins by using decimal notation. Include comparison of measurement. For example, "I see you have 2 pounds of gold," said Fox. "Two is so little and I have lots of gold. I will trade you my 24 individual ounces of gold for your 2 pounds."

Grades 6–8

Change the math in the trickster tale to have students include decimals in measurement comparisons. For example, "I see you have 123.6 centimeters of beautiful ribbon," said Fox. "Centimeters are so short, and I have lots of ribbon. I will trade you my piece of ribbon that is 1.22 meters long."

Students can include examples that involve comparison of expressions and faulty applications of the order of operations or the distributive property. For example, "Look at these eight shiny quarters. I will give you double the number of these quarters for all of your ride tickets. Oh, but I do want to keep two of the quarters for sentimental reasons." The narrator then portrays Fox taking away two quarters first before doubling the number, rather than doubling first and then taking two away.

Grades 9–12

Additional tricks include making the slope negative, increasing intercept while decreasing slope and extending the period of time, or including an error when distributing a negative sign with absolute value. Students also can research attributes of misleading graphs such as truncated graphs, graphs with an inappropriate scale, or graphs that omit the baseline. Students could find a graph that shows information they think is important and then distort it and create a story of a character using that graph in a persuasive manner.

Fox at the Carnival

(Bold words indicate interactive moments.)

One night, Fox was wandering down the road to one of his favorite places, the carnival. He loved the **smell of the popcorn**, the **feel of the jostling crowd**, and the **sight of the bright lights** illuminating the sky as the **rides whirled in circles**. The only problem was that he only had three nickels, and he knew that 15 cents was not enough.

He was busy thinking about how he could get some more money when he saw Dog sitting by the trail. As usual, **Dog's tongue hung out of his mouth as he panted noisily**. Fox asked Dog if he was going to the carnival, and Dog proudly showed Fox his three dimes.

"Those coins are so small," said Fox. "I am rich, so I will give you these three really big nickels for your three small dimes."

"Wow!" exclaimed Dog as he made the trade. "Thank you, Fox. See you at the carnival."

Calculate!

How many cents are three nickels worth? *(15 cents)*

How many cents are three dimes worth? *(30 cents)*

How can we write this comparison mathematically? *(15 < 30)*

How much money has Fox gained? *(15 cents)*

What equation can we write to show this? *(30 – 15 = 15)*

Fox was grinning about his 30 cents when he saw **Gopher standing high on her toes, looking out of her hole**. Fox asked Gopher if she was going to the carnival, and Gopher proudly showed Fox her two quarters.

"You only have two coins," said Fox. "I am rich, so I will give you these three dimes for your two quarters."

"Wow!" exclaimed Gopher as she made the trade. "Thank you, Fox. See you at the carnival."

Fox at the Carnival *(cont.)*

Calculate!

How many cents are three dimes worth? *(30 cents)*

How many cents are two quarters worth? *(50 cents)*

How can we write this comparison mathematically? *(30 < 50)*

How much money has Fox gained? *(20 cents)*

What equation can we write to show this? *(50 – 30 = 20)*

Fox was grinning about his 50 cents when he saw **Spider weaving his silky web**. Fox asked Spider if he was going to the carnival, and Spider proudly showed Fox his one dollar bill.

"You only have paper money that can rip or burn," said Fox. "I am rich, so I will give you these two silver quarters for your dollar."

Wow!" exclaimed Spider as he made the trade. "Thank you, Fox. See you at the carnival."

Calculate!

How many cents is a dollar worth? *(100 cents)*

How many cents are two quarters worth? *(50 cents)*

How can we write this comparison mathematically? *(100 > 50)*

How much money has Fox gained? *(50 cents)*

What equation can we write to show this? *(100 – 50 = 50)*

Fox was grinning about his dollar when he saw **Snake slithering among the tall grass** where she had heard what Fox had been doing. Fox asked Snake if she was going to the carnival. Snake lifted her head and made **a loud hissing noise**. So much air came out of Snake's mouth that it **blew Fox's dollar far, far away**, where Dog, Gopher, and Spider found it.

"See you at the carnival," said Snake, and she slithered back into the grass.

Storytelling Craft Tips

How to Engage the Audience

- Ask a question: "And what do you suppose happened next?!"

- Before the story, choose a gesture or phrase for each character. When the character is mentioned, listeners use the gesture.

- Invite classmates along the journey with you. "Get out your binoculars and come along!"

- Repeat lines to increase audience awareness and add dramatic interest.

- Allow your voice to hold emotion, reflecting what is happening as the story unfolds.

- Use facial expressions and eye contact to help the audience feel connected to the story.

- Pace your speech and add pauses for dramatic effect. Slowing down and speeding up language can intensify the story as the audience follows along.

- Use descriptive details to help the audience picture the story as it is being told.

Name: ____ Date:_________________

Character Development Planner

Directions: Use this chart to develop ideas for the animals your trickster will meet.

Animal 1	Animal 2	Animal 3
Character Traits	Character Traits	Character Traits
Voice	Voice	Voice
Props	Props	Props
Gestures	Gestures	Gestures
Setting Details	Setting Details	Setting Details

Math Plot Planner

Directions: Use this chart to help you plan your mathematical trickster tale.

Who is your trickster? _______________________________________

What does your trickster have? _______________________________________

Why does your trickster want more? _______________________________________

____

Trickster has:	Trickster has:	Trickster has:
First animal has:	Second animal has:	Third animal has:
Mathematical representation of the comparison:	Mathematical representation of the comparison:	Mathematical representation of the comparison:
Trickster's trick:	Trickster's trick:	Trickster's trick:
Trickster gained:	Trickster gained:	Trickster gained:
Mathematical equation:	Mathematical equation:	Mathematical equation:

At the end of the story, how does your trickster lose what has been gained?

____

____

____

Scenarios

Model Lesson: Story Starters

Overview

The story prompt serves as a jumping-off point for developing a story. The story starters in this lesson provide a combination of mathematical prompts (pictures, graphs, and equations) and an introductory scenario to trigger students' thinking about a mathematical story. Students work in groups to create their own stories, sparking their participation in mathematical conversations about the relevance of mathematics to their lives.

Materials

- *Story Starter Cards* (pages 40–43)
- *Story Starter Organizer* (pages 44–45)
- *Elements of Storytelling* (page 25)
- *Storytelling Craft Tips* (page 34)

Standards

Grades K–2

- Communicates mathematical ideas, reasoning, and their implications using multiple representations, including symbols, diagrams, graphs, and language as appropriate
- Identifies ways in which voice and sounds may be used to retell a story

Grades 3–5

- Applies mathematics to problems arising in everyday life, society, and the workplace
- Imagines how a character's inner thoughts impact the story and given circumstances

Grades 6–8

- Uses a problem-solving model that incorporates analyzing given information, formulating a plan or strategy, determining a solution, justifying the solution, and evaluating the problem-solving process and the reasonableness of the solution
- Develops a character by articulating the character's inner thoughts, objectives, and motivations

Grades 9–12

- Understands solving equations as a process of reasoning and explains the reasoning
- Uses personal experiences and knowledge to develop a character that is believable and authentic

Scenarios *(cont.)*

Preparation

Examine the story starter examples given in the Specific Grade-Level Ideas. Reproduce the appropriate cards from *Story Starter Cards* to display for students. If you wish to adapt these prompts or create your own, you will need to create or find a visual prompt that will generate curiosity and provide a catalyst for each story. This could be a bar graph, a line graph, or an image that will prompt mathematical thinking.

Decide how you want to use grouping for this activity. Do you want individual students to think of their own stories to bring to their groups to consider? Do you want students to brainstorm with a group right from the beginning? Do you want groups of students to create a story from the same starter, or do you want some groups to have different beginnings?

Plan working groups so that each group consists of students with a variety of abilities. Students with strengths in telling stories, creating stories, and thinking mathematically all can bring their unique capabilities to the task.

Procedure

1. If students are not familiar with what a story starter is, explain the concept.

2. Ask students to consider and discuss the question "What makes a good story?"

3. Share your chosen *Story Starter Card* with students. Read the story starter aloud and ask questions to help students think about what might happen next and to identify a potential conflict in the story.

4. Draw students' attention to the visual on the card and ask them to identify what it tells them and how it might relate to the story.

5. Review the *Storytelling Craft Tips* with students.

6. In small groups, have students brainstorm ways to connect the starting scenarios with the visual and decide what conflict could arise in the story and how the conflict could be resolved. Use the Planning Questions to guide students' thinking.

7. Have students share their ideas with the class.

8. Tell each group to choose one of the ideas and develop it further. Distribute the *Story Starter Organizer* and have students use the organizer to record their thinking.

9. Provide time for students to develop and practice telling their stories and then present them aloud. Encourage students to develop ways to differentiate their characters with different voices, invite interactive moments for listeners, and use gestures and expression to bring the story to life.

10. Have students identify the different ways in which mathematics was integrated into the stories. Use the Discussion Questions to support conversation.

Planning Questions

▸ What story ideas does this starter spark for you?

▸ What characters are suggested? Events?

▸ How will you integrate this mathematical information into your story?

▸ What mathematical dilemma might your characters encounter?

▸ How might the progression of events in your story build interest, come to a climax, and end in a resolution?

▸ How might you engage with your audience as you tell the story?

Scenarios *(cont.)*

Discussion Questions

- How did you portray your characters?

- What approach did you use to flesh out your story?

- What was the conflict at the heart of the story?

- How did math add to the telling of the story?

Specific Grade-Level Ideas

Grades K–2

You can include the mathematical expressions provided, depending on students' needs and abilities. Invite students to ask questions of the storyteller to develop their thinking. This could be done as "hot seating" a particular character or the storyteller, probing for additional ideas and insights.

Grades 3–5

As an extension, have students build on others' ideas. For example, one group can offer a few sentences to begin the story, ending with "and then," which signals the next group to continue from this point.

Grades 6–8

Have students create a story share with a public audience such as a local nursing home. Challenge students to create creative stories highlighting a variety of mathematical ideas. As an extension, make two spinners, one with random equations, such as $4x + 217 = 281$, and one with random settings, such as a *health club* or *sports stadium*. Students spin both spinners and then combine the two results to tell a story.

Grades 9–12

To encourage students' recognition of mathematics as part of everyday math, have each group of students randomly choose an article from the newspaper or a page from their math text, exchange what they chose with another group, and use what they were given to start a mathematical story.

Story Starter Cards

Grades K–2

It was a bright, sunny day for my birthday party. I was just about to give each friend a cupcake when there was a loud noise behind me.

$$12 - 7$$

Our class had a field day yesterday with lots of contests. The tug-of-war contest was really funny.

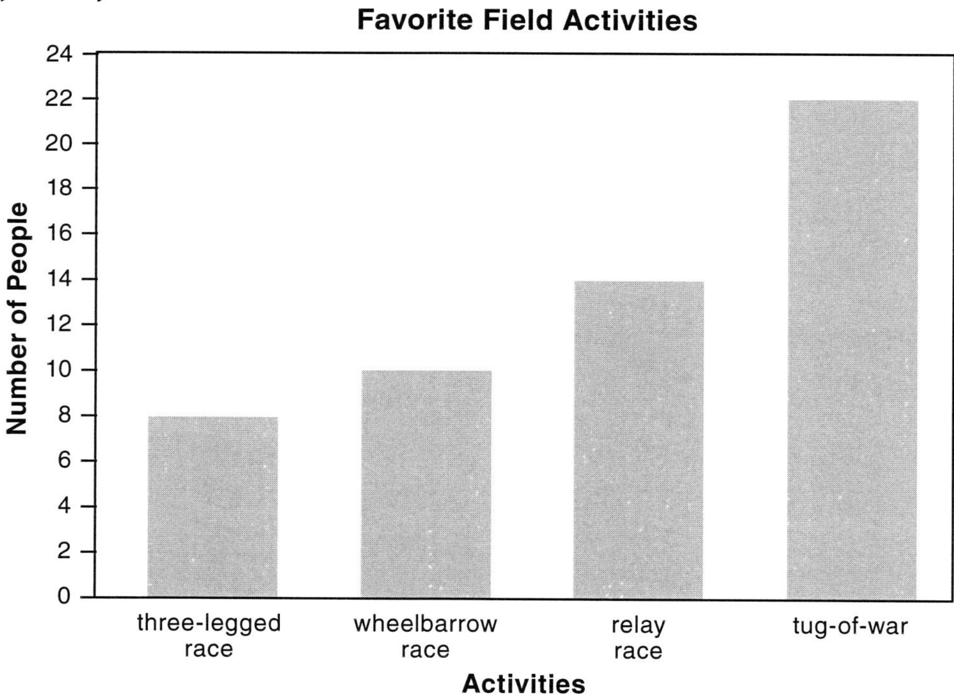

Story Starter Cards *(cont.)*

Grades 3–5

I've always been afraid of dogs, but I need $100, and I need it now.

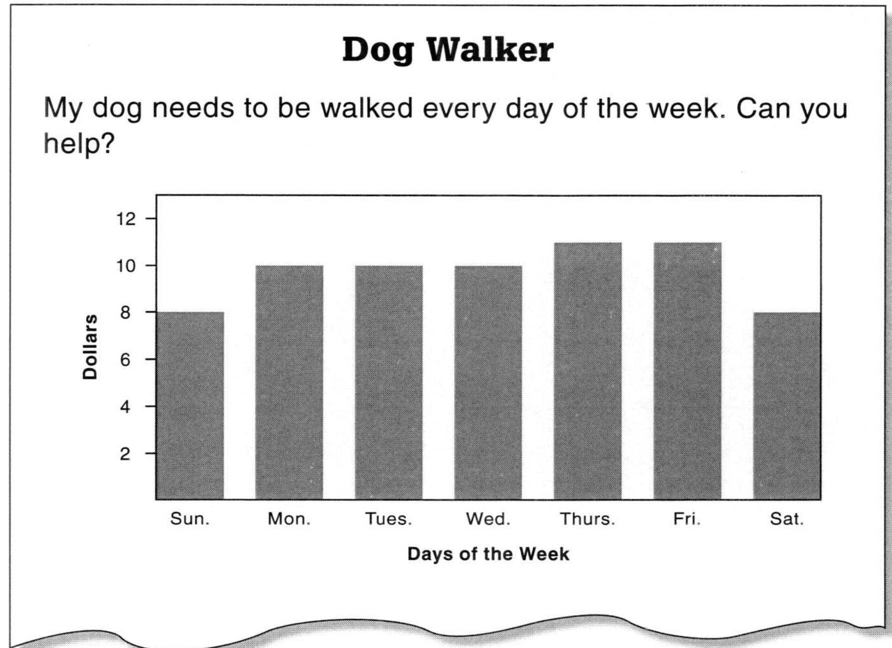

It was going to be the best scavenger hunt ever. I really wanted the teams to be even so that everyone would have a great time, but it didn't work out that way in the beginning.

Scavenger Hunt List

1. a raw egg signed by a police officer

2. a menu from a restaurant

3. a quarter from 1994

$$24 \text{ people} \div 5 = 4 \text{ r}4$$

Story Starter Cards *(cont.)*

Grades 6–8

My name is Chris, and I am a champion skateboarder. Yesterday I was boarding along when something very strange happened.

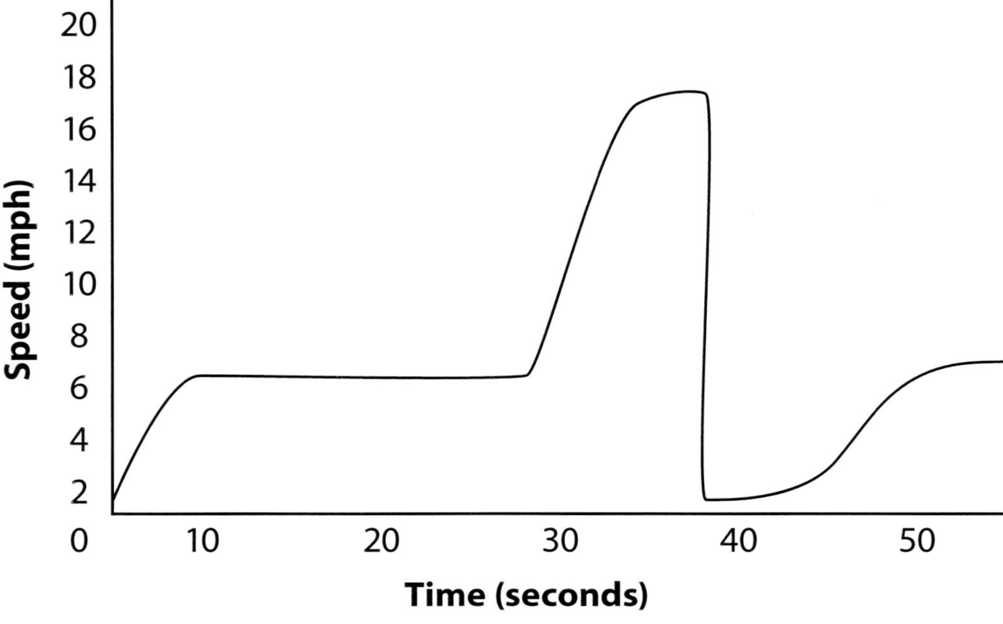

Finally, my mother said I could have a cell phone. She decided this because yesterday it would have really made a difference if I had owned a phone.

Choosing a Plan

Individual Plans

- Unlimited nationwide calling

- Unlimited domestic messages

- No annual contract!

Family Plans

- Unlimited calls and messages nationwide

- Two-line minimum to get started

- One-year contract

Story Starter Cards *(cont.)*

Grades 9–12

I was at the carnival, and I should have been thinking about what to get to eat, but as I looked at the rides across from the cotton candy stand, all I could think about was a trigonometric function.

I was excited to get my license, but now I need to pay for gas. Based on my earnings, I'm in trouble. How can I convince my mother that I need to trade the 10-year-old car I drive for her electric car?

Story Starter Organizer

Directions: Use the questions to help you write your story.

1. How does the story begin?

   ____

   ____

2. What are two important things that will happen in your story?

   ____

   ____

3. What is a moment of climax or conflict?

   ____

   ____

4. What three math ideas will you include in your story?

Name: ____ Date:_________________

Story Starter Organizer *(cont.)*

4. What creative choices will you use to tell the story (use of voice, gesture, and interactive moments)?

____

____

____

____

____

____

5. How will the story end?

____

____

____

____

____

____

____

____

Story Box Tales

Model Lesson: Math Tools Story Box

Overview

In this lesson, students will create and tell a story based on objects placed in a story box. In this instance, the objects will include a variety of math tools, such as a measuring tape, a protractor, a calculator, a sample spreadsheet, graph paper, a stopwatch, and so on.

Storytellers may work with a single object or more than one. As the storytelling unfolds, students integrate math vocabulary, focusing on a day in the life of the object.

Materials

- box to serve as the Math Tools Story Box
- *Story Box Tales Planner* (page 49)
- *Elements of Storytelling* (page 25)
- *Storytelling Craft Tips* (page 34)

Standards

Grades K–2

- Describes and compares measurable attributes
- Uses and adapts sounds and movements

Grades 3–5

- Solves problems involving measurement and estimation
- Revises and improves an improvised or scripted drama/theater work
- Investigates how movement and voice are incorporated into a drama/theater work

Grades 6–8

- Solves problems involving measurement and conversion of measurements
- Uses appropriate mathematical tools strategically
- Articulates and examines choices to refine a scripted drama/theater work
- Develops effective physical and vocal traits of characters in a scripted drama/theater work

Grades 9–12

- Uses appropriate mathematical tools strategically
- Practices and revises a scripted drama/theater work
- Explores physical, vocal, and physiological choices to develop a performance that is believable, authentic, and relevant to a drama/theater work

Story Box Tales *(cont.)*

Preparation

To spark story ideas, gather a variety of objects that connect to mathematical content or could foster a sense of setting, context, and character. Place the items in a box that students will select from.

> "Thinking of math as a creative subject . . . [involves] looking at innovative ways to engage students in math. One way to spice up the subject is by bringing storytelling into lessons."
>
> —Lauren Barack (2019, para. 4)

Procedure

1. Tell students they will select an item from the Math Tools Story Box and plan and tell a story that will illuminate a mathematical idea or concept. Depending on the preferences of you and your students, students can create their stories individually or in groups. Model choosing an object from the story box and then telling a story.

   A measuring tape story might begin with:

   What's the best gift you ever received? No really, think about it. Not what made you happy or inspired, but something you actually used. For me? I was nine years old. I received a small square package. *What could it be?* I wondered. I opened it and—wait for it—it was a measuring tape! I have wanted to be a contractor for as long as I could remember. This was my first real contractor tool, and I LOVED it! I pulled out the tape, reviewed the numbers, and I was off measuring everything.

   A stopwatch story might begin with:

   Have you ever felt fast? I mean, really fast? Have you ever raced someone, blew past them, and felt the wind whipping around your head? Me neither. But then I bought a stopwatch. And I started to practice . . . and practice and practice. Check it out . . .

2. Have students select their items from the Math Tools Story Box. Distribute copies of the *Story Box Tales Planner* and have students sit with their item to brainstorm story ideas.

3. Once students have written notes outlining the frame and approach to their story, have them review the *Storytelling Craft Tips* to give them ideas about how to bring their stories to life.

4. Have students work individually, in pairs, or in triads to create their Story Box Tales. Remind them to think about their main character's traits and the problem they will face and to make mathematical connections part of their stories. Use the Planning Questions to guide students' thinking.

5. Allow time for students to practice telling their stories in their small groups and give each other feedback.

6. Have students share their work in a "story share."

Planning Questions

- What ideas does your object(s) spark for you?

- How will your story begin?

- What problem will your character face?

- What problem solving will you include in your story?

- When might your character speak? How will your voice change to indicate a new speaker?

- What parts of your story will a narrator tell?

Story Box Tales *(cont.)*

Discussion Questions

- What did you learn about the math tool in the process of creating a story about it?

- What interesting ideas do you remember from the stories others told?

- In what ways did storytelling encourage you to delve deep into the use of math tools?

- How did you use the *Storytelling Craft Tips* to engage your audience?

Specific Grade-Level Ideas

Grades K–2

Rulers and measuring tape would be an appropriate focus for students. Encourage students to note when they might use each tool. You also may wish to include common math manipulatives in the Math Tools Story Box.

Grades 3–5

Students can focus on liquid measuring tools, protractors, or calculators. Within their stories, they could describe equivalencies about the liquid measures, identify the types of angles they measure, and comment on when using a calculator is better than pencil and paper and vice versa. Once the story is told, you can invite students to record and illustrate it.

Grades 6–8

You could give students metric and standard measuring tools and have the character describe how to translate among those units. You could include calculators and spreadsheets, with characters exploring the use of each. Stopwatches could support a story involving time, distance, and speed. Students also could respond to pictures of math in nature.

Grades 9–12

You could give students graph paper and graphing calculators and discuss the advantages and disadvantages of each. Students also may wish to create their own boxes and trade them with classmates. As a culminating activity, students could have a story box jam where they tell their stories in a "coffee house."

Name: ____ Date:_____________________

Story Box Tales Planner

Directions: Use the prompts in the chart to help you plan your story.

Your object	
Potential mathematical connections to integrate into your story	
Story line (Map the beginning, middle, and end of your story.)	
Characters in your story (Add a short description of each.)	
Conflict (What is the problem or dilemma explored? Tension or conflict makes a story interesting.)	
Resolution (How is the problem or dilemma solved?)	

The Untold Story

Model Lesson: Math Sidebars

Overview

Numerous stories have been written to purposely combine mathematics and literature, but what about those stories that do not highlight mathematical ideas? In this strategy, students consider mathematical information that may be missing from stories and add it in as a sidebar. A sidebar can be thought of as a story within a story. It is often boxed off and provides details about a related part of a story. Students will create math sidebars that share the relevant mathematics embedded in a story, though perhaps hidden from view, and alert listeners to the pervasive nature of mathematics.

Materials

- book containing sidebars
- *What's Been Untold?* (page 55)
- *Elements of Storytelling* (page 25)
- *Storytelling Craft Tips* (page 34)

Standards

Grades K–2

- Uses objects, pictures, and expanded and standard forms to represent numbers
- Identifies ways in which voice and sounds may be used to retell a story

Grades 3–5

- Understands that numbers and the operations performed on them can be used to describe things in the real world and predict what might occur
- Imagines how a character's inner thoughts impact the story

Grades 6–8

- Understands the general nature and uses of mathematics
- Develops a character by articulating the character's inner thoughts, objectives, and motivations

Grades 9–12

- Understands the general nature and uses of mathematics
- Develops a character by articulating the character's inner thoughts, objectives, and motivations

The Untold Story *(cont.)*

Preparation

Read the Procedure and rehearse telling the well-known story of "Hansel and Gretel." Determine what voice you will to use for your mathematical sidebars. For example, do you want to use the voice of young Hansel or the authoritative voice of a mathematical expert?

Find an example of a book with sidebars to share with students.

Identify stories familiar to students and brainstorm mathematical questions they could ask related to the characters, plots, or settings. Read the Specific Grade-Level Ideas and identify activities that would work well with books or historical contexts appropriate for students.

> "When children listen to stories, they create mental images that belong to them, connecting the content to something personally significant."
>
> —Mary B. Goral and Cindy Gnadinger
> (2006, 4)

Procedure

1. Introduce the idea of sidebars by showing students a book with sidebars and asking them to share what they know about the use of sidebars in a story and any experiences they have had using sidebars.

2. Explain to students that some important facts about the story of "Hansel and Gretel" have been untold but that these facts are now going to be included in mathematical sidebars. Retell the story of "Hansel and Gretel," stopping after Hansel marks the path with white pebbles from his pocket. Say to students, "And here is a part of the story that's untold. Hansel had to think carefully about how many pebbles would fit into his pocket and when to place one on the ground. His thinking went like this:

'I know I only have 15 pebbles to use. If I place one here, when should I put the next one down? Should I place one every 50 feet, every 100 steps, or even farther apart? How will I decide?'"

3. Provide time for students to talk about the problem Hansel faced and how mathematics could help him. Ask: "What investigations can you carry out to help you decide what Hansel should do?"

4. Return to the story and stop again when Hansel uses bread crumbs to mark the trail. You may wish to again provide the related mathematical sidebar or invite a student to do so. The sidebar may be similar to the one about the pebbles, but the bread crumbs also suggest a question of size. How small can the crumbs be and still be effective? You may invite students to consider that animals ate every other bread crumb, leaving more distance between each crumb.

5. Return to the story and stop to discuss a mathematical sidebar about Hansel's placement in the cage, mentioning the probable size of the cage compared to Hansel's height. Have students discuss how these mathematical ideas help them better understand Hansel's thinking and what happened to him. As a class, summarize these ideas by completing *What's Been Untold?* using the story of "Hansel and Gretel" as a model.

6. Challenge students to weave the sidebar information into a retelling of the story.

7. Divide the class into groups and assign them a story they know or a historical period to capture within a story, or allow them to choose a story of their own. Have students brainstorm possible untold mathematical components in their story. Distribute *What's Been Untold?* and have

The Untold Story *(cont.)*

students complete it as they brainstorm their sidebars. Use the Planning Questions to guide students' thinking. Also review the *Storytelling Craft Tips* to help students find ways to bring the story to life.

8. Allow time for groups to practice telling their stories (or sections of their stories) with the mathematical sidebars included. Consider identifying a character who will repeatedly integrate math facts throughout the storytelling.

9. Have groups share their stories, engaging their listeners in solving the mathematical dilemmas. Use the Discussion Questions to debrief with students.

Planning Questions

▸ From whose or what perspective will you tell the story? How will this influence how you tell the story?

▸ What numbers could you use to describe the story's setting?

▸ When will you stop the story to tell the untold mathematical sidebar?

▸ How will you show the shift between the narrator and the character(s) so that listeners know who is speaking?

Discussion Questions

▸ Why did the character in the story need to use math?

▸ What did you discover about how math functions in stories?

▸ How can math add new details to a story?

The Untold Story *(cont.)*

Specific Grade-Level Ideas

All students can benefit from exploring "Hansel and Gretel" as an introductory example. Ideally, this mathematical lens is applied frequently so that it becomes a classroom norm to ask, "How can mathematics help me better understand a story? Character choices? Story events? This setting? This dilemma?" Search within the story for mathematical moments that will encourage students to identify and tell an untold story.

Grades K–2

Using familiar stories, work with students as a class to create mathematical sidebars. Many fairy tales lend themselves to mathematical analysis. "Goldilocks and the Three Bears" is a well-known favorite. Students can further investigate the length of a bed that would be too small or too big for students in the class. Focusing on the moment when Goldilocks discovers the sizes of the different beds, create a sidebar in which Goldilocks takes out a measuring tape she always carries—just in case—and measures the beds against her four-foot length. Students can tell richly detailed descriptions of this moment in the story, or they can add in her discovery of another "too big, "too small," or "just right" comparison.

Students relate easily to *Alexander and the Terrible, Horrible, No Good, Very Bad Day* by Judith Viorst. Younger students can simply count all the horrible things that happen to Alexander in one day and retell the story, referring to the events by number. They can tell a story about another day in Alexander's life that was not shared in the book and elaborate on the details and numbers of events that occur in this untold story. Older students can retell the story using a clock to show the estimated times at which these events occurred. As a follow-up activity, students can create their own horrible-day stories in which they use at least three numbers.

Grades 3–5

A Chair for My Mother by Vera Williams is about family members who save coins in a jar so that they can buy a chair. The focus on money can lead to many questions about savings, the possible size of the jar, and the possible value of the coins.

Engage students in a discussion about matching mood to content in storytelling and treating content that might explore issues with sensitivity.

Have students read a book connected to the westward expansion of the United States, such as *Dandelions* by Eve Bunting. Students can explore questions such as "How much food should a family bring for such a trip? How much space would there be in the wagon for these provisions? How many miles per day would the family have to walk to make the trip?" Students can add parallel stories from their lives that mirror the ideas in the story but draw out their own real-life examples.

There are a variety of books written about emigrants. Quantitative data and relationships can help students better understand cultural differences. Encourage students to retell such a story but to do so with mathematical sidebars. A co-storyteller can weave in mathematical information that compares populations, temperatures, currency, and so forth of the original and current homeland.

The Untold Story *(cont.)*

Specific Grade-Level Ideas *(cont.)*

Grades 6–8

Have students read a book about the Great Depression such as *The Mighty Miss Malone* by Christopher Curtis. Any number of scenes can be considered, or you can have students investigate the financial hardships of this period and compare them with those experienced today.

Applying a mathematical lens to a biography can further amplify the magnitude of that person's success. For example, "How could you estimate the number of miles athlete Wilma Rudolph ran in her lifetime? How many calories did swimmer Michael Phelps need to eat each day when he was in training? How many miles did aviator Amelia Earhart fly, and what calculations did she need to make for her plans for her travel? What percentage of athletes who compete in the Olympics win a medal?" Have students include five key mathematical facts as they tell the story of a sports star's life with rich details that bring the story to life.

Hold an Untold Story Contest. Students tell only the mathematical sidebars, and contestants compete to identify the matching story.

Grades 9–12

Have students make connections to topics in a set of texts about civics or events in history (newspapers, primary source images, videos, podcasts, or oral histories), identifying math sidebars that would help them better understand what they are studying. For example, when studying elections, students might add sidebars related to campaign funds raised and their sources and compare that information to previous eras. Students studying World War II can compare wartime food rations to food consumption in the United States today or to what programs such as the Supplemental Nutrition Assistance Program (SNAP) provides.

Students also can be quite creative in writing math sidebars for popular fiction stories of their choice. For example, they might link comments about probability to *The Hunger Games* books.

Students also can devise their own stories and integrate math sidebars that support their tales.

Name: ____ Date:___________________

What's Been Untold?

Directions: Use the questions to plan mathematical sidebars for a story.

Name of the original story: ____

Record ideas for how math is part of the story that has not been told.

____

____

____

____

What ideas about the setting (time and place of the story) can you include in a math sidebar?

____

____

What ideas about the problems the characters face can you include in a math sidebar?

____

____

How can you integrate the sidebar details into an oral storytelling of the tale?

____

____

How do the math sidebars help you better understand the story?

____

____

____

____

Points of Entry

Model Lesson: Story Enders

Overview

This strategy can be used at any point in a story; students will be entering the story at the end and working backward. Working backward is often used to solve mathematical problems. In this strategy, students are given the last line of a story and have to figure out what happened in the middle and beginning. Like story starters, story enders can help students begin to create, tell, and then enjoy the different stories their peers create from common story enders.

Materials

- *Story Enders Planner* (page 60)
- *Elements of Storytelling* (page 25)
- *Storytelling Craft Tips* (page 34)

Standards

Grades K–2

- Communicates mathematical ideas, reasoning, and their implications using multiple representations
- Contributes to the adaptation of the plot
- Uses and adapts sounds and movements

Grades 3–5

- Communicates mathematical ideas, reasoning, and their implications using multiple representations
- Revises and improves an improvised or scripted drama/theater work
- Investigates how movement and voice are incorporated into a drama/theater work

Grades 6–8

- Communicates mathematical ideas, reasoning, and their implications using multiple representations
- Articulates and examines choices to refine a scripted drama/theater work
- Develops effective physical and vocal traits of characters in a scripted drama/theater work

Grades 9–12

- Communicates mathematical ideas, reasoning, and their implications using multiple representations
- Practices and revises a scripted drama/theater work
- Explores physical, vocal, and physiological choices to develop a performance that is believable, authentic, and relevant to a drama/theater work

Points of Entry *(cont.)*

Preparation

Identify scenarios that will elicit students' thinking about working backward. For instance, ask students questions such as "If someone new to the school were given written directions from the school's front door to our classroom door, how could those directions be used to figure out how to get back to the front door? If you had to be at a special event at 7:00 in the morning, how would you decide when to wake up?"

Identify a piece of writing with which students are familiar. It could be a classic tale or contemporary fiction. Mark a particularly dramatic moment in the text, such as when the clock strikes 12 o'clock in a version of "Cinderella" or when Harry Potter first enters the chamber in *Harry Potter and the Chamber of Secrets* by J. K. Rowling.

Procedure

1. Ask students if they ever work backward to solve a problem. Pose some scenarios in which students can work backward to stimulate further discussion.

2. Choose one of the story enders (see Specific Grade Level Ideas). Tell students you are going to show them the last line of a story. Read the story ender as you display it on the board and ask students to brainstorm what may have happened before the story ended. Have students first brainstorm individually before sharing with partners. Then have students discuss their ideas with one another.

3. Have students share their ideas with the larger group and ask such questions as "What do you think happened before that? What title would you give this story?"

4. Invite students to consider how to tell the resulting story in an interesting way. Share *Elements of Storytelling* and *Storytelling Craft Tips* to generate and test ideas, putting the story on its feet.

5. Have students work alone, in pairs, or in small groups to complete their stories and practice telling them. Distribute the *Story Enders Planner* to help students plan their stories. Use the Planning Questions to guide students' thinking.

6. Invite students to include opportunities for audience interaction in their stories. This may include choral moments, character movements, and shared mathematical calculations.

7. Have students tell their stories to the class. Encourage the audience to pay close attention and identify compelling moments in the story and in the storytelling.

8. Challenge students to note the similarities and differences among the stories with the same endings. Be sure that students compare both the story plots and the mathematics.

9. Use the Discussion Questions to debrief the activity.

Planning Questions

- What kind of story does this ending suggest?

- What mathematical problem or conflict might the character encounter? How will it be resolved?

- What character traits will you give your main character?

- What other roles might you include?

- What specific events will take place to keep the story moving?

Points of Entry *(cont.)*

Discussion Questions

- How did working backward to tell a story work for you?

- What did you discover about the math topic through storytelling?

- How was the experience of hearing stories others created? What did you learn?

- How did your understanding of the math topic deepen?

Points of Entry *(cont.)*

Specific Grade-Level Ideas

Grades K–2

Have students record their stories or draw pictures to help them remember what to tell next. Some possible story enders include the following:

- *I will never forget the day I found all those pennies.*

- *At last, I counted the right number of cookies.*

- *Finally, I had enough ribbon for everyone.*

- *And when I woke up, all the circles were back where they belonged.*

Grades 3–5

Although many students can work independently, allow them the opportunity to first brainstorm ideas with others. Some possible story enders include the following:

- *Finally, I woke up from the nightmare and realized that zero still existed.*

- *If I had known this was going to happen, I would have paid more attention to learning about fractions.*

- *And then I found my watch and realized I hadn't missed the party after all.*

- *I can't believe I earned so much money in one day.*

Grades 6–8

Challenge students to write their own endings to a mathematical story. Their endings can be placed in a hat and drawn by other students. Other possible story enders include the following:

- *And that's how I shared a billion dollars with others.*

- *Finally, I got the hit that would win the game and give me the highest batting average on the team.*

Grades 9–12

You or your students can collect story endings from newspapers, media, or topics being explored in other classes to spark storytelling. Here are two examples:

- *And after discovering that 73 percent of beach litter is plastic, we got to work.*

- *And that's how we figured out how many people we would need to serve at our local food pantry.*

Name: _________________________________ Date:_________________

Story Enders Planner

Directions: Use this organizer to help you plan your story based on a story ender.

Who?

List characters and specific character traits for each character.

Where?

List details about the setting.

Ending

Beginning

Write about what happens in the beginning of the story and how it relates to mathematics.

Middle

Write about what happens in the middle of the story and how it relates to mathematics.

Drama

Drama

Understanding Drama

Students don't always see an immediate connection between mathematical concepts and their lives or interests. Drama can provide engaging contexts for exploring mathematical ideas. By enacting scenes that connect to a mathematical concept or skill, students can apply their learning in real-world settings.

When we integrate drama into the mathematics classroom, we invite students to consider particular situations in which mathematical ideas are embedded. As students explore these scenarios, they uncover and deepen their mathematical thinking, make personal connections to mathematics, and recognize its real-world relevance. Christopher Andersen (2004) notes that drama has the ability to re-create the essential elements in the world; as such, drama can place mathematics in authentic situations that make sense to students.

> "Using drama play as the means of experiencing problem solving, students gain deeper content knowledge through the creative processes they use to develop and enact the stories."
>
> (Masoum, Rostamy-Malkhalifeh, and Kalantarnia, 2013, 2).

When students can explore mathematics through the lens of a character, they are called upon to imagine themselves working through processes, events, and dilemmas. In their roles, they must make choices, solve problems, translate concepts, and articulate ideas. This process requires students to explain, persuade, clarify, and negotiate their thinking (Elliott-Johns et al. 2012). As students investigate perspectives that are different from their own, they expand their worldviews and develop an awareness of their own. Such experiences help students clarify their thinking, understand different perspectives, and consider new strategies for solving problems.

Drama will provide students with contexts in which they can ground their mathematical investigations. And of course, through dramatic explorations, students learn about and develop skills in drama as well.

These drama strategies provide a rich context for mathematical investigations in which students imagine themselves in a variety of math-related situations. Embedding mathematical ideas into dramatic scenarios creates motivation for students to participate eagerly in the exploration of ideas from multiple perspectives.

Elements of Drama

In the field of drama, there are many different ideas about what elements are important in dramatic work. The following definitions are adapted from a variety of sources, including the "Drama Handbook" (International School of Athens, n.d.), "The 12 Dramatic Elements" (Cash, n.d.), and "Elements of Drama" (Windmill Theatre Company, n.d.).

- **Roles:** The characters (people, animals, objects, ideas, and more) in a drama

- **Tension:** Dramatic friction or opposition that emerges from a conflict, struggle, or juxtaposition of ideas or motivations; dramatic tension drives action and generates interest

- **Time:** The pacing of how action moves as the drama unfolds

- **Dialogue:** The words spoken by characters in a drama

- **Situation:** The circumstances that frame the problem and identify what is happening

- **Space:** This is where the drama is unfolding or the use of the performance space; this also refers to the positioning of the body across levels in space (low, medium, and high)

Drama (cont.)

Strategies for Drama

Mantle of the Expert

Developed by dramatist Dorothy Heathcote, this strategy asks students to imagine that they have a particular expertise that informs how they approach the work and how they present their ideas. Inviting students to imagine that they have a specific frame of reference can be a catalyst that deepens their interest and sense of authority in an area of study. Heathcote and Bolton (1995) note, "Thinking from within a situation immediately forces a different kind of thinking. Research has convincingly shown that the determining factor in children's ability to perform particular intellectual tasks is the context in which the task is embedded. In Mantle of the Expert, problems and challenges arise within a context that makes them both motivating and comprehensible."

When students are in a dramatic role, they begin to think through the lens of the character they are playing, consequently developing the attitude and ways of thinking of a mathematical expert. Being asked questions about the decisions they make in their roles, called *hot seating*, can draw evidence of students' mathematical thinking.

Teacher in Role

In process drama, the teacher and students work together to explore a problem or situation in an unscripted manner through improvisation (O'Neill 1995). In this strategy, the teacher takes on the role of a character to introduce a drama. Teachers can model the kind of work that they will ask students to do or set the stage for a dramatic scene. Either way, the strategy serves as an invitation for students to join in the dramatic work, to imagine, or to consider *what if?* There are a variety of ways that the teacher can create this role. For example, the teacher can portray a character in a book who presents their perspectives, become a historical character who shares thoughts at a time when a key choice must be made that will have a significant impact on events, or introduce an investigation by depicting a character who shares the details of a scenario and asks others to participate as related characters. The allure of seeing their teacher be willing to engage in the creation of a scene compels students to suspend their disbelief and join in the dramatic enactment.

Tableaux

Tableau is a French word meaning "frozen picture." It is a drama technique that allows for the exploration of an idea, character, or relationship without movement or speaking. In this technique, students use their bodies to create a shape or full picture to tell a story, literally represent a concept, or create a tangible representation of an abstract concept. Working with physical stance (low, medium, high), suggested relationships (body placement and eye contact), and a sense of action frozen in time allows students to explore ideas and provides a range of ways for students to share what they know about a concept. One student can create a frozen image, or a group can work together to create an image. The process of creating group tableaux prompts discussion of the characteristics of what is being portrayed. The learning process occurs in the translation of ideas to physical representation.

Drama *(cont.)*

Enacting Scenes

The bread and butter of drama is the development and enactment of scenes. Students portray characters that find themselves in particular settings and influenced by specific circumstances. They make choices, solve problems, and react to relationships with other characters. We watch (or participate ourselves) as characters play out choices and deal with implications as the drama unfolds. Scenes are valuable thinking frames and can be used flexibly across content and contexts. Students can enter a scene suggested by someone else or create their own in response to mathematical problems. Drama allows abstract ideas to become concrete and enjoyable, and it increases the pace at which children learn mathematical concepts (Erdoğan and Baran 2009).

Monologue

A *monologue* is a dramatic scene performed by one person. In creating a monologue, students take the perspective of a character (real or imagined), an object, or even an idea. The character must be established without interactions with others (that would be a dialogue) and must speak in a way that engages the audience with this singular focus.

There are often monologues in stories and plays that illuminate what a character is thinking. Most often, a monologue reveals a conflict of some kind that the character is wrestling with, perhaps a choice to be made or a problem to be solved. Note that variations include *soliloquy*, in which a character is speaking to him- or herself. The creation of a monologue provides the opportunity to investigate what Barry Lane (1992) calls a "thoughtshot" of a character's inner thinking.

This strategy allows students to "get into the head" of a particular character. Eventually, the goal is for students to create their own monologues, but you may want to introduce the strategy by having students explore prepared monologues in resources such as *Magnificent Monologues for Kids 2* by Chambers Stevens and *Minute Monologues for Kids* by Ruth Mae Roddy. Students then can develop characters and create and perform monologues for inanimate objects or forces, or they can portray specific characters (a historical figure or a character from a book, newspaper article, or painting), or they can create an imagined character. For a monologue to be dramatic, the character must have some tension or conflict that he or she is wrestling with. This conflict can be an internal or external dilemma. Its resolution or the naming of it will create dramatic interest.

> "Drama [is] recognized as a powerful learning medium because it creates a context for children to relate to their lived experience."
>
> —Anika Stojkovic (2017)

Mantle of the Expert

Model Lesson: Designing Math Exhibits

Overview

In this strategy, students take on the expert mantle of an environmental engineer who uses math to make her case and asks students to do the same. She and her team are invited to present for an exhibit at a local museum to educate the public about an environmental issue. This flips students' usual roles, and they suddenly find that *they* are experts in a particular field, communicating about an environmental issue through a mathematical lens. Students watching the presentations will imagine that they are administrators meeting with museum educators to hear exhibit ideas and further probe each group's vision with questions. Note that while we use the creation of museum exhibitions, the expert mantle can be used with a wide range of other contexts such as being interviewed on a talk show, meeting with other experts at a conference designed to solve a problem, and so on.

Materials

- *Sample Letter of Invitation* (page 70)
- *Great Pacific Garbage Patch Fact Sheet* (page 71)
- *Brainstorming Guide* (page 72)
- *Elements of Drama* (page 63)

Standards

Grades K–2

- Counts whole numbers
- Knows processes for telling time, counting money, and measuring length, weight, and temperature, using basic standard and nonstandard units
- Collaborates to develop a guided drama experience

Grades 3–5

- Multiplies and divides whole numbers to solve problems
- Selects and uses appropriate units of measurement according to type and size of unit
- Collaborates to develop and present a drama/theater work

Grades 6–8

- Understands statistical variability
- Compares, organizes, and displays data using tables, graphs, frequency distributions, and plots
- Demonstrates mutual respect for self and others while incorporating ideas to develop and present a drama/theater work

Grades 9–12

- Uses a variety of models to represent functions, patterns, and relationships
- Analyzes data to best represent functions, patterns, and relationships
- Demonstrates mutual respect for self and others while incorporating ideas to develop and present a drama/theater work

Mantle of the Expert *(cont.)*

> "Mantle of the Expert works by the teacher planning a fictional context where the students take on the responsibilities of an expert team. As the team, they are commissioned by a client to work on an assignment, which has been planned to generate tasks and activities that will involve them in studying and developing wide areas of the curriculum."
>
> —Mantle of the Expert (n.d., para. 1)

Preparation

Identify the exhibit theme you would like groups to work on and the range of expert roles you'd like students to engage with. Possible themes are offered in the Specific Grade-Level Ideas. Read the *Sample Letter of Invitation* and decide how to adapt it for students. If time allows, visit museum exhibits in person or online.

Procedure

1. Invite students to imagine they are an expert environmental engineer. (If you choose a different scenario, have students imagine they are an expert in a relevant field.) Explain that they will receive an invitation from a local STEM museum inviting them and their team to plan and present ideas for a new exhibit highlighting mathematical connections in a problem or field.

2. Tell students that they will receive a letter of invitation from the director of a local STEM museum with an opportunity to pitch an exhibition on the problem of plastics in the ocean, highlighting the issue through an investigation of the Great Pacific Garbage Patch. Use the *Sample Letter of Invitation* as is, or customize it for students, based on a theme you have chosen. Tell them that they will imagine they are environmental engineers and act accordingly as they plan their presentation of exhibit ideas.

3. Divide the class into small groups of three or four so groups can work together to brainstorm and plan their exhibits through the lens of their expertise. Then distribute the *Sample Letter of Invitation* to each group. Have students read the letter in groups and select the idea they will develop. Each group should receive the same concept, which will serve to show how the mathematical idea can be approached from many perspectives. Sharing the same focus also deepens the knowledge of the group in a particular area so that when students are watching other presentations, they will be able to ask in-depth questions about the presentations.

4. Distribute the *Brainstorming Guide* and have students work together to complete it. Check in with groups as they work to hear their preliminary ideas, help them form their design concepts for the exhibit, and prompt them to consider how to present their design ideas. Use the Planning Questions to guide students' thinking. Resource materials can be gathered and shared.

5. Once groups have completed the *Brainstorming Guide*, tell them to plan their presentation and then rehearse it. Watch each group rehearse and provide feedback. Tell students that as each group presents, students who are not involved in the presentation will act as the director of the museum and as a panel of administrators who will be making the selection of what will be included in the exhibit. Then invite the exhibit designers to present their ideas to the panel. Note that following each presentation, members of the panel will ask questions of the experts so that they can make informed decisions about the exhibit.

Mantle of the Expert *(cont.)*

6. Direct each group to introduce the characters on their team and present their ideas in a dramatic presentation. During the presentations, the administrative panel should note questions to ask during a question-and-answer period following the presentation.

7. Facilitate a final conversation in which the experts and administrators note the features of the presentations that were most effective in presenting math in a compelling way. This work could be further developed into real exhibits that are presented to other classes.

8. Debrief, using the Discussion Questions.

Planning Questions

▸ How could you make the numerical data you want to include in your presentation more meaningful to non-experts?

▸ How can you explain the computational strategies you used in your preparation?

▸ What information can you collect to demonstrate your expert role?

▸ How can you explain the ways in which your exhibit will engage the public?

▸ How can you use your expertise as an environmental designer with a specialty in math to communicate key ideas about a topic or issue?

▸ How will you present your ideas to show how the topic might be explored in a museum exhibit?

▸ How might you establish your character with a sense of deep expertise? Is there a prop that will help you step into imagining you have the expertise required?

Discussion Questions

▸ How did "taking on the mantle of the expert" affect the way you approached the task?

▸ What expertise did your character bring to the work?

▸ How did this expertise add to the ideas explored?

▸ What mathematical concepts did you explore?

▸ How was your expertise apparent in how you portrayed your character?

▸ How was your expertise apparent in the way you explored the math concepts?

Mantle of the Expert *(cont.)*

Specific Grade-Level Ideas

Grades K–2

Ask students to imagine they are education experts asked to create a plan for an exhibit that shows math on the playground. As part of their exhibit plan, invite students to sketch a map of their school playground with details, including, for example, the heights of different equipment, the number of steps on specific structures, the height between treads on a climbing wall, and/or what shapes are embedded in the playground equipment. Ask students to note math in techniques for deciding who goes first, such as one potato, two potato; even and odd; and so forth. Invite the team of education experts to share their ideas with an imaginary school committee to get approval for making recommended improvements to the playground (based on their expertise).

Grades 3–5

Ask students to imagine they are expert event planners who have been asked to create an exhibit that features party planning and math. As museum visitors engage with the exhibit, they can create the full menu for the event and figure out how much to order based on guest attendance and how many people each food item will serve (pizza slices, drinks per gallon, and so on). Students also can calculate the cost of each item and how much the overall party will cost. Invite students to present their plan to an imaginary budget department, justifying their choices, and the rationale behind them.

Grades 6–8

Invite students to step into the role of a statistician exploring the role of statistics in a variety of areas, such as data related to the use of social media. Students in the role could document and present their findings to an imagined audience.

Grades 9–12

Ask students to step into the role of a scientist whose area of expertise is mathematical modeling. Provide a real-world example, such as the growth of bacteria. Then have students create related exhibits by choosing themes such as environmental disasters, health epidemics, or "going viral" on the internet. Create a context in which scientists need to share and explain their thinking (e.g., a conference, a special think tank, an interview with the press).

Sample Letter of Invitation

Dr. _________________________________

Environmental Engineer

100 Periwinkle Drive

Lee, MA 01238

Dear Dr. _________________________________ ,

We are writing to invite you to collaborate with the Green Mountain STEM Museum to plan for the design of a new exhibition focused on the importance of math in understanding our world.

We are planning for the opening of a new wing in the museum that will house an exhibit called *Math Worlds*. We are seeking to develop several ideas about what this exhibit might include and how this exhibit will capture the excitement of math in the world in a way that is educational, interactive, and engaging for visitors to the museum.

You and your team are invited to design an exhibit on the Great Pacific Garbage Patch. Your expertise on the effects of plastic debris in the ocean will be important in this design process. We would like you to propose an engaging exhibit that explores the Great Pacific Garbage Patch, highlighting key facts and why we need to focus on how we use and dispose of plastics.

Please draft your preliminary ideas and share them with our administrative team on _________________________________ , 20____. Please be prepared not only to make a compelling case for your proposed exhibit and how it will engage the public, but also to provide a clear rationale for why this exhibit would be beneficial to include in our planning for next year.

Good luck, and I look forward to hearing your creative math ideas.

Sincerely,

Jen Smitherton

Executive Director

Green Mountain STEM Museum

Name: _________________________________ Date: _______________

Great Pacific Garbage Patch Fact Sheet

- About eight million metric tons of plastic ends up in the ocean each year.

- The average American throws away about 185 pounds of plastic every year.

- The Great Pacific Garbage Patch is the name for a huge collection of floating trash. It is twice the size of Texas (617,000 square miles or 1.6 million square kilometers).

- Plastic bags can take 20 years to decompose, plastic bottles up to 450 years, and fishing line 600 years; but in fact, no one really knows how long plastics will remain in the ocean.

- Plastic often breaks down into small pieces known as "microplastics." These can be swallowed by both animals and people.

- About 80 percent of plastic is from the land and is washed or blown into the ocean. About 20 percent is from fishing gear or other sources.

- Plastics can last for centuries. The increased use of plastic has impacted the amount of plastic that ends up in the garbage.

Sources Used

Greenstein, June and Hannah Knighton. 2020. "The Possibilities Are Endless For Reuse of Plastic Ocean Trash." Smithsonian Institution. ocean.si.edu/conservation/pollution/upcycled-ocean-plastic/.

National Geographic Society (n.d.). "Plastic Pollution." Resource Library. Accessed October 30, 2021. www.nationalgeographic.org/topics/resource-library-plastic-pollution/?q=&page=1&per_page=25

Weiss, Kenneth. 2017. "The Pileup of Plastic Debris Is More Than Ugly Ocean Litter." *Knowable*, December 6, 2017. knowablemagazine.org/article/sustainability/2017/pileup-plastic-debris-more-ugly-ocean-litter/.

Wetzel, Corryn. 2021. "This New Installation Pulled 20,000 Pounds of Plastic From the Great Pacific Garbage Patch." *Smithsonian Magazine*. October 19, 2021. www.smithsonianmag.com/smart-news/this-new-installation-just-pulled-20000-pounds-of-plastic-from-the-great-pacific-garbage-patch-180978895/

Brainstorming Guide

Directions: Fill in the chart to organize your ideas for your museum exhibit. Attach sketches of potential layouts for your exhibit.

Your Role/Expertise:	
Math Concept:	
Real-Life Example:	
Initial Ideas for Exhibit:	

Questions to Consider	Ideas
How will this idea be made engaging for the age group attending?	
How will you explain and represent the mathematical ideas?	
How will visitors interact with the exhibit?	

Teacher in Role

Model Lesson: The Math Detective

Overview

In this strategy, you will invite students to imagine they are detectives skilled in identifying fractions. You will begin the scenario by acting as if you are a detective searching for "Real Math." The detectives, or the students, will be convened for a meeting. Identifying places where fractions exist in life will give students a sense of why it's important to understand the math concepts they are learning. The exchange of ideas and sorting of evidence common to detective work will allow misconceptions to be addressed. Although this exemplar focuses on detectives, you may vary your role as a detective to other careers that support a variety of content.

Materials

- *Detective Script* (page 77)
- detective props, one per student (detective hat, magnifying glass, notepad) *(optional)*
- evidence-collection tools (tweezers)
- examples of fractions (a checkerboard, a marked measuring cup, and a clock showing half past the hour)
- box to hold items
- cameras *(optional)*
- *Evidence Chart* (page 78)
- *Elements of Drama* (page 63)

Standards

Grades K–2

- Reasons with shapes and their attributes
- Envisions and engages in a guided drama experience
- Applies skills and knowledge from other content areas in a guided drama experience

Grades 3–5

- Understands the concepts related to fractions and decimals
- Represents equivalent forms of fractions and decimals
- Articulates visual details of imagined worlds while engaging in a drama experience
- Applies skills and knowledge from other content areas in a guided drama experience

Grades 6–8

- Understands the concepts of ratio, proportion, and percent and the relationships among them
- Articulates visual details of imagined worlds while engaging in a drama experience
- Applies skills and knowledge from other content areas in a guided drama experience

Grades 9–12

- Applies geometric concepts in modeling situations
- Imagines and explores multiple perspectives and solutions to problems in a drama/theater work

Teacher in Role *(cont.)*

Preparation

Review the *Detective Script* so you are comfortable in the role. Adapt the script as needed for students and the area of focus. Feel free to use your own script if you prefer; just make sure your manner of speaking is quite different from your usual tone to create a sense of character. You can make the activity more engaging by using a few props, such as a detective hat, magnifying glass, detective notepad, and evidence-collection tools such as tweezers. Your willingness to be dramatic will intrigue students and help them feel comfortable in taking their own dramatic risks.

Gather examples of fractions, such as a checkerboard, a marked measuring cup, and a picture of a clock showing half past the hour, and place them in a box to share with students later. Additional ideas are provided in the Specific Grade-Level Ideas.

Procedure

1. Tell students that you are going to begin a drama that invites them into an investigation of real-world math. They will be asked to join the investigation squad and collect and present their findings as detectives. They will have 24 hours for the search. The idea is to have fun while bringing forward examples of math in their lives. If desired, have students dress the part of a detective presenting "evidence" the next day and work with a partner.

2. Tell students that the scene begins when you say, "Curtain up," and ends when you say, "Curtain down." Then excuse yourself from the classroom for a moment and put on your detective outfit, if desired. Return to the room and say, "Curtain up," letting students know that the drama has begun.

3. Moving into the detective role, use the *Detective Script* to introduce yourself and present the challenge. Ask students to choose a costume item or prop as a way to invite them into the role of co-detectives.

4. End the drama by telling students that their teacher is returning but that you'll be back tomorrow at the same time to see what they've collected. Say, "Curtain down," and leave the room to alert students the drama is ending.

5. Provide time for students to collect evidence of fractions they find in the classroom. Tweezers can be used to handle the evidence with care. Then, extend the activity throughout the day by having students find fractions in other parts of the school and at home. Use the Planning Questions, as needed, to support students' work.

6. Once all evidence is collected, gather students together again to consider their findings. Return to the detective role and invite students to present their evidence. As students present, have other students use the *Evidence Chart* to record additional evidence and continue to probe and ask questions. Invite other detectives to weigh in on the discussion of evidence, developing the collective knowledge of the class. Continue to add words, phrases, and significant ideas to an "evidence wall." Encourage students to report in the role of experts. Challenge them to use their evidence to convince you and their peers of their ideas.

7. Extend students' thinking by continuing the conversation in role, using the Discussion Questions. Note that the questions should be asked in role.

Teacher in Role *(cont.)*

Planning Questions

- How will you portray your detective character?

- How will you engage students to invite them into the drama?

- Where might you begin your search for fractions (or other math concept)?

- How will you document evidence (camera, notepad, collection of samples)?

- How will you recognize fractions (or other math concept) in the world when you see them?

> "Being in the role allows the teacher to keep the drama going by questioning, challenging, organizing thoughts, involving students, and managing difficulties. In role, the teacher can protect the drama from failure, encourage greater language use, point out consequences, summarize ideas, and engage the students in the dramatic action."
>
> —Rosalind Flynn (2019, para. 12)

Discussion Questions

- Could you help me identify the greatest fraction you found?

- It's been said that the parts of a whole can have different areas. What can we say to stop this rumor?

- I am impressed by your abilities as detectives. Can you explain how you were effective in finding so many examples of fractions?

- How did you approach the role of detective?

- I have heard that fractions can be on a number line. Has anyone found evidence of this?

Teacher in Role *(cont.)*

Specific Grade-Level Ideas

Grades K–2

Review the meaning of the word *detective* prior to this activity. Then take time to discuss the characteristics of the math concept they are looking for. For example, "We are searching for examples of squares. How will I know I've found the right shape?"

The master detective can be a puppet that visits regularly during the course of the year, looking for examples of mathematical concepts being studied at that time.

Other evidence that students can find includes objects that help you know the length of an inch or a foot, examples of specific shapes, or different strategies used to add and subtract. Examples can be studied with a real or created magnifying glass to keep the drama going.

Grades 3–5

Prior to beginning the activity, discuss the role of detectives searching for evidence. Ask students what they know about experts and how experts can be identified. Have students identify specific ways they recognize experts so they can call upon these ideas when asked to portray an expert.

Other evidence that students can find includes objects that help you to know mass or liquid measures, properties of specific shapes, or different strategies used to multiply and divide.

Grades 6–8

Have students peruse newspapers and store flyers and collect mathematical evidence involving rates, ratios, and percentages, particularly large or small numbers or articles that depend on proportional reasoning. They also can present their own detective role-play to younger students.

Grades 9–12

You can ask students to create escape rooms where the clues are mathematical. Clues can involve inequalities or geometric relationships (e.g., walk forward the number of inches that the length of the hypotenuse would be in a right triangle with side lengths of 72 inches and 96 inches).

Detective Script

Curtain up.

Detective peers around the corner suspiciously.

Good! You have arrived. Mr(s). (insert teacher's name) told me you would be here and ready to help me with my . . . er . . . yes, my search. I need your help.

You see, I'm a detective. Who knows what a detective is? I've been asked to find (*looks over shoulder as if checking to make sure no one is listening*) fractions! That's right. Fractions. I'm not entirely sure if I know exactly what they are, but never fear! Detectives detect!

I'm hoping—I mean really hoping—that you'll join me as detectives in training. You will learn that it takes great observation and focus to be a detective. You never know what you'll be asked to find. People, things, evidence of all kinds . . .

(*Looks around the room carefully*) Perhaps you know what fractions are. I need your help. I need it desperately. You see, I have . . . um . . . one tiny problem. It's the thing I never quite learned in school. And so, I really don't know what to look for! Will you help? Are you in?

I need to know just what a fraction is and how I'll recognize it. Can you help? Just to make sure we're on the same page, let's list the characteristics of the . . . . er . . . math evidence we'll need.

Discussion ensues as the detective works with students to give a few examples of where they may find fractions. As the "detectives" make relevant points, sharing their knowledge about concepts and examples, the detective takes notes on the board. These words and phrases can be referred to when they return together with evidence of fractions in hand.

Great! I thank you! I now know what I'm looking for. I think I have a few examples in my bag that fit the description of the evidence you've described. Let's see . . .

At this point, the detective can share examples with students to solidify their understanding of what they're looking for and how they might record their findings using the Evidence Chart.

Your job, should you choose to accept it, is to locate and document fractions where they occur! You can work with partners. We'll meet in the morning to share what we've found. OK! I see your teacher is coming back—see you tomorrow. Oh, and good luck.

Curtain down.

Name: _______________________________________ Date:__________________

Evidence Chart

Directions: Complete the chart as you collect evidence.

Math Content:	
Description of Evidence	**Description of Math Concepts**

 117847—Integrating the Arts in Mathematics © Shell Education

Tableaux

Model Lesson: Math Statues

Overview

In this strategy, students use their bodies to create a tangible representation of an abstract concept. Working with level (low, medium, high), suggested relationships (body placement and eye contact), and a sense of action frozen in time allows students to explore ideas and provides a range of ways for them to share what they know about a concept. Students create *tableaux*, or statues, to represent mathematical ideas and then view the various tableaux created by others, trying to identify the concepts depicted.

Materials

- images of tableaux
- *Tableau Tips* (page 84)
- *Gallery Walk Observation* (page 85)
- *Elements of Drama* (page 63)

Standards

Grades K–2

- Analyzes, compares, and classifies simple geometric shapes
- Collaborates to develop a guided drama experience

Grades 3–5

- Classifies basic shapes by their properties
- Understands characteristics of lines
- Collaborates to develop and present a drama/theater workdrama/theater work

Grades 6–8

- Represents patterns, relationships, and functions with verbal descriptions, graphs, tables, and equations
- Demonstrates mutual respect for self and others while incorporating ideas to develop and present a drama/theater work

Grades 9–12

- Analyzes data and selects the appropriate model to represent data
- Communicates directorial choices for improvised or scripted scenes

Tableaux *(cont.)*

Preparation

As you prepare to use this strategy to explore mathematical concepts, think about how to group students so that more complex ideas can be represented. You can ask students to create a single statue or work in small groups to create more statues. Larger groups of five or six might best portray more complex ideas.

Search online for images of tableaux. Select some appropriate images to share with students. Additional suggestions are provided in the Specific Grade-Level Ideas.

Procedure

1. Introduce *tableau* as a French word that means "frozen picture," using the examples of tableaux you selected.

2. After viewing several examples, invite students to consider what makes an interesting tableau (suggested action, interesting composition, contrasting visual ideas, interesting use of space, physical levels, and so on).

3. Select students to help model a tableau. You could, for example, invite one student to stand straight to form one side of the triangle and another student to bend at the waist and form the other two sides with outstretched arms.

4. Have five different students join you. Suggest that they arrange themselves to form a variety of triangles. For example, one student could place their hands on the hips while another bends a leg so that it forms a triangle with the other leg. Have students talk about the differences between making a single sculpture and a group sculpture, and the experience of having a "sculptor" role, directing and facilitating the process of group decision making.

5. Give students a mathematical term to dramatize through tableaux or ask them to identify one themselves. Then describe how students will create their tableaux. For example:

   ▸ Have students work in pairs. One student is the sculptor (directing the action) and the other is clay (actor). The sculptor models for the clay the type of pose that would represent a geometric term, such as the name of a shape. They suggest adjustments as they see the image of the tableau develop.

   ▸ Have students work in small groups. One or two group members go to the center of the room and begin the sculpture with a pose. The rest of the participants add on, one by one, to create a group sculpture until all group members are involved. Suggested terms to explore include *perpendicular*, *equal*, and *symmetry*.

   ▸ For more complex ideas, have students create a "slide show" in which they dramatize multiple tableaux that show a progression. Images are presented one right after the other. The viewers can share their thinking about what they have seen following each slide show. The presenters can say, "Curtain down" and "Curtain up" between images, indicating that the viewers should close their eyes in between "slides" so that they see only the still images and not the movement between images.

Tableaux *(cont.)*

6. As students work, use the Planning Questions for support. Help students understand that they can make their images more dramatic by:

    ▸ exploring the placement of their bodies on different levels, adding visual interest (for example, low-level bending low to the ground, mid-level sitting on a chair, or high-level reaching into the air on tip-toes)

    ▸ including a sense of frozen action

    ▸ using space to enhance the composition

    Also have ready the *Tableau Tips* for creating a compelling image so you can coach students as they're making artistic choices (side-coaching).

7. Once students have completed their tableaux, invite them to participate in a "gallery walk." Each group prepares to share their tableau in a particular location in the room or outside. Introduce the presentations by saying, "Imagine we are in an art gallery. We'll walk around and look at the sculptures. At each stop on our gallery walk, we will talk about what we notice and brainstorm what words come to mind, as well what makes a compelling tableau. If desired, have students stand in a neutral position and then "bring the image to life" at a clap or agreed-upon signal (for example, say, "Curtains up!"). Each group presents their tableau one at a time for the rest of the class.

8. Gather students around one of the tableaux. Ask them to "read" the image quietly first using the *Gallery Walk Observation Sheet.* Then have them say aloud what they notice in the tableau and brainstorm ideas for the theme represented. Continue to move through the gallery walk until all images have been shared. Use the Discussion Questions to guide student thinking.

9. As you move around during the gallery walk, keep a record of the words used to describe the tableaux. You will end up with a rich list of adjectives, synonyms, and metaphors that will challenge students to see the theme represented in new ways. Add to the list as each group describes their process of creating their tableau. This is often where ideas are translated and the richest realizations occur. Documenting students' language will reveal the connections they have made in understanding the vocabulary words and the use of tableau to create meaning.

> "The name of this strategy comes from the term *tableau vivant* which means 'living picture.' In this activity, students create a still picture, without talking, to capture and communicate the meaning of a concept. Students must truly understand the meaning of a concept or idea to communicate it using physical poses, gestures, and facial expressions rather than words. This collaborative strategy is appealing to kinesthetic learners and allows all students to be creative while strengthening their comprehension of a concept."
>
> —The Teacher Toolkit (n.d., para. 1)

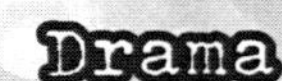

Tableaux *(cont.)*

Planning Questions

- As you think about creating your tableau, what key mathematical concepts are important to include?

- How will you work together with others to show different aspects of an idea?

- How will you make a compelling image that also communicates mathematical ideas?

Discussion Questions

For the viewers:

- What concept do you think the tableau represents?

- What artistic choices did you see in the tableau?

- What words come to mind as you view the sculpture?

- What do you see in the sculpture that suggests the mathematical idea?

- What action is suggested?

- How does this information inform your interpretation of the sculpture?

- What similarities were there in the different sculptures of the same ideas?

- What differences were there in the different sculptures of the same ideas?

For the participants:

- How did you meet your goal(s)?

- What was the sculpting experience like for you?

- What artistic choices did you make in creating your tableau?

- Which math ideas were easy to illustrate? Which concepts were more challenging?

- What was it like to join the tableau?

- How did the descriptions offered by the viewers of the tableau match your ideas of the math concept being presented?

Tableaux *(cont.)*

Specific Grade-Level Ideas

Grades K–2

Provide students with vocabulary or concepts that are concrete and easy to enact. Have students use their bodies to create geometric shapes such as triangles or rectangles, providing them with the opportunity to embody the idea and develop the skills to hold a shape still. Nongeometric ideas to explore include comparative phrases such as *greater than, less than, longer than,* or *shorter than.*

Grades 3–5

Provide students with the names of geometric shapes, types of angles (*acute, obtuse,* or *right*), or *parallel* and *perpendicular* lines to enact. You also can challenge students to enact a term such as *polygon* that will require them to portray a general category and recognize the underlying connection among several examples. Other ideas include *array, area,* or *perimeter.* Nongeometric concepts to explore include *remainder, fraction, equal, commutative,* and *associative.*

Ask students to create group images that show the relationship between ideas and creative visuals.

Grades 6–8

Ask students to select a concept from a list of mathematical concepts you have explored as a class. When working with particularly abstract ideas such as *functions, proportionality, variability,* or *independent variables,* have individual students or pairs of students make a tableau for the same term and then see if the other students can identify the concept.

Grades 9–12

Assign or have students choose terms or concepts related to a unit on statistics and data analysis. Possible terms include *inverse, box plot, random, distribution, correlation, compound event,* and *margin of error.* Invite students to "activate the tableau" with a clap that brings the image to life.

Tableaux Tips

As you create your tableau, consider using focus, action, space, and levels to create a compelling and dramatic image.

Focus: As you create your image, identify where you want the viewers' eyes to go. Create/compose your tableau in a way that creates a sense of focus to help viewers notice what is most important first.

Action: Your image is still, but you want to create a sense of an active moment captured in time. Think of your tableau as an active moment that was paused right in the middle of the action.

Space: Your tableau is a frozen sculpture. Harness the power of a three-dimensional image by using space intentionally.

Levels: Arranging people's bodies on different levels makes the tableau more interesting. See suggestions below.

Using Levels in Drama

Levels	Frozen Movements
low level	crawling, crouching, rolling, crab walking
mid level	bending, walking hunched over, skipping, skating, sliding, swimming through air
high level	reaching, jumping, walking on tiptoes

Source: Monica Prendergast. Used with permission.

Name: ____ Date: ___________________

Gallery Walk Observation

Directions: As you observe the tableaux, record your observations in this chart.

Observation Notes	Tableau 1	Tableau 2	Tableau 3
Words to describe the tableau			
Notes from the sculptor and "clay" about the process			
Math concept that is being represented			
What we've learned about the math concept			

 117847—Integrating the Arts in Mathematics

Enacting Scenes

Model Lesson: Mental Math Commercials

Overview

In this strategy, students imagine they work for an advertising agency and have been invited to create a commercial for a new "Got Math?" campaign. Each advertisement will include a scene in which a math concept is applied within a real-world context. For the audience (the rest of the class, in this case), the scenarios present math problems in engaging ways that trigger interest and curiosity. All students are invited to solve the problems alongside the characters. As a result, students begin to understand why flexible computation and estimation skills are important and required for everyday life.

Materials

- *Scenario Cards* (page 90–93)
- *Scenario Planning Guide* (page 94)
- poster board
- props for scenes (*optional*)
- *Elements of Drama* (page 63)

Standards

Grades K–2

- Represents and solves real-world problems involving addition and subtraction of whole numbers
- Contributes ideas for dialogue and plot while collaborating on a short scene
- Uses voice, gesture, and movement to communicate emotions

Grades 3–5

- Represents and solves word problems and real-world problems involving number operations
- Collaborates to devise original ideas for a drama/theater work
- Makes physical choices to develop a character and create meaning

Grades 6–8

- Selects and uses appropriate computational methods to solve a problem for a given situation
- Develops an improvised character by considering inner thoughts, objectives, and motivations
- Uses various physical choices and character objectives in a collaborative drama/theater work

Grades 9–12

- Understands solving equations as a process of reasoning and explains the reasoning
- Explores physical, vocal, and physiological choices to develop a performance that is believable, authentic, and relevant to a drama/theater work

Enacting Scenes *(cont.)*

Preparation

Read the scenarios provided in the *Scenario Cards* and decide on the tasks appropriate for students, or provide your own tasks relevant to a current curricular unit. Gather props that will encourage students to create rich characters. Then identify a scene in which mental math would be a natural occurrence, such as making purchases, planning a schedule, or keeping records. Additional suggestions are provided in the Specific Grade-Level Ideas.

Procedure

1. Ask students to help you dramatize a model scene. For example, a middle school scenario could include two friends shopping at a thrift store. They discover a must-have item that costs $20. The item is 30% off with a sign that says, "Today Only! Take another 20% off!" The characters have an animated conversation about what a deal this offer provides, and they work to figure out if they have enough money with just $10 in cash. Will they leave with or without the item? Students can create a final caption for their scene, such as "Savvy customers shop for sales. I've saved over $15 in the last two weeks by using mental math in the moment." Have younger students dramatize sharing food items equally at snack time or purchasing simple items.

2. Distribute the *Scenario Cards* and the *Scenario Planning Guide* and provide time for students to work in small groups to analyze the scenario and plan the characters and details of the scenarios they will perform. Use the Planning Questions to guide students' thinking.

3. Have students make two posters to hold up during their performance. One sign should say, "Got Math?" and the other, "You Need to Know Your Math!" Have students practice performing their scenes, identifying when math calculations are needed. At this point in their performance, they will freeze the scene, hold up their "Got Math?" sign, and allow time for viewers to figure out the problem along with them. Then they will signal the end of their scene by holding up their "You Need to Know Your Math!" sign.

4. Have students present their scenes to the rest of the class, stopping as planned and holding up their "Got Math?" sign to indicate to viewers they need to help calculate the math problem presented. Record the solution strategies as they are suggested for students to refer to throughout the lesson. Once several different strategies are recorded, have students continue the scene. The characters should then calculate the math, and the scene moves on to a natural conclusion. The actors should display the "You Need to Know Your Math!" sign to end the scene. Note that scenes may end up with comedic moments, which add to students' enjoyment of the activity.

5. Debrief the scene using the Discussion Questions. Highlight how mathematics contributed to the resolution of the characters' situation and return to the list of suggested strategies. Have students compare the strategies according to their mathematical similarities, differences, and ease of use.

> "Every scene must contain conflict. The purpose of the conflict is to deny the character their goal and to create drama, engaging the audience. Putting obstacles in the way of the protagonist creates conflict. They can be physical or psychological but they must be made visual."
>
> —William MacDonald (2020)

Enacting Scenes *(cont.)*

"Acting out the problem is a strategy in which students physically act out what is taking place in a word problem. When given a written word problem in math, students can discuss the critical elements of the text including what the problem is asking and which aspects are relevant or irrelevant. Then, problems can be acted out by actual students, who may utilize props or manipulatives to illustrate what is taking place in the problem."

—Goalbook Toolkit (n.d., para. 1)

Planning Questions

▸ How might your math problem unfold in a real-life situation?

▸ What characters might find themselves in this situation? When? Where?

▸ What props might you use to help dramatize the need for mathematical information?

▸ What representations might you make to explain the mathematical thinking that is needed?

▸ Is there a different mathematical strategy you could use?

▸ What dramatic strategies might you employ to make the scene feel real?

Discussion Questions

▸ Did the audience calculate the answer in the same way that the characters did?

▸ How else might this calculation be performed?

▸ In what situations do you find mental math helpful?

▸ What math skills do you use when you calculate mentally?

▸ For you, what makes a particular technique easier or more challenging?

▸ How did the dramatization help provide an engaging story?

▸ What artistic choices did you make to bring the scene to life?

Enacting Scenes *(cont.)*

Specific Grade-Level Ideas

Grades K–2

Have students think about what they know about counting, time, and money, and how they use this knowledge in their lives. Once example ideas are explored, students can work on creating characters who can demonstrate the use of math in dramatized scenes. Use actual objects (coins, blocks, toys, and so on) as props to make the concepts concrete for students. See the *Scenario Cards* for grades K–2 for specific scenarios.

Grades 3–5

If you want students to create their own scenarios, provide them with grocery store flyers or menus to trigger ideas. Allowing students to create characters for each scene with interesting props and costume pieces will increase their investment in the activity. See the *Scenario Cards* for grades 3–5 for specific scenarios.

Grades 6–8

If you want students to create their own scenarios, provide them with data related to stocks, sports, or pop culture. See the *Scenario Cards* for grades 6–8 for specific scenarios. Invite students to develop the scenes with an interesting conflict with math problems at the center to increase interest, engagement, and ownership. Adding information about the characters, and their motivations can add nuance and intrigue to the unfolding dilemma being explored.

Grades 9–12

Students at this level can generate their own scenario cards. Challenge students to record their scenes in a Got Math Marathon. Then have them watch and solve each scene's math challenges, acknowledging creative and mathematical innovation in the creation of the scenes. To add depth to the scenes, you can invite students to include a short monologue for their character that reveals what they are thinking and feeling as the scene unfolds.

"A scene is the unit which contains one incident, which informs the journey. If it doesn't contain an incident that informs the journey, it's not a scene. It doesn't belong in the play."

—David Mamet
(as cited in MacDonald 2020)

Scenario Cards

Directions: Cut out the cards and distribute them to students as appropriate. Have students use the information on the cards to create the details of the scenarios they will perform.

Grades K–2

Your friend spilled a box full of crayons on the floor and has asked you to help pick them up. Some of the crayons have rolled under the table. The box holds 10 crayons. You pick up 7 crayons and put them in the box. How many more crayons do you need to find under the table? Discuss with your friend as you search for crayons.

You are buying muffins that come in packs of 3, 4, and 5. You must decide how to buy 10 muffins. What might you buy?

You and your brother are at the store and have just discovered a new robot that lights up, talks, and walks. You have saved $12. The cost of the robot is $25. How much more money do you need to save to buy the robot? Make a plan to convince your parents to pay you to do chores around the house to get the rest of the cash you need. Practice the pitch you will use with your parents, including the pay you should receive for each chore. Which chores will you need to complete to get enough money to buy the robot? Demonstrate scenes in which you imagine you are doing the chores and earning the cash you need.

Scenario Cards *(cont.)*

Grades 3–5

You woke up late for school this morning. It's 7:30 a.m. now. It takes you 20 minutes to eat breakfast, 5 minutes to brush your teeth, and 10 minutes to walk to the bus stop. Will you be able to make the 8 a.m. bus? Your mother is at your door, and she is quite upset. You need to tell her how you will adjust your schedule to make the bus and calm her down!

Your older brother is bragging about how much money he made babysitting and says, "I made $40 for babysitting for one night!" You know that the going rate is $5 an hour. How long were the parents gone if the amount of pay is right?

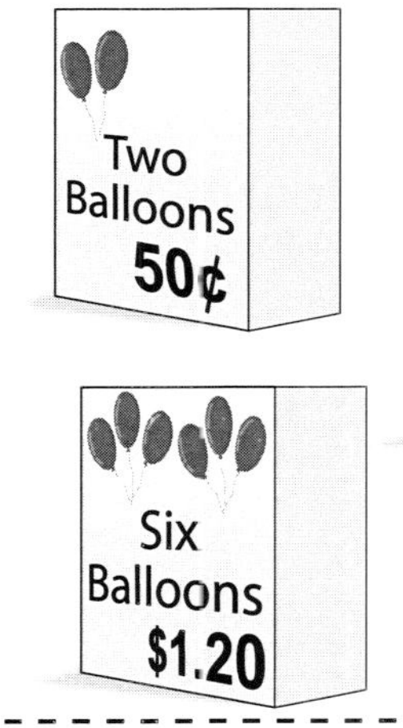

You and your sister are buying 10 balloons for a party. You each have a different idea of which package to buy. What conversation might you have? How will you persuade her that you are right?

Scenario Cards *(cont.)*

Grades 6–8

The local sports store is having a blowout sale where everything is reduced by 30%. You have a coupon for $10 off. About how much will you save if you buy a new baseball mitt that costs $89? Your dad just covered the cost of your baseball uniform and is not interested in spending more. Convince your dad that this is the moment to buy!

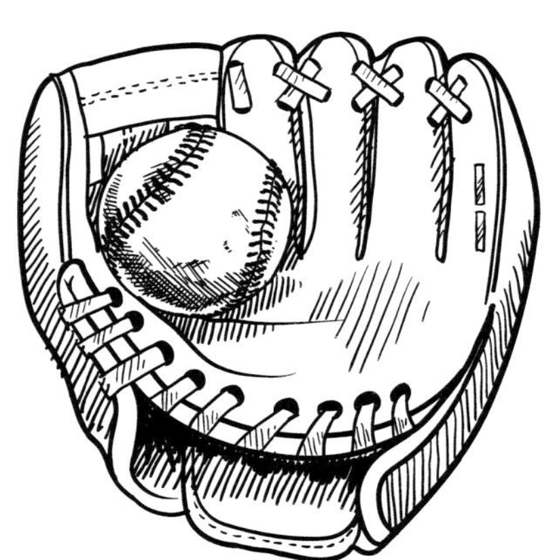

Several sports clubs have a special offer, and you are trying to decide which club to join. You have found three clubs that have facilities that you like. The Play It Now Club charges a $100 joining fee and $4 per visit. The My Fit Club charges $6 per visit with no joining fee. The Health Plus Club charges a $50 joining fee and $5 per visit. Which club should you join? Why might someone else make a different choice?

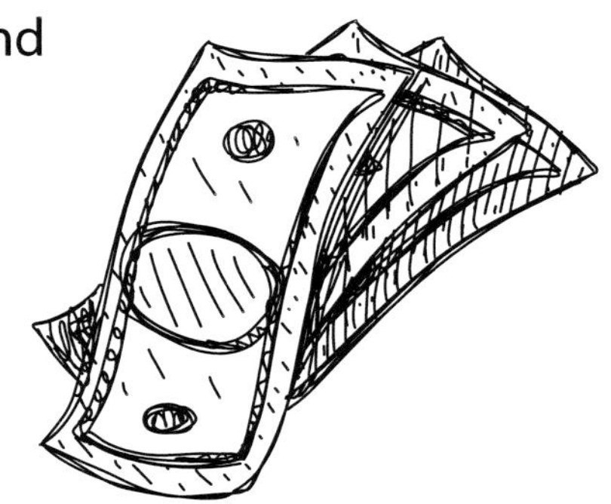

You run 2 miles every day. You ran on Monday and averaged 5.8 minutes per mile. On Tuesday, you had an even better run, averaging 5.6 minutes per mile. Wednesday, you ate an entire large pizza just before running and only averaged 6.8 minutes per mile. Your coach told you that you must average 6.0-minute miles over the course of the week. Share your plan to meet this goal over the next two days with your coach. Convince the coach that you can do it.

Scenario Cards (cont.)

Grades 9–12

 Your friend says she can read your mind. She says she will blindfold herself and you will hold up one or two fingers. Then she will tell you how many you are holding up. She says that she will do it 15 times and that then you will believe she is telling the truth. How many times should she get it right to reasonably prove to you that it was unlikely to only be a matter of luck, even if you think it just means she is peeking? 

There are already 8 gallons of water in the bathtub, which your father is filling for a bath for your little brother. You want him to come and help you find your favorite T-shirt, and he says he doesn't have time to do so because the tub will fill soon. The tub holds 80 gallons of water, but that wouldn't leave any room for your brother. The tub fills at an average rate of 5 gallons per minute. How could mathematics help you convince your father that he has to help you?

Your school's track and field coach has set up a task for the five students on your relay team. She has placed 100 sticks in a line across the football field. The first stick is 1 foot away, the second stick is 2 feet away, the third stick is 3 feet away, and so forth, all across the field. The coach tells the team that the first runner has to bring back the 100 sticks, but do so one at a time, bringing each stick back before going to get the next one. Then the second runner has to return them the same way, one at a time, placing one and coming back before placing the next stick. Then the next three runners continue, alternating picking up or placing back the sticks in the same manner. The coach then announces that the entire task has to be completed in 10 minutes. How will you convince your coach that this is impossible in that amount of time?

Scenario Planning Guide

Directions: Complete the chart.

Character Details Describe your character's age, personality, and other characteristics.	
Character Motive What does your character want in the scene?	
Setting Describe the context for the scene.	
Conflict Give details about a conflict that creates dramatic tension.	
Mathematics Describe the mathematical ideas explored.	
Dialogue What do the characters say to each other?	
Action What happens to spark the scene?	

Monologue

Model Lesson: The Life of a Shape

Overview

There are often monologues in stories and plays that illuminate what a character is thinking. Most often, the monologue reveals a conflict of some kind that the character is wrestling with, a choice to be made or a problem to be solved. Mathematical monologues give students the opportunity to personify a mathematical concept. Students may create monologues that are dramatic, comedic, or a combination of both. The properties of shapes are highlighted in this presentation, but any mathematical concept is appropriate to consider.

Materials

- monologue examples from familiar sources
- *Monologue from a Cube* (page 99)
- *Monologue from an Oval* (page 100)
- chart paper
- *Monologue Planner* (page 101)
- *Elements of Drama* (page 63)

Standards

Grades K–2

- Classifies and sorts geometric shapes using properties, similarities, and differences
- Contributes ideas for dialogue and plot while collaborating on character development
- Uses voice, gesture, and movement to communicate emotions

Grades 3–5

- Classifies and sorts geometric shapes using properties, similarities, and differences
- Collaborates to devise original ideas for a drama/theater work
- Makes physical choices to develop a character and create meaning

Grades 6–8

- Describes and connects the relationships between two- and three-dimensional representations of a figure
- Develops an improvised character by considering inner thoughts, objectives, and motivations
- Uses various physical choices and character objectives in a collaborative drama/theater work

Grades 9–12

- Uses congruence and similarity criteria for triangles to solve problems and prove relationships in geometric figures
- Shapes character choices using given circumstances in a drama/theater work
- Practices and revises a scripted drama/theater work

Monologue *(cont.)*

Preparation

Select a number of shapes for students to use in their monologues. Decide whether you want to assign shapes to specific students or let them choose their own shapes.

Read over the two monologue examples (*Monologue from a Cube* and *Monologue from an Oval*) and select one to use with students. Practice reading the monologue so that you can present it with dramatic interest. You also may wish to select an example of a monologue from literature to share with students. Additional suggestions are provided in the Specific Grade-Level Ideas.

Procedure

1. If students are not familiar with what a monologue is, share a monologue from a familiar play, movie, or book, or share a monologue that has been written for children. Talk with students about how a monologue is different from a dialogue.

2. Read the monologue example you chose to students *without* dramatic flair. Ask students to identify the dilemma or problem that the cube/oval is sharing. Next, reread the monologue again without expression, asking students to close their eyes and visualize the character. Ask: "How might the cube/oval look, talk, move, or behave?" Give students a copy of the monologue and ask them to consider how it could be read dramatically. For example, when might they change their voice, make a gesture, move, pause, or otherwise dramatize the reading?

3. Provide time for students to practice delivering the monologue in pairs. Invite students to share their performances with the whole class.

4. Assign a shape to each student or have students select their own. Have students form groups with others who are working with the same shape. Provide each group with chart paper, and direct groups to brainstorm and record ideas related to their shape. If desired, use the Group Brainstorming Questions to help stimulate ideas.

5. Once a few minutes have passed, direct groups to read their list of ideas and think about which ideas suggest a conflict, which ideas could lead to effective dramatization, and which ideas might suggest humor. Have students share their thinking with their groups and discuss possible ideas to develop into a monologue.

6. Provide time for students to develop their monologues in class or at home using the *Monologue Planner*. Share the chosen monologue example with students to help them see the connection between the planning process and the final product. Use the Planning Questions to help guide students.

7. Invite students to present their monologues to the class.

8. Debrief the monologues using the Discussion Questions.

> "Using theatrical activities to teach math will make learning more appealing and enjoyable for students, and at the same time, it will improve their creative thinking and innovation. It can also help introverted and insecure students come out of their shell. Most importantly, it allows students to observe how math relates to the real world."
>
> —Laura Cole (2013, para. 8)

Monologue *(cont.)*

Group Brainstorming Questions

▸ What do you think of when you see this shape?

▸ What properties does this shape have?

▸ What makes this shape useful?

▸ How might your character bring to life the characteristics of the shape?

Planning Questions

▸ If this shape were a person, what personality traits might you associate with it? Why?

▸ How old is your character? Where does your character live? What does your character like/dislike?

▸ What dilemma does the character have?

▸ What is your character trying to persuade us about?

▸ What gestures would suggest this shape?

▸ How does the shape feel about what it is saying? What facial expressions and body stances would portray this feeling?

▸ How will your voice change during the monologue?

▸ What costume might you wear to help us imagine the character?

Discussion Questions

▸ What mathematical insights did you gain?

▸ What emotions did you feel?

▸ What aspects of shape did your character focus on?

▸ How did you suggest your character's personality?

▸ What dramatic choices did you make in creating a monologue for your shape?

▸ How did you portray the character of your shape?

▸ What interesting choices did you see made in the monologues of others?

▸ What characteristics of shapes were effectively communicated?

Specific Grade-Level Ideas

Grades K–2

This activity can be more improvisational for younger students. When you give students a specific context, it helps them to consider how their character would react in that situation. Assign students a shape and ask them to imagine they are entering a party where nobody knows them. How would they introduce themselves as a triangle, square, or circle? What is important about how they look, where they can be found, or what their life is like? Students can begin their monologues by saying, "Hi, I'm (name of shape). Let me tell you a bit about myself." Students can also pretend to be a particular number.

Monologue *(cont.)*

Specific Grade-Level Ideas *(cont.)*

Grades 3–5

Students may choose to rehearse their monologues and share them with the class or invited guests. Students can use notecards to practice and then improvise. The focus is on sharing their character and shape characteristics, not memorizing the monologue.

Students also can pretend to be a particular number or unit of measure.

Grades 6–8

Assign two- and three-dimensional shapes to students. Invite students with related shapes to present back-to-back to facilitate a discussion about similarities and differences. Or you can emphasize the Platonic solids. Students also can focus on a particular number, measurement unit, measure of central tendency, or distribution display.

Identify a key emotion or feeling for students to connect to the monologue such as longing, fear, or being misunderstood. For example, ellipse-shaped objects may feel misunderstood, as they are seen by too many as only a stretched out circle or as lacking singular focus because of their two foci. A triangle, for example, may long to turn into a cone or be similar to another triangle, or a cylinder may fear losing its faces and turning into a tube. Challenge students to really think about the "life" of their shape (e.g., a circular-shape monologue could reference the dilemma of never being able to stand still without rolling or falling down, the magnificence of pi, or the need to serve as a sewer cover because the top can't fall down the hole).

Grades 9–12

You may have some students explore ideas within the suggestions for grades 6–8. Others can focus on inscribed circles or quadrilaterals in a circle. They also could consider the relationship between central, inscribed, and circumscribed angles. An inscribed angle could bemoan its sense of feeling captured, perhaps even suffering from claustrophobia. An inscribed quadrilateral might speak proudly about how to find its angle measures. Challenge students to identify with the inscribed shapes and make listeners want to learn more about them.

Students also could explore triangle equality with a triangle using each of the SAS, SSS, and so forth theorems trying to find a match. There can be frustration as it looks like congruence is found, but then not, until finally a perfect match is identified.

Monologue from a Cube

I love that so much about me is the same size. I mean, I can wear my clothes any way I want. I can put my tops on the bottom and my bottoms on the top. And I adore my right angles. They fit together so well. I mean, if I get together with my cube friends, we can make a wall and none of us have to stand upside down or sideways! And how about my symmetry? There are four different ways that my faces can fold themselves in half and match perfectly.

Sometimes I think my other-shaped friends are jealous of me. I think they wish they had my properties, too. But I'm going to confide in you. The thing is, sometimes I wish I were just a bit more irregular, a bit more mixed up! I mean, what would it be like to see a whole different side of myself just by looking at a different face or edge? Or what if I weren't always being called on to make walls and had a bit more free time? Really, the thing I wrestle with most is . . . dare I say it? Why can't I think "outside the box"? Sometimes I feel like a blockhead!

Monologue from an Oval

Why do things have to
be so hard? I don't seem to
fit in anywhere. I look at all those
polygons with their straight sides and
angles, mixing it up with different cliques. All
those shapes with four of everything can go to
the Quadrilateral Club or the Quadrangle Hangout
anytime they want. And those triangles! With their
three angles and vertices, they are used all the time
in structures like bridges! Triangles are as strong as an
ox! Even the polygons with five or more sides, like the
pentagon, hexagon, and octagon, are so hip—as house
templates for preschoolers, stop signs, and more. I have no
straight sides and no angles or vertices! Oh, circle and I hang
out sometimes, given that we're both made up of one long
closed curve. I feel like I see the shape of a circle more
than me, like in smiley faces, Frisbees, and rotaries. And
circles have an infinite number of lines of symmetry,
while mine are limited to two. But wait a minute. I
guess I should feel lucky. After all, who wants to
be lumped in with everyone else all the time?
Being different is awesome!
Look out, world!
Here I come!

Credit: Denise Chesbro, Third-Grade Teacher

Monologue Planner

Directions: Fill in this planner to help you create your monologue.

Properties:	Things this reminds me of:	Facts about my character:

Math Topic:

My character's personality:	What my character wants or is bothered by:	Ways I can add drama (use of voice, gesture, props):

Poetry

Poetry

Understanding Poetry

"Poetry is about as ancient as mathematics in human culture. Its language can be whimsical, somber, joyful, beautiful, concise, thought-provoking, and inspirational."
—American Mathematical Society (n.d.-b)

The lessons in this chapter invite students to investigate the ways in which math is essential to the creation of certain types of poems such as the cinquain, fib, and lune. They discover how math ideas, such as the number of syllables or words, enhance the meaning expressed by the poet. Students explore collections of poetry and write poems to experience how poetry is a way to communicate their thoughts, wonderings, and findings about mathematical concepts.

In this chapter, we offer opportunities for students to explore all different types of poems so they can decide which styles they prefer as they integrate poetry and math learning. As Polly Collins stated, "When students create poems about topics of study, they enhance their comprehension through the connections they have made between the topic and their own lives, the topic and the world around them, and the poetry and the content texts they have read" (2008, 83). Developing mathematical understanding through the creation of poems allows students to consider math concepts in new ways and share their understanding through language and metaphor.

Often students enjoy creating poems but are not sure how to begin. The strategies in this section provide guidance that will help students identify and work with rich language to explore mathematical ideas. Students are invited to put words together in fresh ways, drawing on evocative language, playful juxtaposition of ideas, and the creation of images through words as they read and write poems about concepts in math. This active engagement changes students' relationships with math as they find their own language to describe what they know.

We tend to think about mathematics as working with numbers, and yet theoretical structures of math, vocabulary, and application of math to real-world situations are equally important for students to understand. By working with poetic language, symbolism, and metaphor, students can deepen their understanding of mathematical ideas. Kwame Alexander wrote, "A poem is a small but powerful thing" (2019, 28).

Using language to explore mathematical ideas builds conceptual understanding. When students become poets, they fine-tune their writing and explore the use of patterns, rhythm, and metaphor. Writing poems allows students to use language in fresh ways to develop a deeper understanding of mathematical ideas.

Elements of Poetry

The following list of terms related to poetry is informed by the Academy of American Poets (n.d.), and the work of Kwame Alexander (2019), Georgia Heard (1999), and Mary Oliver (1994).

- **Sound:** The creation of meaning with sound, often through the use of onomatopoeia, assonance, consonance, alliteration, and more.

- **Rhythm:** The beat of the poem, created through pattern, repetition, rhyme, syllables, and more.

- **Imagery:** Precise word choices and figurative language create an image in the reader's mind by evoking the senses and imagination.

- **Structure:** The organization of ideas. Some poems are free verse, others follow a specific form. Intentional line breaks and use of space on the page create meaning.

- **Density:** What is said (or can be said) in how little space. Density often distinguishes poetry from regular speech and prose.

- **Audience:** Poets write with their audience in mind, revealing tone or attitude toward the message, subject, and more.

Poetry *(cont.)*

Strategies for Poetry

Poems for Two Voices

Compare and contrast is one of the most effective instructional strategies that teachers can use (Marzano 2007). A dialogue poem encourages students to explore two different perspectives on a topic. This form of poetry works well with opposite but related concepts or perspectives. Similarities and differences between concepts can be explored, giving the rhythm and feel of a dialogue. The poem is constructed by two writers, encouraging conversation about the content being explored and the ways to best translate ideas into poetic form. This collaborative work allows students to share what they know with their peers and deepen learning. These poems also prompt students to better differentiate between two concepts they're learning at the same time.

Poetry Collections

When students are given the opportunity to explore a variety of poems of different structures, styles, and craft strategies, they can determine what they would like to try themselves. Students decide what they like about rhyming and non-rhyming poems. Jan LaBonty and Kathy Everts Danielson note that "a preference for rhyme and rhythm is contained in the linguistic make-up of all humans. There is pattern and measure in every language and in the way we structure our lives" (2004, 40). Some students may find they prefer poems that do not rhyme. Students will find their own poet voices and ways to communicate meaning, drawing upon ideas from mentor poems as a way to synthesize learning and distill the essence of concepts and ideas.

Found Poetry

This strategy prompts students to find and collect words and phrases from a variety of sources. Students collect and record these words on paper and place them in a "word bowl." Students draw out words and phrases, playing with the juxtaposition of the words. They experiment with line breaks and the creation of meaning in unexpected ways, revealing fresh language and insights into the concepts of study. McKim and Steinbergh (1992) note that with word-bowl poetries, "The very fact of manipulating the words, discarding some, trading others, adding what one needs for sense, can teach us something about selection and choice in making poems. Joining two or three words that normally don't appear together can make fresh images, charging them with new energy and excitement." This strategy allows students to work with descriptions of concepts to create poems that reveal relationships and ideas about content in unique and enlightening language. Putting words together through juxtaposition allows students to boil ideas down and reveal new fresh insights to their essence. Students benefit from having a range of words available from which to draw.

> "Both mathematicians and poets strive for economy and precision, selecting exactly the words they need to convey their meaning."
>
> —Evelyn Lamb (2018, para. 9)

Poetry *(cont.)*

Structured Poems

Many forms of poetry are created within specified formats. The structure of a certain number of words and syllables or a given pattern of rhythm helps students plan and organize their writing. JoAnne Growney (2009) notes, "Long traditions embrace the fourteen-line sonnet with its ten-syllable lines. Five-line limericks and seventeen-syllable haiku also are familiar forms. Moreover, patterns of accent and rhyme overlay the line and syllable counts for even more intricacy" (12). The possibilities are endless as students engage with different patterns and writing within a particular structure, enabling mathematical concepts to be viewed through a new lens. Furthermore, Corie Herman (2003) suggests that the structured nature of these poems supports diverse students' abilities to succeed in writing them.

"I Am From" Poems

"I Am From" poems often follow a pattern and can be created through student responses to prompts (Kuta 2003). Using the senses to reflect on what has been seen, heard, smelled, touched, and tasted, students become aware of how they (or characters, fictional or real) have been shaped by their unique experiences. This biographical strategy allows students to investigate traditions, attitudes, environmental influences, and commonly held perceptions about a particular idea or within a particular era. The observations and reflections help students become aware of how time and place can influence perspective. When written about themselves, students' "I Am From" bio poems can provide teachers with relevant background information, offer insights on how to best work with individual students, and enhance student–teacher communication.

When integrating mathematics and poetry, it's helpful to remember the words of Georgia Heard (2021):

> Poets . . .
> Observe the small moments around us
> Find poetry in the ordinary
> See beauty in the ugly
> Are curious and filled with wonder
> Love the meaning the sounds of words
> Look at the world in a new way
> Pay attention to and write from all our feelings
> Give voice to the unspeakable
> Are empathetic

Poems for Two Voices

Model Lesson: Mathematics in Two Voices

Overview

In this strategy, students read a poem written for two voices, brainstorm a list of mathematical topics for this type of poem, and then work individually or in pairs to create their own poems for two voices. As they do so, they gain a deeper understanding of the similarities and differences between two mathematical ideas. These poems also prompt students to better differentiate between two concepts that are learned at the same time, for example, factors and multiples.

Materials

- *Sample Poems for Two Voices* (page 111)
- sample poems for two voices from websites such as *The Poem Farm* (**www.poemfarm. amylv.com/**)
- math texts or related resources
- *Poem for Two Voices Plan* (page 114)
- *Elements of Poetry* (page 105)
- *Poetry Craft Tips* (page 112)
- *Tips for Performing Poetry* (page 113)

Standards

Grades K–2

- Counts whole numbers
- Writes a poetic narrative in which they recount events

Grades 3–5

- Represents and solves multistep problems involving the four operations with whole numbers using equations
- Produces clear and coherent writing appropriate to poetic form

Grades 6–8

- Represents and solves multistep problems involving the four operations with rational numbers using equations
- Produces clear and coherent writing appropriate to poetic form

Grades 9–12

- Represents and solves multistep problems involving the four operations with rational numbers using equations
- Produces clear and coherent writing appropriate to poetic form

Poems for Two Voices *(cont.)*

Preparation

Think about mathematical ideas that are related but have different characteristics, such as even and odd numbers, positive and negative numbers, or prime and composite numbers. Brainstorm characteristics of each idea in preparation for a discussion with students.

Familiarize yourself with the example provided in the *Sample Poems for Two Voices*, or try writing one of your own. Note that each part of the poem should be read by a different voice.

Procedure

1. Display the *Sample Poems* or share your own creations. Have two students read the different parts of the poem aloud.

2. Ask students, "What do you notice about how these poems are formed? What do you learn about each concept? How does the poem reveal contrasting ideas?"

3. As a class, brainstorm a list of possible math topics for writing poems for two voices. Record responses for students to refer to throughout the lesson. See the Specific Grade-Level Ideas for additional suggestions. Encourage students to use their math textbooks or math literature to draw out more ideas and language that might be incorporated into the poems.

4. Assign or let students choose partners and ask them to choose an idea from the brainstormed list that they would like to explore in their poem for two voices. Use the Planning Questions to guide discussion. Distribute the *Poem for Two Voices Plan* and provide time for students to write their poems. Encourage students to create an image or provide mathematical examples to further exemplify the concepts. If written over time, students can use collaborative technology such as Google Docs™ for their collaboration.

5. Provide time for students to practice performing their poems aloud in two voices.

6. Have students make audio recordings of their performances and listen and discuss them afterward. You also can share these poems on a class blog or by using software that supports voice recording.

7. Have partners present their poems and images to the rest of the class. Use the Discussion Questions to debrief.

Planning Questions

- What words or phrases are associated with each idea?

- What could you write that the voices could read together?

- How will you embed examples of the math within the poem?

- How can you illustrate the poem to exemplify the differences between the concepts?

- What ideas will you use from *Tips for Performing Poetry*?

Discussion Questions

- What differences did you identify between the mathematical concepts?

- What did you learn by writing your poem?

- What artistic choices did you make in creating your poem?

- What feedback could you give the teams of authors?

Poems for Two Voices *(cont.)*

Specific Grade-Level Ideas

Grades K–2

Have students draw from a brainstormed list of ideas about differences between the chosen math concepts. Possible topics include addition and subtraction, particular numbers such as 1 and 2, and particular shapes such as triangles and squares. Students are likely to focus on examples such as 1 nose, 2 eyes, and more.

Grades 3–5

Have students work with a partner to write a poem for two voices after a group brainstorming session. In addition to the ideas for grades K–2, students can consider multiplication and division, factors and multiples, even and odd, area and perimeter, numerator and denominator, and part and whole.

Grades 6–8

In addition to the ideas for grades 3–5, students can consider negative and positive integers, decimals and fractions, rate and ratio, center and variation, and slope and intercept.

Grades 9–12

Have students create poems about independent and dependent variables, linear and quadratic functions, domain and range, surface area and volume, simple and compound interest, and positive and negative correlations.

Sample Poems for Two Voices

<table>
<tr><td valign="top" width="50%">

Math Tutor

Hello. I'll be your math tutor.
    Yay Math
    My favorite

Your brother traveled 117 miles in 2.25 hours.
What was his average speed?
    I don't have a brother
Well, if you did?
    Then you can ask him

OK, let's try something different.
It takes 6 cubes to build a staircase with 3 steps.
How many cubes are needed for 11 steps?
    First of all
    Who uses cubes to make a staircase?
    It would be structurally unsound
    Unless they are granite cubes
    But that would be ridiculously expensive
    Secondly
    Why not a ramp?
    A ramp would be more accessible for all

Ugh. Julia has $\frac{1}{2}$ pizza left in the fridge.
At breakfast, she ate $\frac{1}{3}$ of it.
What fraction of the original pizza is left for lunch?
    She has bigger problems than math
    Seriously
    Eating pizza for breakfast, lunch, and dinner?

Argh. Let's try something hands on, shall we?
In a packet of 40 Skittles, 30% are red.
How many are not red?
And please don't tell me that you are color-blind.
Or that candy rots your teeth.
    Om Nom Nom
    Gulp
    What was the question again?

        —Joe Metz

</td><td valign="top" width="50%">

**Positive and
Negative Numbers**

Negative numbers
           Positive numbers
Less than zero
           More than zero
In the red
           In the black
Below sea level
           Above sea level
Below freezing
           Above freezing
Debt
           Profit
We balance
each other out

      We give symmetry to the
        number line

      Zero is not one of us

</td></tr>
</table>

Name: ____ Date:___________________

Poetry Craft Tips

Directions: Read the tips below and choose one or more to try out in your poem.

- Help readers make a mental image in their mind by choosing **precise words**.
  Example: *periwinkle* instead of *blue*

- Use words that show one or more of the **five senses.**

- The decision of where to use **line breaks** impacts meaning.
  Example: Set a word or phrase on a line all by itself for impact.

- Use **alliteration** with purpose.
  Example: To show the mood or to create pacing (how quickly or slowly the reader reads a section of your poem)

- Try a **circular ending**. Begin and end your poem by repeating a word, phrase, or idea.

- **Vary the length of your stanzas**. Follow a long stanza with a short stanza (or the reverse) to show a change in events, a change within a character, the passing of time, and more.

- Repeat words or phrases to create rhythm and beat.

- Repeat words or phrases to show that an idea is important.

- Convey feelings, motivations, and action with **strong verbs.**
  Example: *dip into the water* is different from *cannonball into the water*

- Use a **metaphor** or **simile** to compare, enhancing meaning and imagination.

Source: Adapted from "Writing Strategies Used in Poetry" (pages 48–49) of *Writing Is Magic, or Is It? Using Mentor Texts to Develop the Writer's Craft* by Jennifer M. Bogard and Mary C. McMackin (2015).

Tips for Performing Poetry

Directions: Consider these helpful tips as you play around with different ways to recite a poem.

Tips to Consider

- Think about how you want your audience to feel as you recite your poem.

- Find parts that might be spoken loudly, quietly, quickly, or slowly.

- Find a place in which you can pause for added effect.

- Use facial expressions to match meaning.

- Match the tone of your voice to the meaning of the lines.

- Find places for big or small movements.

Name: _______________________ Date: _______________________

Poem for Two Voices Plan

Directions: Brainstorm ideas for your poem before you begin writing. Use this planner to organize your ideas.

Summary of Event: ____

Poem Title: ____

Voice 1: _______________________ Voice 2: _______________________

Thoughts and Ideas

Shared Thoughts and Ideas

Thoughts and Ideas

Poetry Collections

Model Lesson: Mentor Math Poems

Overview

In this lesson, students explore a collection of math poems with rhythm and beat, some with end rhyme and some without end rhyme. Students experience how rhythm and beat help us recall facts or explore math themes. As students explore math poems, they might find that a poem with a repeating word or a catchy beat helps them recall facts or remember ideas, whereas others might prefer a poem with end rhymes.

Materials

- collection of math-themed poems
- *Sample Mentor Poems* (pages 118–119)
- *Observing My Mentor Poem* (page 120)
- *My Math Poem* (page 121)
- *Elements of Poetry* (page 105)
- *Poetry Craft Tips* (page 112)
- *Tips for Performing Poetry* (page 113)

Standards

Grades K–2

- Represents and solves problems using addition and subtraction of whole numbers
- Demonstrates understanding of word relationships and rhyme in writing

Grades 3–5

- Represents and solves problems using addition and subtraction of whole numbers
- Demonstrates understanding of language, word relationships, and rhyme in writing

Grades 6–8

- Selects and uses appropriate computational methods for a given situation
- Demonstrates understanding of language, word relationships, and rhyme in writing

Grades 9–12

- Understands solving equations as a process of reasoning and explains the reasoning
- Demonstrates understanding of figurative language, word relationships, and nuances in word meanings

Poetry Collections *(cont.)*

Preparation

Gather a collection of math-themed poems appropriate to students' grade level; you can use the *Sample Mentor Poems* or select your own examples. The mentor poems should be a variety of styles and topics about math. The purpose is to expose students to the idea that poems can be created about math.

Procedure

1. Distribute a collection of math-themed poems to small groups. Have them read and enjoy the poems together and ask them the following questions: "What did you enjoy about the poems? What math ideas are shown in the poems? What do you notice about how the poems are created?"

2. After discussing students' thoughts about the poems as a class, have individuals choose the poem they enjoyed best and would like to use as a mentor poem for their own writing.

3. Using the math content you are studying or have studied in the past, have students analyze their poem using *Observing My Mentor Poem* to help guide students' thinking. Use the Planning Questions to help support students, as needed.

4. Distribute copies of *My Math Poem* and provide students with time to write their own poem, using their mentor poem for ideas about craft. Use the *Tips for Performing Poetry* to help students as they practice reciting their poems.

5. Place students back in their small groups and invite them to share their poems with their peers.

6. Offer students an opportunity to revise their poems and share them with the class. Use the Discussion Questions to debrief

and have students think about how poetry allows them to explore mathematical ideas.

Planning Questions

▸ What craft techniques did the poet use to create rhythm and beat?

▸ How does rhythm and beat amplify meaning?

▸ Which mentor poem did you enjoy the most and why?

▸ What does the collection of math-themed poems reveal about math ideas?

▸ What math topic would you like to explore through poetry?

Discussion Questions

▸ What craft strategies did you use in your poem? (Consider: line breaks, word choices, rhythm, alliteration, metaphor)

▸ What math content did you explore and why?

▸ How did writing a poem about math help you to understand a math concept?

"Model how to collect words you love; poems you don't want to lose; and interesting phrases to remember. Model how to stop in the moment, and add them to your collection."

—Jenn Bogard (personal communication, July 15, 2021)

Poetry Collections *(cont.)*

Specific Grade-Level Ideas

Grades K–2

Choose a math topic and work with students to create two different poems: a poem that rhymes and a poem that does not rhyme. Have a class discussion about which they prefer and why.

Have students create poems for other mathematical concepts such as geometric shapes or units of measurement.

Share math-focused poems such as "∞" ["Infinity"] and "Math," both by Amy Ludwig VanDerwater. These poems can be found at *The Poem Farm* website (**www. poemfarm.amylv.com**).

Grades 3–5

Students might enjoy noting the rhyme schemes, meter, and rhythmic patterns of poems. For example, "One Inch Tall" by Shel Silverstein has an AABBBC rhyme scheme. For this poem, the number of syllables in each line is also consistent: 14-14-8-8-9-6. This regularity supports memorization.

Students can create rhymes for multiplication facts and fact strategies as well as other mathematical concepts such as three-dimensional geometric shapes, the rectangular coordinate system, or how to construct or read a graph.

Poems about math for this level include "My Birthday" by Amy Ludwig VanDerwater (**www.poemfarm.amylv. com**) and "Nature Knows Its Math" (**poetryfoundation.org**) by Joan Bransfield Graham.

Grades 6–8

Students can create poems to help them recall mathematics concepts such as the order of operations, working with positive and negative integers, statistical data (mean, median, mode), or the defining properties of geometric figures.

Students at this level will enjoy poems such as "Problem in a Math Book" by Yehuda Amichai (**poetryfoundation.org**) and "Living in Numbers" by Claire Lee (**poets.org**).

Grades 9–12

Students at this level can explore word problems with complex steps by creating poems using found poetry or other poetic strategies. Then invite them to take their mentor poems and freshly written work and perform them through spoken word.

Math poems for this level include "Zero Plus Anything is a World" by Jane Hirshfield, "Calculations" by Brenda Cárdenas, "Applied Geometry" by Russell Libby, and "Pythagorean Silence [excerpt]" by Susan Howe. These can be found at **poets.org** or **poetryfoundation.org**.

> "Metaphors and similes are to poetry what sorrow and hope are to the Blues, what salt and butter are to popcorn—they add the flavor."
>
> —Kwame Alexander (2019, 56)

Sample Mentor Poems

These are examples of poems that support students' automaticity and fact fluency.

Brother

Ten candies wrapped in silver
Waiting just for me
My brother grabs seven
Now there are only three.

Make a Ten

$5 + 7$ needs to be
$5 + 5 + 2$ for me.
Make a ten, and add two more.
Get to twelve, and get out the
    door.

Distribute It

8×3 just needs to be
5×3 and 3×3.
Add the fifteen to the nine.
Twenty-four, and all is fine.

New Books

Went to the library to pick out
    eleven
Exciting new books to read.
Found eight right away.
They were not enough for me,
How many more should I get?
I can subtract or I can add.
$11 - 3 = 8, 8 + 3 = 11$.
Either way is what I say and it
    makes me glad
That I'll have 11 new stories to
    read.
They take me to other times and
    places, it's heaven.

The Doubling Dance

The doubling dance
The doubling dance
Can't leave products up to chance.
2×8 is . . .
16!
Do the doubling dance and find
4×8 is . .
32!
What can doubling do for you?

Sample Mentor Poems *(cont.)*

Poems for Mathematical Wonderings and Findings

These poems model mathematical wonderings and findings.

Shape of the comb,
Hexagon—how?
Working, working, always working,
Miles traveled, sac full, time to head home,
Why so little reward? But so rich . . .

—Elizabeth Melino

Where did you come from?
What size is the hive?
So many bees, so many jobs, so many perfections.
What is your reason?
A week, a month, a year?
Yummy honey,
Where did you go?

—Megan Dodge

Perfect precision
Golden sweetness
Waggle dance
How do you do it?
Beautiful bee

—Kate Lynch

Observing My Mentor Poem

Directions: Use this chart to plan your math poem.

Mentor Poem Strategies	My Notes
Style What do you notice about the style of your mentor poem. Is it free verse? Does it use a particular form or structure?	
Message What does the poet communicate about math?	
Craft How does the poet use craft to help convey this message (line breaks, precise word choices, alliteration, metaphor; images, and so on)?	
Ideas for Your Poem What ideas would you like to use in the creation of your poem?	

Name: ____ Date: _______________

My Math Poem

Directions: Complete each section to brainstorm and write your own math concept poem.

Math Concept
Explain the math idea that you would like to explore through your poem. Include details about the math concepts.

My Craft Ideas
Write ideas for creating rhythm and beat using word choices, line breaks, and possible rhymes.

My Poem
Write your own poem inspired by the mentor poem. Use mathematical content of your choice.

Found Poetry

Model Lesson: Mathematical Word Bowls

Overview

In this strategy, students brainstorm words they associate with mathematical concepts and put the terms together in new ways to create poems that depict mathematical understanding. Students are encouraged to experiment with a variety of ways to juxtapose the words and may add others as needed.

Materials

- reusable containers or shoe boxes
- chart paper
- scissors
- *Poetry Word List* (page 125)
- *Elements of Poetry* (page 105)
- *Poetry Craft Tips* (page 112)
- microphone (*optional*)

Standards

Grades K–2

- Represents and solves problem situations for a given mathematical number sentence involving addition and subtraction of whole numbers
- Links events in a poetic narrative
- Demonstrates understanding of word relationships and rhyme in writing

Grades 3–5

- Represents and solves multistep problems involving the four operations with whole numbers using equations
- Organizes clear and coherent writing appropriate to poetic form
- Demonstrates understanding of language, word relationships, and rhyme in writing

Grades 6–8

- Solves real-world and mathematical problems using numerical and algebraic expressions and equations
- Organizes clear and coherent writing appropriate to poetic form
- Demonstrates understanding of language, word relationships, and rhyme in writing

Grades 9–12

- Understands solving equations as a process of reasoning and explains the reasoning
- Produces clear and coherent writing in which the development, organization, and style are appropriate to task, purpose, and audience
- Demonstrates understanding of figurative language, word relationships, and nuances in word meanings

Found Poetry *(cont.)*

Preparation

At the top of a sheet of chart paper, write mathematical concepts that students are familiar with but about which they need to deepen their understanding. Collect reusable containers or shoe boxes if you wish to have them serve as word bowls. Other suggestions are provided in the Specific Grade-Level Ideas.

Procedure

1. Have students brainstorm all the words they associate with the chosen concept. Record students' words on chart paper. You will be cutting the words apart, so be sure to leave space between words.

2. Cut the chart paper apart so that each word is on a separate slip of paper and place the words in a bowl or other container. Ask students to help you draw several words from the bowl and create a group poem by arranging the selected words. The idea is to put the words together in a variety of ways until they create a clear sense of the idea students are exploring. As appropriate, encourage metaphors, similes, imagery, sensory descriptors, and feeling words.

3. After you have completed an example together, students are ready to prepare for their own poems. Divide the class into groups of two or three. Assign each group a mathematical concept or allow groups to choose their own. Have groups work with the *Poetry Word List*, writing words in the spaces provided to build their own lists.

4. Give each group a word bowl (reusable container or shoe box). Have students cut their words apart and place them into the word bowl.

5. Have groups exchange word bowls, making sure that no team receives its original word bowl. Direct students to take 25 words from the bowl and work together to juxtapose them in different ways until they are satisfied with their poem. Tell groups that the selected words are a starting point to spark ideas, so they can exchange words that don't work in the poem or add words they prefer. They also can create phrases, including metaphors and similes, around the words.

6. Once the poems are complete, have students write out a final copy to share with the class. Students also can add images and numbers to illustrate the ideas.

7. Remind students that some poems are meant to be heard. Allow group members to rehearse reading their poems aloud to bring them to life.

8. Plan a poetry slam where students present their poems to one another. Bring in a microphone and invite other classes to hear the poems.

9. Use the Discussion Questions to debrief the class.

Found Poetry (cont.)

Planning Questions

▸ Reviewing the *Poetry Craft Tips*, what techniques would you like to try?

▸ What materials will you use and why?

▸ What words will you choose and why?

Discussion Questions

▸ Why is it important to describe mathematical ideas in words?

▸ After you brainstormed your ideas, how did you identify the words you selected?

▸ What did you learn through the process of creating your own poem?

▸ What unique or fresh language came out of the exploration of juxtaposing different words and phrases?

▸ What did you learn from listening to the other groups' poems?

Specific Grade-Level Ideas

Grades K–2

Have students work in small groups to brainstorm a small number of words. Write student-generated words on slips of paper to add to the word bowl.

Students also could write their words on objects that can be easily moved around to try out different arrangements. For example, students might write one word per rock, paper cube, or full piece of construction paper.

Poetry themes might include language related to order and spatial terms and terms such as *tens*, *equal*, and *inches*.

Grades 3–5

Invite students to work in small groups, each taking a turn to add, remove, or rearrange a word to form new poems that vary slightly. Have them record all the different variations of poems using the same words in different arrangements.

Possible themes for the poems include fractions, geometric shapes and properties, area, perimeter, and place value.

Grades 6–8

After exploring the task as a whole class and giving each group their assigned concept, students can create their initial list of words using the *Poetry Word List*. Then you can provide time for students to combine their ideas at the end of the week. Have students provide copies of their first drafts as well as their final poems, along with individual reflections on the process. Challenge students to delight in descriptive language. Possible themes include slope, average, intercepts, ratios, and percent.

Grades 9–12

Adapt this activity according to the ideas for grades 6–8. Possible themes include inequality, periodicity, margin of error, and complex numbers. Invite students to generate lists of words based on their understanding of a particular mathematical concept. Have them cut the words apart and place them in a plastic bag. Next, they exchange bags with another student and create a poem using the words. Share the poems with the class in a poetry jam.

Name: _________________________________ Date:_______________

Poetry Word List

Directions: Use the spaces to record and collect words and phrases. Then cut out the words and place them in your word bowl. Play with the arrangement of the words and phrases to create meaning, mood, and rhythm.

Our Collection of Words and Phrases

Structured Poems

Model Lesson: Poems Using Math

Overview

Poems with specific structures or formats can be mathematical adventures in and of themselves. Some poetic formats employ math to create and guide the development of a poem by inviting the writer to use a prescribed sequence of words, types of words, or syllables in each line. In this strategy, students choose from a variety of different formats that involve the use of math to create the poem, such as a cinquain, lune, or Fib.

Materials

- *Types of Structured Poems* (page 130)
- *Word-Count Lune Planner* (page 131)
- *Fib Planner* (page 132)
- *Cinquain Planner* (page 133)
- *Elements of Poetry* (page 105)
- *Poetry Craft Tips* (page 112)

Standards

Grades K–2

- Counts whole numbers
- Recognizes regularity in a variety of patterns
- Writes a poetic narrative
- Demonstrates understanding of word relationships and rhyme in writing

Grades 3–5

- Identifies a wide variety of patterns and the rules that explain them
- Organizes clear and coherent writing appropriate to poetic form
- Demonstrates understanding of language, word relationships, and rhyme in writing

Grades 6–8

- Represents a given situation using verbal descriptions, tables, graphs, and equations
- Organizes clear and coherent writing appropriate to poetic form
- Demonstrates understanding of language, word relationships, and rhyme in writing

Grades 9–12

- Represents a given situation using verbal descriptions, tables, graphs, and equations
- Produces clear and coherent writing in which the development, organization, and style are appropriate to task, purpose, and audience
- Demonstrates understanding of figurative language, word relationships, and nuances in word meanings

Structured Poems *(cont.)*

Preparation

Try writing a poem yourself so you can experience working within the structure. You can use *Types of Structured Poems* to support you as you write. Gather samples of each type of poem to inspire students.

Procedure

1. Display examples of your chosen structured poem or share your own creation. Read the poems to students, have them read along with you, or ask student volunteers to read the poems. Then read the poems to students again, asking listeners to keep their eyes closed and visualize what they hear.

2. Ask, "What do you notice about how these poems bring mathematical ideas to life? What do you learn about each concept? How are these poems alike?" Allow time for students to identify ideas related to the number of lines, the number of words in each line, the types of words in each line, the common mathematical theme, and the shape of the poems.

3. Distribute whichever planner (*Word-Count Lune Planner, Fib Planner,* or *Cinquain Planner*) is most appropriate for your grade level.

4. Choose a mathematical topic as a class and invite students to brainstorm words associated with this topic. You also can refer students to a mathematics word wall, if there's one in your classroom.

5. Once a topic is chosen, brainstorm ideas for the different lines of the poem as a class. Use the Planning Questions to lead the discussion. Encourage students to think of examples of the mathematical concept to include a broad range of ways to think about its relationship to real life.

6. Continue as a class, or have students create a poem in small groups, building on the ideas generated.

7. Have students work individually or in pairs.

Planning Questions

▸ What word will you choose to start your poem?

▸ Close your eyes and think about your word. What do you see? What do you feel? What does this word remind you of? Which words on your list do you like best?

▸ Brainstorm actions that connect to your word. Which action words give new insights about the mathematical ideas?

▸ What memories do you associate with this mathematical term?

> "Pincus came up with Fibs while pondering a haiku writing exercise. A confessed math geek, he sought a form that offered added precision and was intrigued by Fibonacci numbers. In nature, the sequence is evident in the spirals of nautilus shells, waves, pinecones, and sunflower seeds, to name a few."
>
> —Deborah Haar Clark (n.d.)

Structured Poems *(cont.)*

Specific Grade-Level Ideas

Grades K–2

Gather a variety of examples of lunes. Ask students what they notice about how the poems are created. Ask, "How many words are on line one? How many words are on line two? Line three?" Create a lune together as a class using ideas from a shared experience such as caring for a class pet or building with blocks. Invite students to create a lune poem about a topic of their choosing. Discuss how the required number of words on each line impacts their word choices. Ask students "What was the experience of having to choose just one word for line one? How did you decide which word to choose?"

Possible topics include the following:

- **Operations and Algebraic Thinking:** *addition, difference, equal, equation, sum, subtraction*

- **Number and Operations in Base Ten:** *thousand, hundred, ten*

- **Measurement and Data:** *length, time, ruler, clock, hour, inch, foot, centimeter, meter, minute, graph*

- **Geometry:** *circle, cone, cube, cylinder, hexagon, quadrilateral, rectangle, sphere, square, trapezoid, triangle*

Grades 3–5

Invite students to try the format of a cinquain and then ask them what a decaquain would be (10 lines) and how many total words it would have.

Possible mathematical topics:

- **Operations and Algebraic Thinking:** *array, division, estimation, multiplication, product, equation, quotient, remainder, unknown*

- **Number and Operations in Base Ten:** *digit, million, billion, trillion, decimal, tenths, hundredths, thousandths*

- **Number and Operations—Fractions:** *numerator, denominator, whole*

- **Measurement and Data:** *area, volume, perimeter, degree, kilometer, gram, kilogram, pound, ounce, mass, mile, second, volume, protractor*

- **Geometry:** any name of a shape as well as *angle, endpoint, origin, pentagon, parallel, perpendicular, polygon, point, ray, rhombus, symmetry*

Structured Poems

Specific Grade-Level Ideas *(cont.)*

Grades 6–8

In the development of a cinquain consider challenging students with these questions:

- How many syllables would there be if this were an eight-line structure?

- How many lines would there be if there were a total of 112 words?

- Can you write an equation to predict the number of syllables if you know the number of lines?

Students may also wish to create Fib poems.

Possible mathematical topics:

- **Ratios and Proportional Thinking:** *unit, rate, ratio, percent, proportionality*

- **Expressions and Equations:** *coefficient, equivalent, exponent, inequality, intercept, integer, linear, slope, variable*

- **Geometry:** any name of a shape as well as *circumference, congruence, diameter, dilation, face, edge, net, prism, radius, reflection, rotation, surface area, translation*

- **Expressions and Equations:** *coefficient, equivalent, exponent, inequality, intercept, integer, linear, slope, variable*

Grades 9–12

Students can use the same suggestions as those provided for grades 6–8, or they could try the format of a Fib, using the structure of Fibonacci numbers.

Possible mathematical topics:

- **Statistics and Probability:** *center, chance, distribution, frequency, mean, median, sample, variability, histogram*

- **Geometry:** any name of a shape as well as *circumference, congruence, diameter, dilation, face, edge, net, prism, radius, reflection, rotation, surface area, translation, tangent, arc, angles, chords*

Types of Structured Poems

Lune

"To make a lune, write three words in the first line, five in the second, three in the third, and you're done. In counting words rather than syllables, the lune is more flexible than its ancestor, the haiku. Also, lunes have no necessary association with nature or season or even images. It's just eleven words arranged 3/5/3; anything goes" (Collom and Noethe 2005, 122).

Line 1: Three words

Line 2: Five words

Line 3: Three words

Fib

A six-line poem that follows the Fibonacci sequence for syllable count per line:

Line 1: One syllable

Line 2: One syllable

Line 3: Two syllables

Line 4: Three syllables

Line 5: Five syllables

Line 6: Eight syllables

Cinquain

A short poem consisting of five lines (usually unrhymed).

Option 1:

Line 1: One word—title, noun

Line 2: Two words—adjectives, description, or examples

Line 3: Three words—action words (-ing words) or further description

Line 4: Four words—feelings or further description

Line 5: One word—synonym of first word or related word

Option 2:

Line 1: Two syllables

Line 2: Four syllables

Line 3: Six syllables

Line 4: Eight syllables

Line 5: Two syllables

Name: ____ Date: _________________

Word-Count Lune Planner

Directions: Collect words and use this planner to create a meaningful lune.

Mathematical idea for my poem:

____

____

____

Words that describe this idea:

____

____

____

____

My poem:

Title: ____

Three words:

________________________ ________________________ ________________________

Five words:

____________ ____________ ____________ ____________ ____________

Three words:

________________________ ________________________ ________________________

Name: ____ Date: _________________

Fib Planner

Directions: Collect words and use this planner to create a meaningful Fib poem.

Mathematical idea for my poem:

____

____

____

Words and phrases that describe this idea:

____

____

____

My poem:

Title: ____

1 syllable: _______________________________________

1 syllable: _______________________________________

2 syllables: ______________________________________

3 syllables: ______________________________________

5 syllables: ______________________________________

8 syllables: ______________________________________

Cinquain Planner

Directions: Collect words and use this planner to create a meaningful cinquain poem.

Mathematical idea for my poem:

____

____

____

Words and phrases that describe this idea:

____

____

____

____

My poem:

1 word or 2 syllables: _______________________________

2 words or 4 syllables: _______________________________

3 words or 6 syllables: _______________________________

4 words or 8 syllables: _______________________________

1 word or 2 syllables: _______________________________

"I Am From" Poems

Model Lesson: Where I'm from Mathematically

Overview

"I Am From" poems were developed by teacher and writer George Ella Lyon (2010) and suggest a simple writing prompt for exploring personal histories. An adapted format is used here for exploring mathematical bio poems. Students begin each line with the phrase *I am from* and then introduce specific details of their mathematical histories. The reflective process provides students with the opportunity to find connections among their past experiences, note how they solve problems and learn best, and perhaps recognize biases they may bring to the learning of mathematics.

Materials

- *"Where I'm from Mathematically" Examples* (pages 138–139)
- *"Where I'm from Mathematically" Planner* (page 140)
- *Elements of Poetry* (page 105)
- *Poetry Craft Tips* (page 112)
- *Tips for Performing Poetry* (page 113)

Standards

Grades K–2

- Displays, explains, and justifies mathematical ideas and arguments using precise mathematical language in written or oral communication
- Links events in a poetic narrative
- Demonstrates understanding of word relationships and rhyme in writing

Grades 3–5

- Displays, explains, and justifies mathematical ideas and arguments using precise mathematical language in written or oral communication
- Organizes clear and coherent writing appropriate to poetic form
- Demonstrates understanding of language, word relationships, and rhyme in writing

Grades 6–8

- Displays, explains and justifies mathematical ideas and arguments using precise mathematical language in written or oral communication
- Organizes clear and coherent writing appropriate to poetic form
- Demonstrates understanding of language, word relationships, and rhyme in writing

Grades 9–12

- Displays, explains, and justifies mathematical ideas and arguments using precise mathematical language in written or oral communication
- Produces clear and coherent writing appropriate to the task, purpose, and audience
- Demonstrates understanding of figurative language, word relationships, and nuances in word meanings

"I Am From" Poems *(cont.)*

Preparation

Read the *"Where I'm from Mathematically" Examples* to become familiar with how the format can be used to write a mathematical autobiography or math bio-poem. You may wish to write a "Where I'm from Mathematically" poem yourself to share with students. Additional suggestions are provided in the Specific Grade Level Ideas.

> "Poetry personalizes information."
>
> —Georgia Heard
> (as cited in Borris 2016, para. 12)

Procedure

1. Introduce the notion that we all have diverse backgrounds, traditions, and experiences of being "from" someplace. Have students tell how they would respond to someone who asks casually, "Where are you from?" Then have them discuss what would be different if a good friend asked, "So, how did you get to be you?"

2. Explain to students that they're going to think and write about their mathematical biography or their life story as it relates to math. Read aloud the "I Am From" poems provided in *"Where I'm from Mathematically" Examples* and have students discuss the ways in which the writers described their mathematical experiences.

3. Distribute the *"Where I'm from Mathematically" Planner* and have students discuss the various categories and some possible responses. For example, they might think about their family members' or parents' attitudes toward math, interests in math, or expectations for learning math. They may need to interview a family member to inform their responses. You may wish to review the poems you read in relation to this graphic organizer. Use the Planning Questions to facilitate discussion.

4. After this overview, allow time for students to reflect and record words, phrases, or sentences about their mathematical memories.

5. Have students use their brainstormed words and phrases to create their own "Where I'm from Mathematically" poems. Make sure students understand that they don't have to include all the topics or all the words they brainstormed.

6. Provide time for students to revise, edit, or critique their poems in pairs. If this is to take place on the following day, encourage students to talk with their families or caregivers about this topic before returning to school. For example, younger students may enjoy learning about how they used to always count when they went up or down stairs. Older students may wish to learn about their family's mathematical experiences.

7. Have students practice presenting their poems orally, providing them with opportunities to rehearse reading a few times through or with a peer. Use the *Tips for Performing Poetry* as a resource to support students as they practice.

8. Have students share and discuss their poems. Use the Discussion Questions to lead a discussion about the poems.

"I Am From" Poems *(cont.)*

Planning Questions

▸ What can you tell us about mathematical moment(s) in your life?

▸ What are some other words that would help us understand how you felt about math as you were growing up?

▸ Was there a teacher who influenced you mathematically? If so, how?

▸ Are there stories in your life that relate to math?

▸ Can you include descriptions of mathematical moments in your life that make us feel as if we are there?

▸ Are there poetic devices you can use (repetition, metaphor, alliteration)?

Discussion Questions

▸ What did you learn about your relationship with math?

▸ What are some ways our poems are different? The same?

▸ What do our poems suggest about how we think about mathematics?

▸ What are some words or phrases that helped us understand another person's experiences?

▸ What might cause your poem to change significantly at the end of the year?

"I Am From" Poems *(cont.)*

Specific Grade-Level Ideas

Grades K–2

Students are likely focusing on learning to count. Encourage them to recognize building with blocks and identifying patterns as relevant mathematical experiences.

Create a class poem titled "We Are from Math" in which each student contributes a line for the poem. Repeat the line "We are from math" every few lines to add rhythm and a beat.

Grades 3–5

Students can interview one another to complete the *"Where I'm from Mathematically"* Planner. They can imagine they are reporters trying to get the real story about their classmates' mathematical lives. Memories of learning basic facts may be prominent at this age.

Grades 6–8

Encourage students to explore the thinking of several members of their family through math interviews. Students also might interview local community members to find out about the role of math in their lives. Have them write interview questions to prepare.

Students can take on the persona of a mathematical concept and write an "I Am From" poem from that perspective (for example, "I am from a coordinate plane . . .").

Grades 9–12

In addition to the ideas for grades 6–8, students can write "I Am From" poems from the perspective of a present-day or historical mathematician, exploring their childhood, early life, and adulthood in relation to math experiences and inspiration.

"Where I'm from Mathematically" Examples

I am from the candy counter
At Katie's country store
A wooden case displaying sweets of every kind
candy necklaces on a string
chunky caramels in twisted wax paper
rock candy on a stick
I am from pressing my face against the glass
To see the collection, pink, red, orange
Hard yellow candies dressed in sparkling sugar and chocolates
calling my name
I am from quick calculations
Three Swedish fish for a nickel, two pops for a quarter
Fifty percent off gummies today
Makes my head spin as I figure
How far will my dollar go
My mouth waters as I hold my paper bag
My mom calls me sugar tooth
But I also love to share with my 3 best friends

I am from a father who says,
"I don't do math" and a mother who loves to solve jigsaw puzzles with a
    thousand pieces.
She says, "Try again and again until you find a fit."
I am from playing mystery, card, and strategy games.
The suspect is in the dining room with a rope and give me all your twos.
I am from "Solve this problem" and "Tell how you know."
I am from friends who think math is not hot.
I tell them they're wrong and that I'll be rich someday.
I am from solving problems by writing equations and making drawings.
I am from using manipulatives and working in groups.
Pattern blocks, tangrams and geo boards.
I am from feeling proud when I solve a problem that is as hard as stone.

"Where I'm from Mathematically" Examples *(cont.)*

I am from my father who hiked the Appalachian Trail
Georgia to Maine
15-20 miles a day
2,190 in total
We mailed supplies to fill his backpack
Weighing peanut butter tubes and boxes of mac and cheese
Calculating how heavy his pack would be to carry

I am from a mother who manages grants
Bringing ideas into action
She predicts the costs then moves money around to make things balance
Noting important insights in pencil along her columns

I am from working at the supermarket
Making change
Helping customers with mental math
as I help fill carts

I am from learning to sail
counting how fast we go in knots
Watching the wind speed
on an app on my phone
predicting when the wind will
Be just right for my level of skill

Name: _________________________________ Date: _______________

"Where I'm from Mathematically" Planner

Directions: Fill in the boxes to brainstorm ideas for a "Where I'm from Mathematically" poem. Then, on a separate sheet of paper, write your poem, beginning each line with "I am from . . ."

My family and math:	What I do in my free time and math:
Words or quotes I've heard about math:	My friends and math:
How I solve math problems:	How I learn math best:

Music

Music

Understanding Music

Music has played a significant role in every culture since the beginning of time. Now with recent technology, our favorite tunes are readily available, and music has become even more prevalent in our lives. Dr. Howard Gardner (2011) has identified musical intelligence as one form of intelligence. His theory of multiple intelligence suggests that students learn in different ways, and for some students, connecting with rhythm, beat, and melody provides access to learning. And as any adult who has introduced a cleanup song knows, music can motivate children and help them make transitions from one activity to another. Recently, attention has been given to the benefits of music in academic performance. It has been suggested that early music training develops language skills, spatial relations, and memory (Perret and Fox 2006).

Music and mathematics have long been linked. After all, it was the famous mathematician Pythagoras who first noted that the pitch of a string was directly related to its length. "Mathematics is also universal, crosses cultural, historical, and intellectual boundaries, and is reflected in music. The interconnectedness of math and music pulsates with a rhythm and harmony of its own" (Garland and Kahn 1995).

In the following strategies, students explore mathematical ideas alongside the basic elements of music. Students engage in singing, playing, and composing music as well as using everyday objects as nontraditional instruments. The focus is on deepening mathematical knowledge while experiencing the joy of creating music together in ways that all students can participate. Along the way, students develop a deeper understanding of and skills in creating music. No previous musical training is needed for you or students.

Exploring mathematical ideas through music engages and motivates students. As they identify, apply, and generalize ideas to real-world situations, mathematics becomes meaningful and purposeful. Abstract ideas are connected to concrete models, and students' representational fluency deepens. The more avenues we provide for students to experience mathematics, the more likely we are to connect with the variable ways in which they learn.

> "Every musical experience that we offer our students affects their brains, bodies and feelings. In short, it changes their minds permanently."
>
> —Claudia Cornett (2007, 463)

Elements of Music

The most basic accepted definition of *music* is "organized/intentional sound and silence."

According to Jacobsen (1992) and Estrella (2019), the basic elements of music from a Western perspective include the following:

- **Pitch:** Highness and lowness on a musical scale

- **Harmony:** Notes of different pitches played at the same time

- **Melody:** How notes are put together in a sequence

- **Dynamics:** Loudness and quietness of composition (musical piece) and transitions between the two

- **Rhythm:** How time is controlled in music (beat, meter, tempo)

- **Timbre/tone color:** The sound quality of a note

- **Texture:** The number of layers in a composition (musical piece)

Music *(cont.)*

Strategies for Music

Experimentation

The sound of musical instruments changes depending on different variables. In this strategy, students experiment with a variety of variables that affect the quality of sound in a rain stick (material, angle of rain stick, length of the tube, number of nails or placement of foil, and so on).

Experimentation is essential to problem solving. It involves students identifying variables, making predictions, collecting and analyzing data, drawing conclusions, and communicating results. A post on classroom experiments from the Science Education Resource Center (2018) states, "If the result of an experiment is surprising yet convincing, students are in position to build ownership of the new idea and use it to scaffold learning" (para. 1). As a result, this active approach to learning allows students to revise their thinking and deepen their conceptual understanding.

Songwriting

When students sing, a deep connection is created with the melody, rhythm, and lyrics of the song. Further, creating and making music supports academic achievement (Deasy 2002). Although students have opportunities to sing in school, far less attention is given to their ability to create their own songs. This strategy invites students to become songwriters, and as they do, become more familiar with the importance of tone, rhythm, and beat. Students can begin on an intuitive level or simplify the task, for example, by creating new lyrics for a song they already know. As songs can help us remember things, these adaptations can help students retain important mathematical information. Also, writing lyrics prompts students to discuss, synthesize, and categorize curricular concepts. Students can explore rhythms on a drum or experiment with notes on a keyboard. As their musical knowledge expands, they can create original melodies as well as score their compositions.

Scoring

When music is composed, it needs to be scored so that others can perform it. Scoring is the communication of the sounds that are to be made and the timing of those sounds. Scoring music can be done in nontraditional ways so that all learners are able to participate; for example, students can record a word in writing, such as *clap*, or draw a hand to indicate when such a sound is to be made. Such scoring techniques encourage students to construct the symbols and their meanings. Traditional scoring also can be considered, allowing students to experiment with the common language of musicians. "Musical elements such as steady beat, rhythm, tempo, volume, melody, and harmony possess inherent mathematical concepts such as spatial properties, sequencing, counting, patterning, and one-to-one correspondence" (Geist and Geist 2008).

Call-and-Response

Used for centuries around the world, call-and-response is a musical pattern of phrases exchanged between musicians. There is a conversational pattern with the second musician (the "response") responding to the first musician (the "call"). This pattern has rich cultural roots in African, African American, Indian classical, and Cuban traditions, among others. In the United States, such songs are most familiar as sea chanteys and maritime work songs.

The cadences and rhythmic patterns involve learners and support memory. This strategy supports full participation as students pose and answer questions in an engaging way to review information, reinforce skills, and expand ideas (Plessinger 2012).

Music *(cont.)*

Chants

Chants involve the rhythmic repetition of sounds or words. They can be sung or spoken. They can be a component of spiritual practices or heard on a football field. By combining different dynamics (ranging from soft to loud), pitch (variations from high to low), and different notes (length of duration), students can create engaging sound effects that help them learn and remember ideas. According to Sonja Dunn (1999), "A chant is a rhythmic group recitation" (para. 7). Chants can be used in a variety of ways. They can be created with catchy rhythms that make the associated words easy to learn and remember. When this form of chant is emphasized, students retain important mathematical information. Chants also can be constructed by layering phrases on top of another that are then spoken or sung simultaneously. In this format, the use of differing rhythms and pitch creates interest and suggests relationships among the chosen phrases and thus the content being considered.

Experimentation

Model Lesson: Rain Sticks

Overview

In this lesson, students create their own musical instrument of a rain stick. By creating rain sticks, students experiment with the qualities of sound, including variations in volume, timbre, and duration; they also use mathematical skills such as estimation, prediction, measurement, and the recording of data.

Materials

- measuring tools (measuring tape, stopwatch, measuring cups or large jars, scale)
- *Directions for Making a Rain Stick* (page 150)
- items from materials list of *Directions for Making a Rain Stick* (page 150)
- *Experiment Log* (page 151)
- *Elements of Music* (page 143)
- centimeter graph paper (*optional*)
- small bowl

Standards

Grades K–2

- Understands the basic measures of length, width, height, weight, and quantity
- Makes quantitative estimates of familiar linear dimensions, weights, volume, and time intervals and checks them against measurements
- Plays with a variety of musical instruments

Grades 3–5

- Selects and uses appropriate units of measurement, according to type and size of unit
- Uses specific strategies to estimate quantities and measurements
- Performs simple patterns on percussion instruments

Grades 6–8

- Understands the relationships among linear dimensions, area, and volume and the corresponding uses of units, square units, and cubic units of measure
- Selects and uses appropriate estimation techniques to solve real-world problems
- Performs a varied repertoire of music on instruments, alone and with others
- Understands the relationships among music and history and culture

Grades 9–12

- Makes inferences and justifies conclusions from sample surveys, experiments, and observational studies
- Explains volume formulas and uses them to solve problems
- Translates between the geometric description and the equation for a conic section
- Understands the relationships among music and history and culture

Experimentation *(cont.)*

Preparation

Read the *Directions for Making a Rain Stick* and make one as a model. Choose materials that best fit your access and grade-level goals. You can find additional suggestions in the Suggested Grade-Level Ideas.

> "It doesn't matter if it's a flute or a piano or a guitar, all musical instruments work because of one simple scientific principle; they vibrate. . . . That buzzing sound you feel in your fingers are the vibrations in your vocal cords. The faster the vibrations, the higher the pitch of the sound."
>
> —Steve Tomecek (n.d.)

Procedure

1. Begin by asking students what they already know about rain sticks. Share that traditional rain sticks are made from hollowed cactus stalks. The thorns of the cactus are removed and then pushed inward into the stalk. The cactus dries into a hard shell. Pebbles, small gravel, sand, or grit is placed inside the stalk and a piece of cactus is used to close off each end. When tipped vertically, the pebbles striking the thorns sound like rain. Hollow bamboo reeds also might be used. Discuss the ways natural resources are used to make traditional rain sticks and consider why there might be interest in creating the sound of rain.

2. Tell students that they are going to create a rain stick and explore and experiment with the relationship between the amount and types of materials used and the sound produced.

3. Demonstrate the rain stick you made and invite students to listen to the sound as you turn it vertically. Begin by asking students questions: "What's in it? What makes the sound go slowly/quickly?" Have students estimate the amount of time the "rain" lasts and then check their predictions with a timer.

4. After students predict what's inside the rain stick, open one end and empty the filling into a bowl. Have students peer inside of the stick and note the configuration of the nails. Ask, "What role do the nails play? Does the number of nails or the placement of the nails affect the duration of sound? What is the function of the nails? Does the type of filling or amount affect the sound?"

5. After investigating the filling, ask: "How much filling do you estimate is there? How can you test your guess?" Distribute the *Experiment Log* and have students complete the first two columns in the first row. Ask, "Do you think it affects the volume or duration of the sound if only one type of material is used or a mix of materials?" Show students the materials available to them and give them a copy of *Directions for Making a Rain Stick*.

6. Have students begin to make their own rain sticks. Encourage them to make individual decisions about how many nails to put in their rain stick and in what manner (spiral, random, and so on). Have measuring tools available as students experiment with different materials. (You also can have the class work together to make one rain stick, encouraging group input as to the number of nails used, amount and types of filling, and so on.)

7. As students continue to work, divide them into pairs or groups of three to complete the *Experiment Log*. They can listen to each other's rain stick and compare notes and then think of questions to test out. Be sure to have students count the number of nails they used so they can also investigate whether the number of nails used affects the volume or duration of sound.

Experimentation *(cont.)*

8. Use the Discussion Questions to engage students in a conversation about their discoveries.

9. Finally, provide time for students to decorate their rain sticks and share the sounds their rain sticks make. Rain sticks can be covered with a variety of materials: dye-fast tissue paper, newsprint, magazine images, images from the comics, and so on. Covering the paper with Mod Podge makes it more durable.

Planning Questions

‣ What materials do you plan to use and why?

‣ What kinds of math skills do you anticipate using and why?

‣ What might you change about your rain stick to make different sounds? What predictions can you make about what will happen based on your change? What measurements will you make to check your predictions?

‣ How might the results of one experiment help you decide on another change to investigate?

‣ What could you learn from listening to and comparing two rain sticks?

‣ As you experiment, how will you keep track of the changes you make and their outcomes?

Discussion Questions

‣ What strategies did you use to make predictions?

‣ What conclusions did you make about time (velocity, sound, number of nails)?

‣ How would you describe the sounds you like? How did your choices in making the rain stick influence the quality of the sound? (e.g., volume of material, angle of the rain stick)

‣ How might you alter your rain stick design to change the sound or change the duration of the sound?

Experimentation *(cont.)*

Specific Grade-Level Ideas

Grades K–2

Have students use informal units of measure. For example, to evenly place the nails along the spiral, students can place two fingers between one nail and the next. Students can measure time by finding out how high they can count while the sound is made or watch a second hand on a clock or use a stopwatch. Have on hand a variety of measuring cups for predicting the amount of filling.

Grades 3–5

Encourage students to ask questions, be curious, and experiment. For example: "What happens if I put my nails in randomly instead of a spiral? What happens if I use 25 nails? 50 nails? What happens if I use only one type of filling? Or mix types of fillings?" It is fine for students to dump out the filling and change it as part of the experiment. Provide measuring cups, a scale, and a timer to assist in answering questions.

Grades 6–8

Students can focus on the ratio of the amount of the filling to the volume of the tube. They can measure the amount of the filling by using measuring cups or placing the filling on graph paper and estimating the area it covers. They also can make graphs that summarize relationships between two variables, for example, length

Grades 6–8 *(cont.)*

of the tube and time the sound lasts. They can explore volume, density of materials, or angles (does tilting the rain stick at a 45-degree angle versus a 90-degree angle change the velocity? Discuss the validity of their experimentation. If timing the rain stick, for instance, is it important to time it at least three times and average the times to get a more accurate answer?

Students can search the internet to find the various beliefs about the origin and uses of rain sticks. Research indicates rain sticks have been used as a ritual to bring rain, a musical instrument, and a toy.

Grades 9–12

Encourage students to explore relationships among the variables they are considering and complete statements such as *As the volume of the filling decreases . . .*

Have students attempt to estimate relationships among the data and estimate margins of error.

Students can measure conic sections of the container. Have them record justifications for their conclusions.

Students at this level also can search the internet to learn about the various beliefs about the origin and uses of rain sticks.

Directions for Making a Rain Stick

Materials

- 12" or 24" length x 2" diameter cardboard mailing tube or other heavy tube (ideally with covers for the ends)

- #6 common nails (need to have a head on them—don't use finish nails)

- masking tape or clear packing tape (2" wide)

- beads, pebbles, or other non-food materials (Although you can use a variety of grains in your rain stick, we recommend non-food materials due to the prevalence of food insecurity in communities.)

- hammers or stones

- contact paper (*optional*)

- dye-fast tissue paper (*optional*)

- Mod Podge or Elmer's Glue diluted with water (*optional*)

- cups

- foam brushes

Directions

1. Gently hammer the nails about 1/2 inch apart all the way around the tube. You can follow the spiral line on the tube or randomly decide where to put them. Feel free to experiment with this and discover different sounds. Ask yourself the following questions: "What happens if I use fewer nails? What happens if I spread the nails way apart? Or close together?" **Note:** The closer the nails are together, the richer and longer-lasting the sound will be. The size of the tube can vary, but the nails must not be longer than the diameter of the tube.

2. Use masking or clear tape to cover all the nails. This creates a smooth surface and assures that the nails stay in place and don't fall out. This is important because the nails loosen when the rain stick is shaken.

3. Fill the rain stick on one end with the filling of your choice. Use approximately 2 cups of filling for a 2" x 24" rain stick. However, you want to experiment with the sound. Notice the volume, size, and weight of the material will affect the sound.

4. Decorate the entire rain stick, if desired, with contact paper, newsprint, tissue paper, or paint.

Tips

If hammering is too difficult, you can use a rock to tap in the nails. You also can tightly roll up aluminum foil and put it inside the rain stick to avoid hammering altogether.

You can create rain sticks with paper towel tubes and toothpicks, although they are not very sturdy. The firmer the tube, the better the sound quality. Fish gravel, small pebbles, seeds, and other natural objects can be substituted for food items. Avoid using items that will crumple or fall apart (for example, cereal) or that are too large (for example, buttons) and might jam.

Name: _______________________________________ Date: _________________

Experiment Log

Directions: Complete the table with information about your experiment.

Idea to Test	Prediction	Findings	Conclusion

Songwriting

Model Lesson: Adaptation

Overview

Students express mathematical knowledge by writing new lyrics to familiar songs. The result is sometimes called a *piggyback song* as it is built or rides on a song that already exists. Adapted songs can be simple (one verse) or involve several verses separated by a repeating chorus. In such cases, the chorus can represent central ideas worth repeating, and the verses can be constructed to expand ideas, consider different examples, or suggest a sequence. In this strategy, students explore an adapted song and then create their own.

Materials

- *Song Exemplars* (pages 157–158)
- *Lyric Brainstorming Guide* (page 159)
- *Chorus and Verses* (page 160)
- *Elements of Music* (page 143)

Standards

Grades K–2

- Represents and compares whole-number relationships
- Demonstrates how a specific music concept (melody) is used for a specific purpose
- Demonstrates and explains reasons for personal choices of musical ideas

Grades 3–5

- Understands the correct order of operations for performing arithmetic computations
- Demonstrates and explains how responses to music are informed by the structure and elements of music like melody
- Describes the connection between personally created music and expressive intent

Grades 6–8

- Represents a situation using verbal descriptions, tables, graphs, and equations
- Demonstrates and explains how responses to music are informed by the structure and elements of music, such as melody

Grades 9–12

- Interprets functions that arise in applications in terms of the context
- Demonstrates and explains how responses to music are informed by the structure and elements of music, such as melody

Songwriting *(cont.)*

Preparation

Decide how you will group students as they plan for their song adaptations. Identify the mathematical theme of the song on which you would like the groups to focus. Refer to the *Song Exemplar* for your grade level to familiarize yourself with these models. Consider having a rhyming dictionary handy for students to consult, if appropriate. Additional suggestions are provided in the Specific Grade-Level Ideas.

Procedure

1. Tell students they are going to adapt a song to incorporate the facts and ideas they have learned. Sing or have students sing the *Song Exemplar* for your grade level as a model.

2. Distribute the *Lyric Brainstorming Guide*. As a class, brainstorm key ideas and descriptive phrases or instructions that students may like to include in their lyrics related to the content you have selected. Have students record this information using the *Lyric Brainstorming Guide*.

3. Have students go back through the list and regroup their ideas into categories, recording their thinking on the *Lyric Brainstorming Guide*. This categorization can help organize the lyrics. During this process, encourage students to decide which lyrics are most relevant and which may be too tangential to include.

4. Ask students to brainstorm familiar songs that might be used for the melody. These can include childhood songs, holiday songs, songs they have heard on the radio or online, or advertising jingles. Brainstorm songs that everyone in the class knows, keeping in mind students who may have different traditions and consequently may not be as familiar with some of the songs. You might learn or review a common melody with the whole class such as "If You're Happy and You Know It Clap Your Hands," "This Land Is Your Land," or "Itsy Bitsy Spider." The songs will take on new meaning once the words have been changed.

5. Focus on some of the key terms and brainstorm rhyming words, having students record them on the *Lyric Brainstorming Guide*. However, remind students that not all lines have to rhyme and that sometimes it is repeated words and rhythm that make a song work.

6. Introduce the terms *chorus* and *verse*. Ask students to think about the structure of the song "Old MacDonald Had a Farm." Explain that the lines about the different animals are verses and the repeated phrase "Old MacDonald had a farm, E-I-E-I-O" is the chorus. Ask students to identify what core idea(s) might be included in a chorus so that it is repeated throughout the song.

7. Have the class try a few different melodies until they find one that fits the content in both mood and rhythm of the words. Choose a few lines from the *Lyric Brainstorming Guide* that might work and try them with each melody to identify the right fit. Encourage students to use the same structure that the song uses in terms of rhythm and number of syllables. In some cases, they might elongate a syllable or adjust their singing of syllables to make the rhythm work.

8. At this point, students can work in small groups to complete their adaptation. If they are including a chorus and two verses in their adaptation, distribute *Chorus and Verses* and have them complete it. They can then refer to it as they sing their song. As students work, use the Planning Questions to support their thinking.

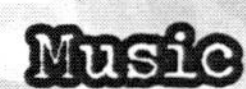

Songwriting *(cont.)*

9. Provide time for groups to share and discuss their songs. Debrief, using the Discussion Questions.

> "Teachers harness the mnemonic power of music by teaching students how to put curricular information into songs, raps, and chants. Learning how to write original songs that transform content information builds student confidence and grows creative thinking."
>
> —Claudia Cornett (2007)

Planning Questions

- What melody will you work with?

- Are there mathematical ideas that you could include?

- When might you use this math in a real-world situation?

- Does it make sense to keep some of the lines from the original song?

- Have you checked to make sure your new lyrics match the structure of the original song?

- Is there a word you could add (or take away) to make the rhythm work better?

Discussion Questions

- How did you decide which mathematical idea to focus on?

- How did you decide on the song you would "piggy back?"

- What artistic choices did you make in writing the lyrics?

- What did you learn about songwriting?

- What was easiest/most challenging about writing your song?

- What did you learn from listening to the songs your classmates wrote?

Songwriting *(cont.)*

Specific Grade-Level Ideas

Grades K–2

As a class, brainstorm ideas to create lyrics and adapt a song that students know well. Work with students to learn the song and sing it together. Topics may include counting songs, shapes, or addition and subtraction. Share the Grades K–2 *Song Exemplar* with students as a model. Students can use their hands to demonstrate the changes in number as they sing, and the song can continue to higher place values with the trading theme of the song.

Grades 3–5

Have students create a song to help them remember rules such as the order of operations. Such a song may only contain one verse and a chorus. Note that students often use a mnemonic device to remember this order, such as **P**lease **E**xcuse **M**y **D**ear **A**unt **S**ally (**p**arentheses, **e**xponents, **m**ultiply and **d**ivide, **a**dd, and **s**ubtract). Unfortunately, the result is that they may conclude incorrectly. For example, they may think that they must multiply before they divide and add before they subtract. Consider the adaptation of "Jingle Bells" in the Grades 3–5 *Song Exemplar.* It emphasizes the left-to-right component of the convention; for example, you add or subtract in the order the operations occur from left to right. You can teach students this song as a way to remind them of this important fact. Then, students can create other songs for vocabulary or procedures they need to remember. When students help write the song, they synthesize and express their knowledge through the creation of lyrics.

Students also can explore conceptual ideas. For example, students can create an adaptation that focuses on what to do with remainders, something that many students find challenging. Students can begin with a stanza that provides an example of when the remainder can be divided into fractional parts. Students can then create other verses that describe a situation in which remainders are omitted or one in which they are rounded up to the next whole number. Remind students that they can create a chorus to sing after each verse.

Songwriting *(cont.)*

Specific Grade-Level Ideas *(cont.)*

Grades 6–8

Students can explore ideas for lyrics and song melodies to be used. They can find and download popular songs and lyrics from the internet. Listening to them and seeing the words may help them replace the words and identify the patterns of the rhythm.

For the Grades 6–8 *Song Exemplar,* have students use gestures to indicate the directions of the slope as uphill (from left to right), downhill (from right to left), horizontal, or vertical.

Grades 9–12

Invite students to focus on a variety of functions such as trigonometric, direct, inverse, and exponential. Have students explain the functions as well as their applications in the real world. At this level, you also can invite students to create harmonies for their songs.

Song Exemplars

Grades K–2

Sung to "She'll Be Coming 'Round the Mountain"

She'll be trading her 10 ones when she has 'em
She'll be trading her 10 ones when she has 'em
She'll be trading her 10 ones
She'll be trading her 10 ones
She'll be trading her 10 ones for 1 ten

Grades 3–5

Sung to "Jingle Bells" (Starting with *Dashing through the snow...*)

We must all agree
On the order to compute
Otherwise you see
We might pay too much loot
Follow the same rule
Working left to right
What fun it is to use this tool
An equation done just right

Chorus

Oh, left to right, left to right
Whatever you first see
Powers and parentheses
In the order that they be
Left to right, left to right
Multiply, divide
Left to right, add, subtract
We do it all in stride.

Song Exemplars *(cont.)*

Grades 6–8

Sung to "Three Blind Mice"

(Chorus)
Rise over run
Rise over run
What is the slope?
What is the slope?

(Verse 1)
With negative slope
It goes downhill
Like a bank account
After paying bills
Take the change in y
Over the change in x
To find the slope

(Verse 2)
With positive slope
It goes uphill
Like the water's height
In a glass you fill
Take the change in y
Over the change in x
To find the slope

(Verse 3)
Horizontal lines
Have a zero slope
With vertical lines
Its undefined slope
Take the change in y
Over the change in x
To find the slope

Grades 9–12

Pythagorean Theorem
(sung to "London Bridge is Falling Down")

Pythagoras found a helpful rule,
Helpful rule, helpful rule
Relationship among the sides
Of right triangles.

Off three sides you make a square,
Make a square, make a square
Hypotenuse square tells the sum
That's all you need.

Square of A plus square of B,
Square of A, square of B
These together give you square of C
Missing lengths discovered.

Algebra and your fine mind,
Your fine mind, your fine mind
Gets the answer every time
Pythagorean theorem.

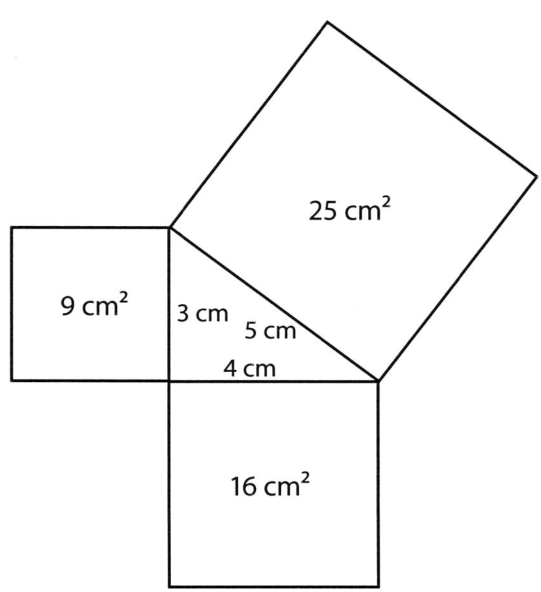

Name: ______________________________________ Date:__________________

Lyric Brainstorming Guide

Directions: Use the chart to help you plan your song lyrics.

Math Concept:	
Key Ideas to Include:	**Descriptive Phrases to Include:**
Categories:	**Potential Rhymes (optional):**

Name: _________________________________ Date: _______________

Chorus and Verses

Directions: Use the chart to help plan your song structure.

Title of Song

Chorus

Verse 1

Verse 2

Scoring

Model Lesson: Clock Music

Overview

In this strategy, students work together to identify a variety of sounds, such as tapping a pencil on a desk and rubbing their feet on the floor, and then play the sounds at particular intervals within a one-minute time limit. Students must create a score to remember the choices they make about the sounds they will use and when the sounds will occur during the minute interval. The mathematical emphasis is on counting, the second hand on a clock, multiplication and division, and fractions.

Materials

- large analog clock with a second hand
- *Individual Musical Score* (page 165)
- *Elements of Music* (page 143)

Standards

Grades K–2

- Measures and estimates lengths in standard units
- Demonstrates and explains reasons for personal choices of musical ideas
- Presents a final version of personal musical ideas

Grades 3–5

- Compares and orders rational numbers
- Explains selected and organized musical ideas
- Describes connection of personally created music to expressive intent

Grades 6–8

- Understands the relationships among equivalent number representations and the advantages and disadvantages of each type of representation
- Explains how knowledge relates to personal choices and intent when creating and performing music
- Demonstrates the relationship between music and another discipline

Grades 9–12

- Creates equations that describe numbers or relationships
- Demonstrates how sounds and musical ideas can represent concepts or texts

Scoring (cont.)

Preparation

Draw a large clock (without hands but with numbers and minute marks) on the board. Leave enough room to record a key or legend. Refer to the Specific Grade-Level Ideas for additional suggestions.

Procedure

1. Ask students to think about different ways a minute can be separated into equal intervals of time (for example, 60 intervals of 1 second, 2 intervals of 30 seconds, 3 intervals of 20 seconds, and so forth). Provide time for students to work with neighbors to identify possibilities. Record students' responses, taking suggestions from students, such as "Let's play something once every five seconds." Tell students that as a class, they will create a composition highlighting these different durations of time.

2. Show students the analog clock and have them clap out the seconds with the second hand for one minute. Have them identify sounds other than clapping that they might make, such as tapping the desk with a ruler. Once students decide on a sound that everyone can make, ask them to create a simple symbol to represent the sound of that "instrument." Mark the symbol (for example, *R* for *tapping ruler*) outside each of the minute marks on the drawn clock to indicate when the instrument is to be played within the one-minute interval.

3. Tell students that they also need a key to help them remember the meanings of the symbols. In a corner by the drawn clock, record *R* and *tapping ruler*.

4. Ask students to identify another time interval from their list. Again, have them identify an instrument and a symbol. Record this in the appropriate positions around the clock and add the information

to the key. Have students practice making the sound at the correct intervals as they watch the analog clock. Repeat for two to four more time intervals.

5. Divide the class into the appropriate number of sections and assign each of them one of the "instruments." Point out to students that they are sitting in sections and responsible for playing their parts like members of an orchestra. Distribute the *Individual Musical Score* and have them make a score that shows only their assigned part. Have groups practice their parts a few times. Use the Planning Questions, as needed, to support students as they work.

6. Remind students to sit where they can see the analog clock so that they know when their parts should be played. You might find a website that allows you to project a live clock on the wall. Tell students to begin their performance when the second hand reaches the 12. Although you can act as a conductor and point to a section to signal that they are about to play, encourage students to watch the clock to determine when they should play their instruments. Have students perform their composition a few times for practice.

7. Suggest that at the 60-second mark, all players create a special sound as the culminating moment of the piece, such as slamming a book closed, and have students practice making that sound once. Have students add this ending to their *Individual Musical Score.*

8. Perform the complete piece two or three times through and then use the Discussion Questions to help students reflect on the experience.

Scoring *(cont.)*

Planning Questions

- How long will your music last?

- What sounds will be in the music you are creating?

- At what times will you play your sound?

- How will you layer sounds to make your composition?

- What are other ways a conductor leads an orchestra (when to play softly, loudly, or to stop playing)? What hand signals might we use for these directions?

> "Counting, rhythm, scales, intervals, patterns, symbols, harmonies, time signatures, overtones, tone, pitch. The notations of composers and sounds made by musicians are connected to mathematics."
>
> —American Mathematical Society
> (n.d.-a, para. 1)

Discussion Questions

- How did the score help you perform?

- If you played for 32 seconds, what intervals might you use for striking your beat?

- When were the greatest number of instruments playing? (All intervals are a factor of 60, so all instruments were playing at that time.)

- Without a score, how could we predict when more than one section would be playing? (Examine the common multiples of the factors of 60.)

- What artistic choices did you make in creating and scoring your composition?

- What was the effect of layering of sounds, use of silence, and solo performances?

Scoring *(cont.)*

Specific Grade-Level Ideas

Grades K–2

Students can practice counting by ones around the drawn clock as well as skip counting by fives and tens. A few students may suggest 30-second or 15-second intervals based on visual familiarity with a clock face or ways to divide a circle into halves or fourths. You could give each small group a score to explore and practice.

Grades 3–5

After students experience this activity, have them develop their own scores in small groups and perform them for the class, providing their own conductor. Students also can experiment with an interval longer than 60 seconds, perhaps indicated on a number line or with a circle drawn for each minute, to gain additional practice identifying all factor pairs and using common multiples to predict when different sounds will be played at the same time. Ask students to intentionally plan for moments of solo sounds, silence, and sounds played at the same time for a texturing effect.

Grades 6–8

Encourage students to create their own scores, distribute them to the class, and conduct their performance. Extend the mathematics in the activity by asking questions such as "What fraction (or percent) of the time is the (name instrument) playing? For what fraction (or percent) of the composition is only one instrument playing?"

Grades 9–12

Students can define their own time frame, create their own scores, conduct their own performance, and use algebraic equations and graphs to communicate the relationships among the amount of time each instrument is played. They also may want to consider how a piece of music is transposed so that it may be played by a different instrument.

Name: ____ Date:_______________

Individual Musical Score

Directions: Write the musical score for your part in the performance. Be sure to complete the key.

Key

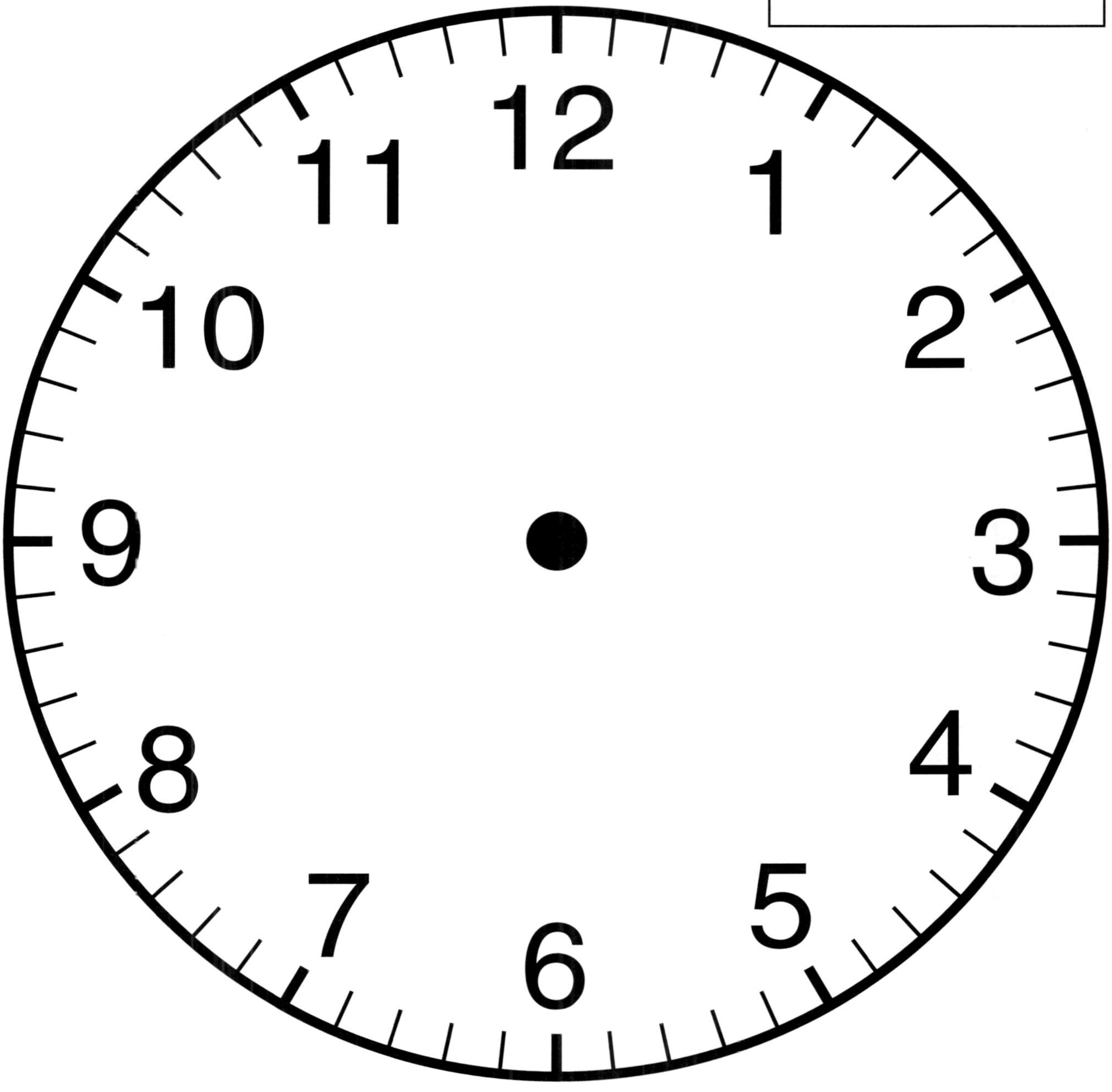

Call-and-Response

Model Lesson: Answer Me in Rhythm

Overview

This strategy reinforces mathematical ideas and engages students in testing their knowledge by posing questions and answering them in a rhythmic pattern. Call-and-response encourages collaboration and group problem-solving. Students will work in pairs to create their own call-and-response song to demonstrate their knowledge about mathematical content. The focus is on equivalence, but this strategy can be used with any content.

Materials

- *Call-and-Response Examples* (page 169)
- *Planning Chart for Call-and-Response* (page 170)
- *Elements of Music* (page 143)

Standards

Grades K–2

- Knows processes for telling time, counting money, and measuring length, weight, and temperature, using basic standard and nonstandard units
- Describes how specific music concepts are used to support a specific purpose
- Demonstrates and explains reasons for personal choices of musical ideas

Grades 6–8

- Understands the relationships among linear dimensions, area, and volume and the corresponding uses of units, square units, and cubic units of measure
- Solves problems by estimating quantities and measurements
- Explains how knowledge relates to personal choices and intent when creating and performing music
- Demonstrates the relationship between music and another discipline

Grades 3–5

- Identifies and uses appropriate units of measurement, according to type and size of unit
- Solves problems by estimating quantities and measurements
- Demonstrates and explains how responses to music are informed by the structure and elements of music
- Describes the connection of personally created music to expressive intent

Grades 9–12

- Applies trigonometric ratio methods to solve mathematical and real-world problems
- Shares music and demonstrates how the elements of music have been employed to realize expressive intent

Call-and-Response *(cont.)*

Preparation

Decide how to divide the class into small groups. Practice a marching-type cadence for the call-and-response examples given on *Call-and-Response Examples* (page 169), or create examples of your own. Note that the first example is simply recall and can be used to reinforce the ability to remember facts. In the second example, the caller should take a step while singing the first call, and the responder has to estimate before making a response. Other suggestions are provided in the Specific Grade-Level Ideas.

> "Research has found that music can help prepare students for the day's lessons by energizing them and stimulating the brain. Incorporating music into math can change the dynamic of mathematics making it a more enjoyable experience for everyone."
>
> —Amanda Johnson (2017, para. 1)

Procedure

1. Share examples of call-and-response (maritime cadences, work songs, sea chanteys, and so on) and discuss the historical and cultural aspects of this musical form. Ask older students, "What purpose did this form of music serve?" Younger students can respond to the question, "How is this way of singing like a conversation?"

2. Display the *Call-and-Response Examples* or use your own examples. Tell students that you will sing/call the question and they will respond in the same rhythm and melody. Then practice the call-and-response with students, using the examples.

3. Divide the class into two groups, one for call and one for response. Have students practice the call-and-response technique independently.

4. Organize students into small groups and tell them they will create their own call-and-response. Note that students can organize their phrases in one of three ways: They can match the melody of a tune or sea chantey, organize their phrases within a certain number of beats, or find an interesting rhythm, much as they do with rap. Also note that a group of students can call the question—it's not limited to one leader.

5. Distribute the *Planning Chart for Call-and-Response* and have students use it to plan their call-and-response. Tell students that rhyming is optional. Encourage each group to create up to five questions to call to the class. Use the Planning Questions to guide students' thinking.

6. Have students present their call-and-response plan to you in writing. Give students informal feedback and have them revise as necessary.

7. Give each group the opportunity to present and perform their call-and-response with the class.

8. Use the Discussion Questions to guide students as they reflect.

Call-and-Response (cont.)

Planning Questions

- What mathematical questions interest you?

- What mathematical concepts will you explore?

- How might you pose a question to generate a short, quick answer?

- How might you phrase a question so that it has an interesting rhythm?

- Do you want to end the question with words that are easy to rhyme or with a memorable rhythm?

- What musical elements will you use to add meaning and emphasis to your call and response?

Discussion Questions

- What strategies did you use to create the rhythm?

- What did you notice when the call-and-response was done with a group?

- What call-and-response might you use to help you remember a mathematical idea?

- What mathematics did you learn by participating in another group's call-and-response?

- Describe your use of the elements of music in creating your call and response. How might you make your call-and-response more mathematically interesting or challenging?

Specific Grade-Level Ideas

Grades K–2

Create group call-and-responses about shapes. For example, "How many sides to a triangle?" This could be followed by "Three sides to make that shape." You also can teach a melody or rhythm and ask a series of basic-fact questions using call-and-response. Students can march in place as they chant responses or add gestures.

Grades 3–5

In this strategy, clapping the beats will help students recognize and follow the rhythm. Include questions about measurement related to length, volume, and mass. This technique also could be used for basic-fact practice and knowledge of geometric shapes.

Grades 6–8

Have students focus on how a change in side length affects perimeter, area, or volume, as well as more complex rhythms. They can ask open-ended questions that can be repeated until the responders run out of ideas. For example, the question might be "What can you tell me about slope?"

Grades 9–12

Students can use the call-and-response strategy to reinforce concepts related to the Pythagorean theorem or trigonometric ratios. They also can experiment with the rhythm of the call-and-response.

Call-and-Response Examples

Money

CALL: How many pennies in a dime?

RESPONSE: 10 pennies work out just fine!

(repeat lines 1 and 2)

CALL: How many pennies in a quarter?

RESPONSE: 25 pennies all in order!

CALL: How many pennies in 10 dimes?

RESPONSE: 100 and the dollar's mine!

ALL: Know your money equivalents.

Measurement

The caller should move while singing the first call, and the responder should estimate before making a response.

CALL: How many inches did I step?

RESPONSE: ___ inches I did step.

(repeat lines 1 and 2)

CALL: How many centimeters did I jump?

RESPONSE: ___ centimeters I did jump.

CALL: How many feet did I walk?

RESPONSE: ___ feet I did walk.

ALL: Know your measures and estimate.

Name: _______________________________________ Date:__________________

Planning Chart for Call-and-Response

Directions: Complete the chart to plan your call-and-response.

Call: Possible Questions	Response: Possible Answers and Rhymes

Chants

Model Lesson: Length of Notes

Overview

Students investigate the duration of different musical notes, focusing on the role of fractions in music. Through a process of adding one layer or phrase on top of another in a chant, the different durations of the notes and the relations among them become particularly noticeable. To create the chants, students combine interesting phrases to be spoken/sung at the same time with different dynamics (ranging from soft to loud), pitch (low to high), and notes (short to long).

Materials

- musical score *(optional)*
- *Chant Reflection* (page 175)
- *Elements of Music* (page 143)

Standards

Grades K–2

- Understands the concept of a unit and its subdivision into equal parts
- Demonstrates knowledge of music concepts and contrasts
- Demonstrates and describes music's expressive qualities

Grades 3–5

- Compares, orders, and represents rational numbers
- Demonstrates understanding of structure and elements of music
- Demonstrates and describes how intent is conveyed through expressive qualities of music

Grades 6–8

- Solves real-world and mathematical problems using numerical and algebraic expressions and equations
- Demonstrates and describes how intent is conveyed through expressive qualities of music
- Demonstrates the relationship between music and another discipline

Grades 9–12

- Creates equations that describe numbers or relationships
- Demonstrates and describes how intent is conveyed through expressive qualities of music
- Demonstrates the relationship between music and another discipline

Preparation

Reflect on students' understanding of fractions and how you might want to group them for this activity. If your school has a music teacher, talk with that teacher about how you might connect this exploration with lessons or a musical piece within the music curriculum. Select sheet music that is written in $\frac{4}{4}$ time to use as a model with students. As you preread the Procedure, think about where to display the initial words and diagrams so that others can be added. Other suggestions are provided in the Specific Grade-Level Ideas.

> "Besides the power of the music itself and the connections with other content areas, word play is at the heart of chants and the lyrics of music."
>
> —Nancy Reif and Leslie Grant (2010, 108)

Procedure

1. Write the following list of food items on the board so students can see them.

   ravioli
   sushi
   soup

   Have students say the words aloud as they clap the syllables. Record the number of syllables next to each word.

2. Explain to students that they are going to create a chant by saying these words at the same time, using the same amount of time. Have the whole group say the word *ravioli* as they clap out the four beats or syllables. Tell students that having four beats to one measure is common in music. Display the musical score written in $\frac{4}{4}$ time and draw students' attention to the time signature and how the measures are identified.

3. On the board, draw a long horizontal line at a height that will allow two additional sections to be added. (You may wish to use the circle model with younger students. See the K–2 Specific Grade Level Ideas.) Tell students to think of this line as representing the time it took to say the word *ravioli* (the whole measure). Ask, "How many beats did this take?" *(4)* "How many beats did each syllable get?" *(1)* "What fraction of the whole measure did each syllable get?" *($\frac{1}{4}$)* Divide the line into four equivalent segments and write one of the syllables of the word *ravioli* below each segment along with the fractions. (See the following diagram.) Ask, "What number sentence could we write to show this?" *($\frac{1}{4} + \frac{1}{4} + \frac{1}{4} + \frac{1}{4} = 1$)*

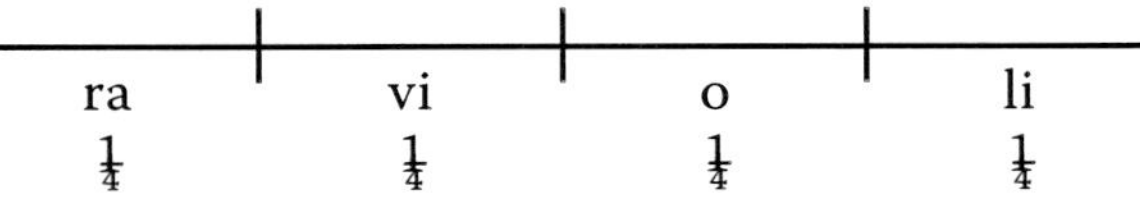

4. Tell students, "We are going to say the word *sushi* in the same amount of time as *ravioli*." Ask, "How many beats will we use?" *(4)* "How many beats will each syllable get?" *(2 beats)* "What fraction of the whole measure will each syllable get?" *($\frac{1}{2}$)* Draw a second line and write the syllables and fractions below. Ask, "What number sentence could we write to show this?" *($\frac{1}{2} + \frac{1}{2} = 1$)*

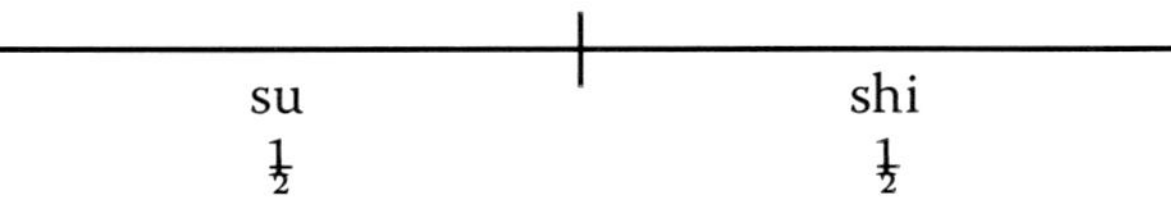

5. Lead students in saying the word *sushi*. Then divide the class into two groups and have one group say the word *ravioli* while the other says the word *sushi*. Have student groups repeat the phrases four times in a row, keeping the correct tempos.

Chants (cont.)

6. Have students say the word *soup* in a drawn-out manner, lasting four beats or claps, draw another line, and record the data.

soup
1

7. Divide the class into three groups. Have the first group say the word *ravioli*. After that word is repeated twice, have the second group join in with the word *sushi*, and after two repetitions of these words, direct the third group to join in with the word *soup*. Once all three layers are included, have the whole group repeat the chant several times.

8. Now, write the phrase *corn tortillas and bean salad* and have students talk with a neighbor about how to represent this phrase on the line. Have students agree on what should be shown and record the new representation at the top of the expanded diagram. Ask, "What number sentence could we write to show this?" ($\frac{1}{8} + \frac{1}{8} + \frac{1}{8} + \frac{1}{8} + \frac{1}{8} + \frac{1}{8} + \frac{1}{8} + \frac{1}{8} = 1$)

corn	tor	till	as	and	bean	sa	lad
$\frac{1}{8}$	$\frac{1}{8}$	$\frac{1}{8}$	$\frac{1}{8}$	$\frac{1}{8}$	$\frac{1}{8}$	$\frac{1}{8}$	$\frac{1}{8}$

9. Divide the class into four groups and have students perform the four layers of the chant.

10. Tell students you will give each group time to elaborate on their layer of the chant. Use the Planning Questions to guide their thinking. When each group is prepared, have students practice their parts together and then present the chant. Ask, "What feedback could you give to other groups about the ways they embellished their part of the chant? What struck you about the sound and rhythms produced in the chants?"

11. Have students create their own chants. Tell students to identify a category of words that interests them and then to choose words to fit the beat. Distribute the *Chant Reflection* for students to complete.

12. Invite a few students to share their explanations of how to use fractions to represent a phrase. Use the Discussion Questions to further probe their thinking about fractions and music.

Planning Questions

- What pitch (high or low) do you want to use?

- How loud (dynamics) do you want to be?

- What other sound effects might you add to give your layer more interest (clapping, stomping, slapping the desk, and so forth)?

- Are there gestures you could add to emphasize your tempo (slow, curved motions or quick, jagged movements)?

Discussion Questions

- Why are all the equations equal to 1?

- If we created a word bank to help us write our explanations, what words would we include?

- What do you notice about the fractions that are and are not used in music?

- How can you predict the number of times each layer of your chant will be repeated?

- Describe the effect of using words of different length, numbers of syllables, and tempos to create a layered chant.

Chants *(cont.)*

Specific Grade-Level Ideas

Grades K–2

Create a list of two or three food items, exploring wholes, halves, and/or fourths. Students don't need to record number sentences with the fractions. Some students will do better with a parts-of-the-whole circular model of fractions rather than a linear one. In such a model, the fractions would be represented as shown.

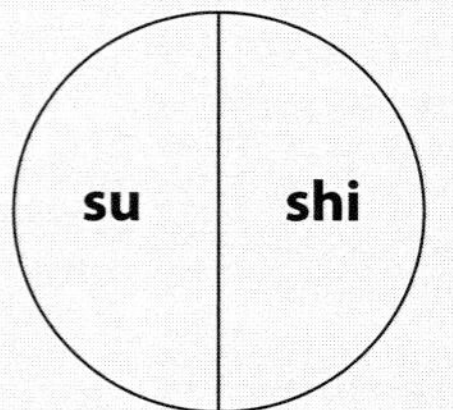

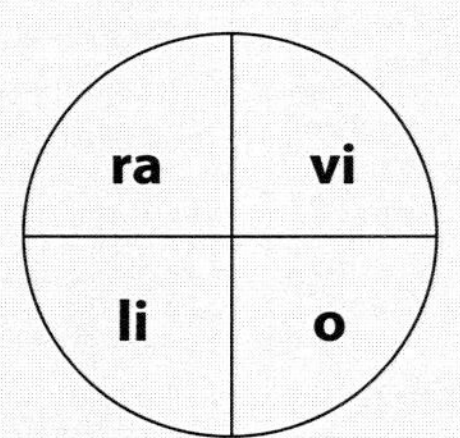

Lead students in creating their own chants using other types of foods or topics such as animals, names, or curricular topics.

Grades 3–5

To have students connect more formally to names of musical notes, you also can record the following on the diagram:

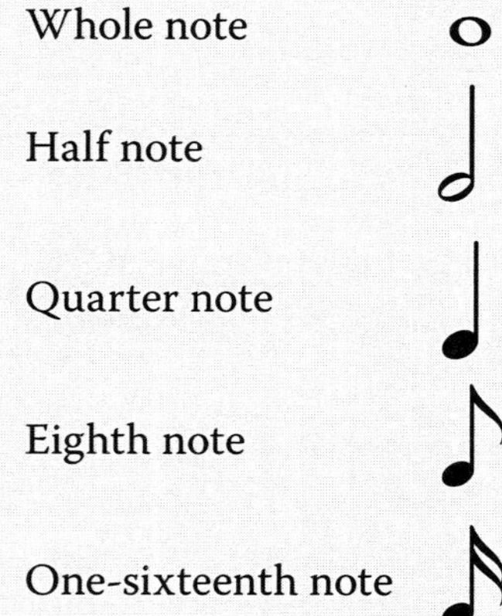

Whole note

Half note

Quarter note

Eighth note

One-sixteenth note

Fifth-grade students can also explore the grades 6–8 ideas.

Grades 6–8

Students can experiment with alternating beats in addition to investigating steady beats. To do so, they would assign a variety of durations for different syllables within a word or phrase. For example, they can say or sing the words *chicken fricassee* by assigning the first three syllables a value of one beat, or quarter notes, and the last two syllables a value of one-half of a beat, or eighth notes. Students can then record the number sentence $\frac{1}{4} + \frac{1}{4} + \frac{1}{4} + \frac{1}{8} + \frac{1}{8} = 1$ to record this combination. Have students write equations to identify 10 different ways (different order doesn't count as a different way) to combine notes within a $\frac{4}{4}$ measure. Also, have students record these combinations symbolically with music notes.

Grades 9–12

These students can create chants with arithmetic and geometric sequences. In groups of four they can identify four sequences that differ, but will share the same number at the end, when they choose to stop. If sequences are shorter, they will need to hold their notes; if longer, the notes will have to be shorter. They can use a rap rhythm to name the numbers in the sequences and decide on a special sound to make when they merge.

Name: ____ Date:_______________

Chant Reflection

Directions: Answer each question.

1. Write your chant on the lines.

   ____

   ____

   ____

   ____

2. Complete a number sentence for each line of your chant to show how the syllables make one measure:

   ____ = **1**

   ____ = **1**

   ____ = **1**

   ____ = **1**

3. What would you say to someone who asked you to explain how to use fractions to represent syllables in a new phrase?

   ____

   ____

   ____

4. Write two new phrases for your chant.

   ____

   ____

Visual Arts

Visual Arts

Understanding Visual Arts

We are bombarded with images on a daily basis, and although we have become more skilled at reading the nontextual representation of ideas, our visual-literacy abilities need to develop further. Why, then, is education so often text based? Working with images can provide opportunities for students to observe, notice details, and make meaning. Visual work can communicate nuances that words cannot. In this section, we see how students can use visual art as a language that is more unstructured than text.

Particular to visual arts is hands-on work with various materials. Visual artists use their art in many ways to create narratives, observe, explore patterns, translate, represent, and juxtapose ideas using visual communication. Using the elements of art—*line, form, shape, color, texture,* and *pattern*—students can investigate and create visual representations of ideas. They also can create images as a way to tell what they know.

Integrating the visual arts is a method to help students see and express mathematical principles visually. "Just as illustrations help students understand the meaning of a story, visual representations help students understand math situations (Dacey, Hopping, and Salemi 2018).

Also, when students process visual information as well as verbal, they use different parts of the brain. Allan Paivio suggests that learning can be expanded by the inclusion of visual imagery, allowing for what he termed "dual coding" (as cited in Reed 2010).

"Moving between visual and numerical concepts can develop representational fluency and enhance students' ability to work with symbol systems. The visual arts are a natural fit with mathematics as images challenge students to work in new ways with ideas of scale, perspective, patterns, and more. As students translate mathematical ideas into visual form, they draw on higher-order thinking skills such as synthesis and evaluation" (Dacey and Eston 2002). All curricular areas have visual aspects, so providing students with the opportunity to work with multiple representations of content is easy to incorporate and will give students new ways to engage with and access mathematical ideas.

Elements of Visual Art

The elements of visual art were informed by a review of the field, including the J. Paul Getty Museum (Getty, n.d.-a), the Institute for Arts Integration and STEAM (Riley 2017), and the Kennedy Center (Glatstein 2019).

- **Line:** A mark made by the path of a point moving in space. Lines can be horizontal, vertical, or diagonal; they can vary in width, direction, and length.

- **Shape:** A closed line. Shapes can be geometric, often made up of straight edges, or they can be organic and made up of irregular, free-form edges; shapes are flat and can be defined by length and width.

- **Color:** The response of the eyes to different wavelengths of light reflecting off objects. Color can be defined by any of its three properties: hue (or name, like red, blue, or green), intensity, and value.

- **Form:** A three-dimensional shape that can be expressed by length, width, and depth.

- **Texture:** The quality of a surface that can be seen and felt, such as rough, smooth, bumpy, and so on. Texture can be real or implied, meaning that a surface can be either physically felt, as having a texture, or visually appear to have a texture, even though the surface is flat.

- **Value:** The lightness or darkness of a color.

- **Space:** The area between, around, above, below, or within objects. Space can be defined as negative (like the emptiness of holes) or positive. Space also describes depth or the illusion (idea) of depth.

Visual Arts *(cont.)*

Principles of Design

These are informed by the J. Paul Getty Museum (Getty, n.d.-b), the Institute for Arts Integration and STEAM (Riley 2017), the Kennedy Center (Glatstein 2019), and PBS Learning Media (KET, 2014).

- **Balance:** Arrangement of art elements with attention to visual weight. Symmetrically balanced artworks feel stable; asymmetrically balanced artworks can create a feeling of instability or movement.

- **Movement:** An artwork can be composed to suggest a sense of action. The elements of art can be intentionally placed in ways that guide the viewer's eyes around the work.

- **Repetition:** Applying art elements so that the same elements are used again and again; repeating elements in a predictable way creates pattern.

- **Proportion:** Size relationships between objects or elements in an artwork

- **Emphasis:** The part of the artwork that stands out in an eye-catching way; the center of interest

- **Contrast:** The juxtaposition of elements in an artwork showing differences that makes them stand out from one other; can include colors, shapes, textures, and more

- **Unity:** The use of elements of art to create harmony in a composition

- **Variety:** Combining art elements in ways that create visual interest

> "When mathematics and art come together, students are often inspired and they can start to see mathematics as a beautiful and creative subject."
>
> —youcubed (n.d., para. 1)

Strategies for Visual Arts

Visual Narrative

In this strategy, students create and arrange images in sequence to tell a story or create a narrative. The story can be told through images alone, or the pictures can interact with text. Students' understanding of curricular content is enhanced as they create visual narratives that demonstrate and/or apply their learning. Often, creating a visual narrative makes it easier for students to grasp connections and clarify their thinking, which they can then translate into text. Students can illustrate mathematical concepts, translating their understanding into visual form.

Visual narratives can culminate in the creation of simple books, digital image essays, magazines, storyboards, comics, and other formats that are easy to make. This allows students to compose content, applying and articulating their knowledge in new ways. Teaching artist and researcher Wendy Strauch-Nelson (2011) notes that students "seemed drawn to the complementary relationship between the linear style of words and the layered nature of images" (9).

Visual Patterns

Lynn Steen (1990), in the classic book *On the Shoulders of Giants: New Approaches to Numeracy*, describes mathematics as the language and science of patterns. Artists often work with patterns. Pattern is considered one of the fundamental communication elements in the visual-arts principles of design. These design elements include line, shape, form, texture, pattern, and color. Through the visual arts, students can demonstrate a variety of curricular concepts by creating and manipulating patterns. Working with patterns can guide observations, and shifting patterns can generate interest and curiosity. Students can track and document patterns in the world through artistic representations that capture cycles of change. In mathematics, students can use visual patterns to deepen and extend their understanding of numbers and operations.

Visual Arts *(cont.)*

Representation

Students investigate the ability of the visual arts to communicate information and ideas in compelling ways, to direct our attention, and to add layers of meaning. When students represent concepts through visual art, they translate their understanding into new forms, taking ownership of ideas and engaging with symbolism and metaphor. In this strategy, students create visual work, such as visual essays or infographics, to depict information.

One example of the power of representation comes from Adam Hollanderk. He created an installation on the National Mall of the Washington Monument of 857 desks representing the number of students who drop out of school every hour. Adeshina Emmanuel (2012) commented, "Everybody hears that 857 number, but it doesn't really mean anything until you're able to see it." The image of hundreds of empty desks prompted visitors to sign a petition demanding that politicians address this trend.

Visual Observation

Visual images can provide opportunities for students to observe, attend to details, and make meaning. As cited by Hilary Landorf (2006), Housen and Yenawine found that close observation and discussion of works of art "measurably increases observation skills, evidential reasoning, and speculative abilities, and the ability to find multiple solutions to complex problems" (29). Students can focus and expand their observations, both through the study of the works of others and in the creation of their own visual work. Through deep observation of the work of a variety of well-known artists, students can investigate how artists use mathematical concepts in the preparation, creation, and representation of visual ideas. Through this strategy, students can recognize the natural fit between mathematics and the visual arts.

Mixed Media

This strategy allows students to experiment with putting a range of materials together in new ways. Students manipulate materials, experiment with the juxtaposition of materials, and create two- or three-dimensional pieces such as mobiles, collages, assemblages, dioramas, and digital installations. Students test and explore ideas in experiential, hands-on ways; make choices about how they will use materials to communicate; and explore cause-and-effect relationships in the process of working with different media. The use of multiple representations is essential to the development of flexible mathematical strategies.

Visual Narrative

Model Lesson: Storyboards

Overview

In this strategy, students use visual narrative as a problem-solving tool. Students decide how to break up a problem into meaningful scenes. Then they combine text with artwork to solve and explain the problem. Students may break up their problems into three scenes with three pieces of artwork, or they can have many scenes and choose to present their narratives through digital storytelling.

Materials

- visual narrative sample (comic, graphic novel, storyboard)
- chart paper or butcher paper
- scissors, glue
- *Storyboard Planner* (page 186)
- *Elements of Visual Art* and *Principles of Design* (pages 179–180)
- sticky notes (*optional*)
- art supplies (markers, crayons, paint, clay, and so on)
- access to a computer with software that can combine text and visuals (*optional*)

Standards

Grades K–2

- Creates and uses representations to organize, record, and communicate mathematical ideas
- Explores uses of materials and tools to create works of art or design
- Describes what an image represents

Grades 3–5

- Creates and uses representations to organize, record, and communicate mathematical ideas
- Creates personally satisfying artwork using artistic processes and materials
- Determines messages communicated by an image

Grades 6–8

- Creates and uses representations to organize, record, and communicate mathematical ideas
- Demonstrates openness in trying new ideas, materials, and methods in making works of art
- Analyzes multiple ways that images influence specific audiences

Grades 9–12

- Analyzes mathematical relationships to connect and communicate mathematical ideas
- Understands connections between equivalent representations and corresponding procedures of the same problem situation
- Analyzes multiple ways that images influence specific audiences

Visual Narrative *(cont.)*

Preparation

Choose mathematical problems you would like students to solve and write them on chart paper. Be sure the problems are at the right level of challenge so that students will wrestle with mathematical ideas but not so challenging that they become frustrated. Identify one problem to solve as a class to model the strategy. Identify an example of visual narrative to share with students, such as a comic, graphic novel, or storyboard. Find possible ideas for exemplars by exploring artists' work on the internet, such as Trenton Doyle Hancock and Liza Donnelly, or graphic novel illustrators such as Art Spiegelman (*Maus*) and Marjane Satrapi (*Persepolis*). Other suggestions are provided in the Specific Grade-Level Ideas.

> "Humans are visual creatures. Where text requires time and mental processing, images are often instant and visceral."
>
> —Workerbee (2014, para. 7)

Procedure

1. Explain that a visual narrative is a story told in a sequence of images and text. Display the visual narrative example that you chose. Have students share their experiences with reading such visual narratives. Discuss how the artist may have decided to break the story or information into panels and explain how to sequence the panels.

2. Tell students they will create a storyboard to help them solve a mathematical problem and explain their thinking. Present the problem you have identified.

3. As a class, decide how to break the problem into sections. Ask students questions, such as "What do we know? What do we need to find?" Mark up the chart paper to show where the problem will be divided.

4. Cut the problem apart and glue each section in sequential order on a long piece of butcher paper. Display the sectioned problem for the class.

5. Introduce students to the definition of *illustration*: "visual imagery that interprets or explains ideas often in books and media." Discuss as a class how illustrations could help make each section of the problem more meaningful. Above the text on the butcher paper, draw a sketch of what the artwork might look like. Refer to the example that you shared earlier and discuss how those illustrations make the comic book/graphic novel more meaningful.

6. Have individual students or pairs solve a new problem using the visual narrative strategy. Distribute the *Storyboard Planner* for students to record their thinking. Print two pages of the planner page: one for drafting ideas and one for students to use as the final copy to go with their artwork. Use the Planning Questions to guide students' thinking.

7. Introduce the art media available to students for their illustrations, such as markers, colored pencils, pencils, or illustration pens. Ask students to make intentional choices about which medium they will use. They should consider which medium will most effectively communicate their message. Share *Elements of Visual Art* and *Principles of Design* to support students' artistic decisions.

8. Have students review their storyboards to evaluate how well they conveyed the strategy for solving their problem. Have students edit or add visual details as necessary.

Visual Narrative *(cont.)*

9. Have students finalize their work by creating a story page for each scene they planned using their desired art materials. Staple the pages together to make a book. Or have students complete this step using software that allows for the combination of text and illustrations.

10. Provide time for students to share their work with one another.

11. Consider having students share their visual narratives with fellow students, omitting the problem-solving information to challenge them to decipher the problems shown in the images.

12. Have students discuss the process of making their visual narratives, using the Discussion Questions.

Planning Questions

▸ How will you break the problem into meaningful parts?

▸ What images might you create to help you solve the problem?

▸ What images or text might you use to explain your solution process?

▸ What medium will you choose to create your artwork (colored pencils, photographs, or drawing programs on a computer), and why?

Discussion Questions

▸ How did you choose your illustration?

▸ How did the images you used influence the text you included?

▸ How do your images and text work together?

▸ What did you learn about problem-solving from creating your storyboard?

▸ As you were reading and viewing the work of others, what did you realize about problem-solving in math?

▸ Why was it necessary to break your math problem into several parts?

Visual Narrative *(cont.)*

Specific Grade-Level Ideas

Grades K–2

Have students focus on the vocabulary associated with different uses of addition and subtraction. For example, students can illustrate the different actions of separating from or adding to, allowing images to add visual details to the story.

Students can use this strategy to explore time. They can add numbers and hands to clocks and create visuals that illustrate and annotate what they do at different times of the day.

Grades 3–5

Have students turn their storyboards into digital stories. In addition to problem-solving, students can create a visual and compelling narrative, explaining particular computational strategies and why they work.

Grades 6–8

Students can use visual narratives to reflect on mathematical concepts such as variability or to tell stories of how mathematics is used in the workplace. Students can do research online, video or photograph examples, and interview people in the field, adding images and text that capture the essence of mathematical concepts. If time allows, they can then create digital storybooks or use presentation software to present their narratives.

Grades 9–12

In addition to the ideas for grades 6–8, students can create storyboards to explore mathematical ideas such as sequences or functions. They also can create tutorials that are not lectures but truly visual essays for other students. They can create a classroom video library of such resources.

Name: _________________________________ Date:_________________

Storyboard Planner

Directions: Plan your scenes using this storyboard.

Text	Illustration

Visual Patterns

Model Lesson: Curve Stitching

Overview

Curve stitching, or string art, was popularized in the 1960s. It involves sewing colored thread through holes or wrapping thread around nails or pins. The positioning of the holes, nails, or pins leads to the creation of geometric patterns and the recognition of algebraic relationships. Straight lines are combined in ways that can create the image of a curve. A wide range of students will be able to participate in this craft. Discussion can support students in discovering the mathematical concepts in this strategy. In the classroom, a variety of materials can be used, including the simple combination of colored pencils and paper.

Materials

▸ *Circle with 10 Points* (page 192)

▸ rulers

▸ *Circle with 12 Points* (page 193)

▸ *Circle with 23 Points* (page 194)

▸ *Elements of Visual Art* and *Principles of Design* (pages 179–180)

▸ colored pencils, colored chalk, ribbons or streamers, thread or yarn, cardboard or wood, paint, nails, hammer (*optional*)

Standards

Grades K–2

▸ Extends simple patterns

▸ Uses observation and investigation in preparation for making a work of art

▸ Interprets art by identifying subject matter and describing relevant details

Grades 3–5

▸ Recognizes a wide variety of patterns and the rules that explain them

▸ Identifies and demonstrates diverse methods of artistic investigation

▸ Interprets art by analyzing characteristics of form and structure and visual elements

Grades 6–8

▸ Understands various representations of patterns and functions and the relationships among them

▸ Develops criteria to guide making a work of art that meets an identified goal

▸ Interprets art by analyzing subject matter and characteristics of form and structure

Grades 9–12

▸ Understands the concept of a function as the correspondences between the elements of two sets

▸ Knows specific techniques and skills used in different art forms

Visual Patterns *(cont.)*

Preparation

Decide on the materials you want students to use; colored pencils on paper, colored chalk on blacktop, ribbons or streamers held by students, thread or yarn on cardboard, paint on paper, as well as nails and embroidery thread on wood are all potential options. Make choices that best fit students and your supplies. Note that paper and pencil are readily available, although nails and yarn challenge students to explore a variety of options on the same frame by unwinding the yarn and starting again. If curve stitching is new to you, take time to explore some ideas yourself through an online search.

For differentiation, you can assign number rules (for example, +5 or +6) or have students make the choice. These activities can be completed in pairs or individually. Other suggestions are provided in the Specific Grade-Level Ideas.

> "The interesting thing is that because the straight lines meet at an angle, there is an illusion that you have created a curved line by drawing straight lines. And the more subdivisions you make in the original two lines, the smoother the curve looks."
>
> —Veronika Irvine (2012, para. 2)

Procedure

1. Display the *Circle with 10 Points* to demonstrate for students how to connect the dots using a +3 number rule. Start at 0 and, using a ruler or other straight edge, draw a line from 0 to 3. Then, do the same from 3 to 6, 6 to 9, 9 to 2, and so on until all the unique connecting lines have been drawn.

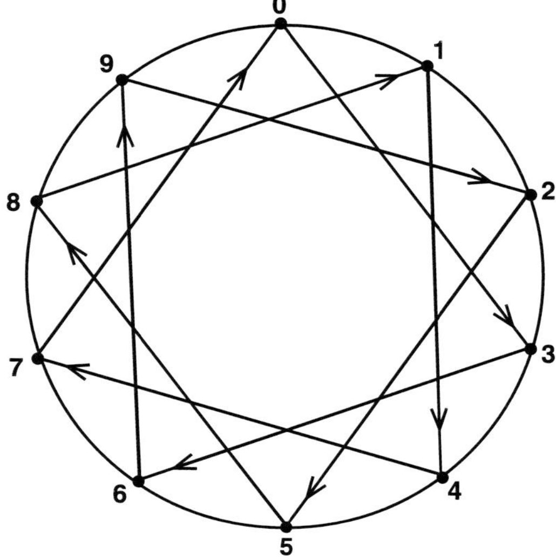

2. Ask students to share anything they noticed or discovered about the pattern. Record responses for students to refer to throughout the lesson.

3. Tell students they will explore other number rules by creating their own patterns. Assign or have students choose a number rule. Have them brainstorm a list of "I wonder . . ." statements about the new rule and record these ideas so they can reference them throughout the lesson. For example, say, "I wonder if it will use all the points," or "I wonder if it will make a pattern."

4. Distribute several copies of *Circle with 10 Points* to students. Use the Planning Questions to discuss. Provide students time to explore their number rules, using pencils and rulers to skip-count and draw lines to connect the dots on their circle.

Visual Patterns *(cont.)*

5. Have students gather to discuss their findings and link back to their initial "I wonder . . ." statements whenever possible.

6. Display the *Circle with 12 Points*. Have students suggest number rules and explain any predictions they can make about the designs that will result. Encourage them to discuss and justify their predictions.

7. Distribute several copies of the *Circle with 12 Points* and have students explore their ideas. This time, suggest the use of colored pencils and the notion of repeating rules on the same circle. For example, a +3 number rule could be placed on the same circle with a +4 number rule, or a +4 number rule that begins at 1 could be placed on the same circle as a +4 rule that begins at 0, using a different color for each rule. Encourage students to explore a variety of colors and combinations. *Circle with 23 Points* is available for students who wish to explore a greater number of points.

8. Have students choose the combination that they find most artistically pleasing and write an explanation of why they chose it and the mathematics illustrated within it. Discuss the *Elements of Visual Art* and *Principles of Design* with students. Invite students to use these to inform their artistic choices.

9. If possible, have students create a more permanent artifact. Have them place the *Circle with 23 Points* on a piece of wood and use a pencil to make a hole through the paper at each point to mark on the wood below. Hammer a nail into the wood at each mark and wind colored yarn or embroidery thread around the nails to create lines. Then have students paint their artifacts so the pattern remains intact once the paint dries.

10. Use the Discussion Questions to help students articulate the mathematical concepts in this activity.

Planning Questions

▸ What number rule do you want to use? Why?

▸ What do you predict will happen in the design next? How will the *Elements of Visual Art* and *Principles of Design* inform the artistic choices you will make for your composition?

Discussion Questions

▸ What do you notice about the numbers you land on for the +3 rule on the *Circle with 10 Points*?

▸ What connections can you make between these numbers and the multiplication table for 3?

▸ What do you think a +5 design would look like on a circle with 15 points?

▸ What must be true for a polygon to emerge from a + rule?

▸ How many different designs do you think there could be on a circle with 8 points? What would you predict about a circle with 29 points?

▸ Does it matter if the number of points is prime or composite?

▸ How could you use math to design specific aesthetic features in your next creation?

Visual Patterns (cont.)

Specific Grade-Level Ideas

Grades K–2

Students can focus on counting, skip-counting, and addition and subtraction. Introduce students to curve stitching by giving 10 students a number sign (0–9) to wear. Then have students arrange themselves in order in a circle. Give an 11th student a roll of string, ribbon, or crepe paper, and identify that student as the designer. Direct the designer to give the end of the ribbon to the student wearing the 0 sign and then to follow a +2 number rule (that is, the designer counts two students and has the second student hold on to the ribbon). The designer continues around the circle until they are back at the starting point. Have the other students count "2, 4, 6, 8, 10" as the stitching is formed. Ask students if they notice anything about the numbers they are saying aloud and the numbers the students are wearing. Point out to students that only the 1s digit is given, so for 10, they only see the 0. Then, explore +1 and +5 rules.

Students can explore number rules using the *Circle with 10 Points* on paper, as described in the activity. Encourage extensive discussion as students discover patterns. For example, the +8 pattern is the same as the +2 pattern, because each time, the 10 points are being separated into a group of 8 and a group of 2. Or as one second-grade student observed, "When you go back 8, it is the same as going forward 2. So, they are the same but backward."

Provide hands-on practice by giving students cardboard that has 10 holes punched in a circle. Have them lace yarn or embroidery thread through the holes to create curved stitching patterns.

Grades 3–5

Students can connect the designs that are the same in the circles to the inverse relationship between addition and subtraction. They also can use their understanding of multiples and factors to make predictions about designs if they know the number rule, the number of points, and that the rule starts at 0. For example, they know that $4 \times 5 = 20$, so they should be able to predict that a +4 rule will result in a regular pentagon on a circle with 20 points. Differences between prime and composite numbers also can be discussed.

Students can explore designs that result from using right angles and focus on measurement and the relationships among lines and curves. Have students trace an index-card corner to make a right angle and measure the same number of equidistant points on each line segment. Students then draw lines from one segment to the other. Have students begin by connecting the top point on the vertical segment with the first point on the horizontal segment. An example is shown below. Students can then investigate the design possibilities when they combine these configurations or when they change the measures of the lengths and angles. Invite students to consider how the use of complementary colors can bring their composition to life in new ways.

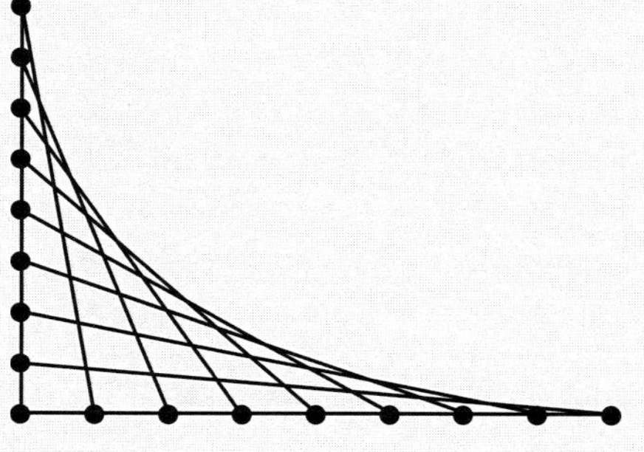

Visual Patterns *(cont.)*

Specific Grade-Level Ideas *(cont.)*

Grades 6–8

In addition to the ideas for grades 3–5, students can explore linear algebraic relationships. For example, if students start at 5 on the *Circle with 10 Points* and follow a +6 number rule and do not stop when drawing over the same line, at what number would they be after drawing 15 lines? Help students identify the $y = 6x + 5$ equation to describe the relationship between the number of times the +6 number rule is applied, starting at 5, and the number at which they end. After generating several such rules, have students explain the meaning of the slope and the y-intercept in this real-world application.

Students also can use their knowledge of circumference and their ability to measure internal angles around the center to mark their own equidistant points on the circle.

Grades 9–12

Some students may want to do research online about modular arithmetic developed by Leonhard Euler and later advanced by Carl Friedrich Gauss and connect the notion of equivalent classes to these circles. Encourage students to consider a variety of designs and not limit themselves to circles or right angles.

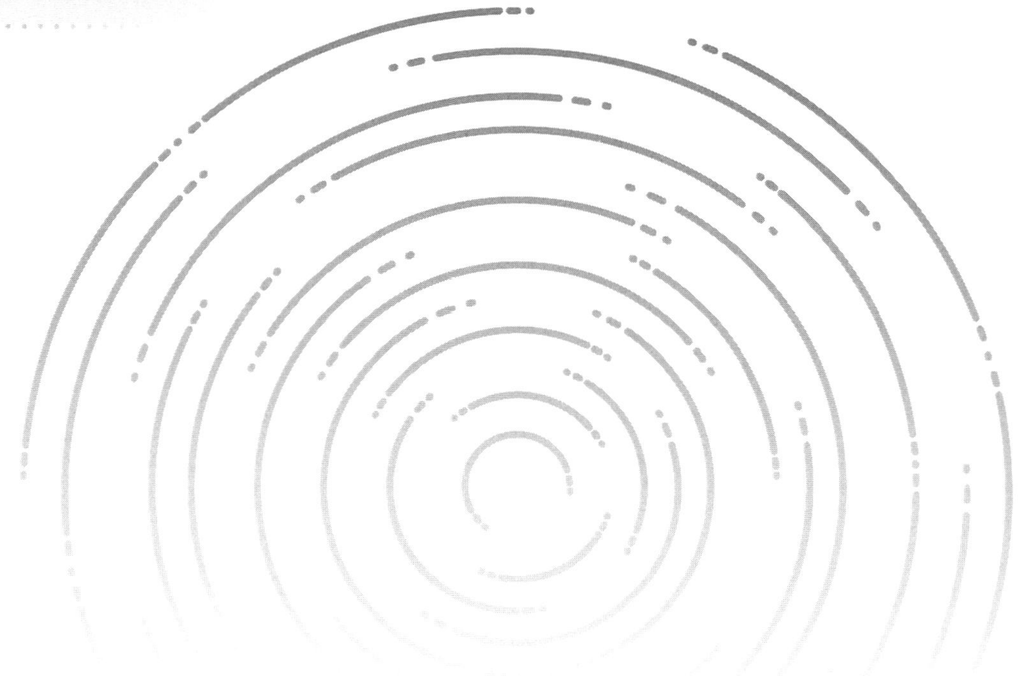

Name: ____ Date:_________________________

Circle with 10 Points

Directions: Make a pattern using a number rule of your choice. Then, on a separate sheet of paper, explain why you chose this rule and the mathematics illustrated by your rule.

0

9

1

8

2

7

3

6

4

5

Name: ___________________________________ Date: ________________

Circle with 12 Points

Directions: Make a pattern using number rules of your choice. Then, on a separate sheet of paper, explain why you chose those rules and the mathematics illustrated by each rule.

0

11

1

10

2

9

3

8

4

7

5

6

Name: _______________________________________ Date:__________________

Circle with 23 Points

Directions: Make a pattern using number rules of your choice. Then, on a separate sheet of paper, explain why you chose those rules and the mathematics illustrated by each rule.

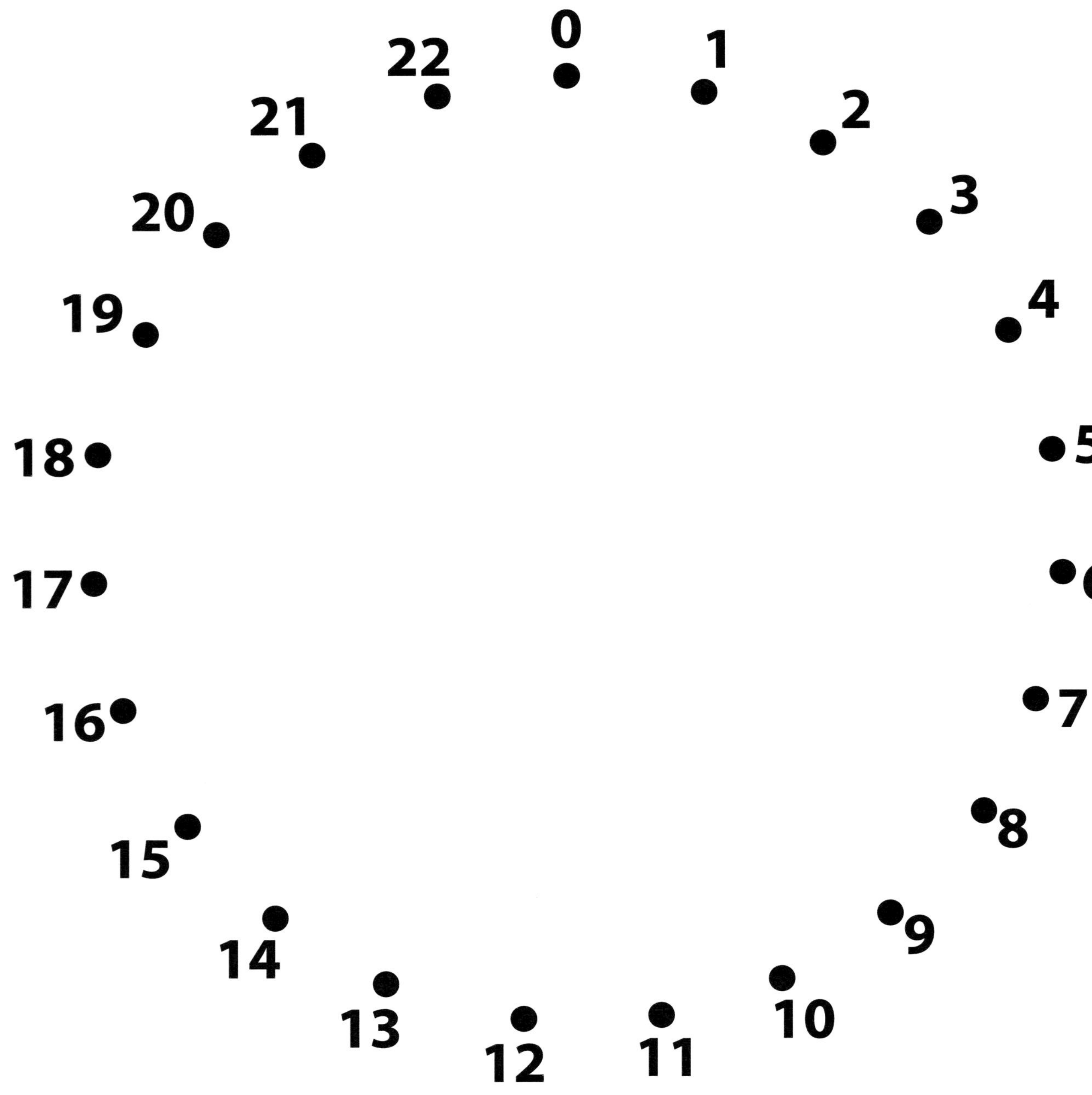

Representation

Model Lesson: Creating an Infographic

Overview

Translating data into visual form through the visual arts can help tell the story of data in fresh ways. In this strategy, students collect data and use visual art to highlight ideas within the numbers, incorporating visual means to provide context, comparison, and even commentary. Students collect data and then create their own representations of that data, thinking about multiple ways their quantitative data can be represented. This process allows students to act as mathematicians and artists as they create their own visual-information maps.

Materials

- art supplies (paper, colored pencils, markers, paint, scissors, crayons, paper, magazines, and so on)
- *Infographic Sample* (page 200)
- *Data Collection Planner* (page 201)
- *Data Collection Summary* (page 202)
- *Infographic Planner* (page 203)
- *Elements of Visual Art* and *Principles of Design* (pages 179–180)

Standards

Grades K–2

- Collects, organizes, and represents information about objects or events in simple graphs
- Describes what an image represents
- Uses observation and investigation in preparation for making a work of art

Grades 3–5

- Organizes and represents data in simple bar graphs, pie charts, and line graphs
- Determines messages communicated by an image
- Identifies and demonstrates diverse methods of artistic investigation

Grades 6–8

- Represents a given situation using verbal descriptions, tables, graphs, and equations
- Analyzes multiple ways that images influence specific audiences
- Develops criteria to guide making a work of art that meets an identified goal

Grades 9–12

- Selects and uses the best method to represent and describe a set of data
- Identifies intentions of those creating artworks

Representation (cont.)

Preparation

Collect a wide range of artistic materials for students to use, as well as reference books for the topic appropriate for your grade level and of interest to students. Find at least two examples of data represented visually from the books you collect. For younger students, Dacey, Hopping, and Salemi (2018) suggest that this strategy be used following Calkins and Tolan's unit on research (2015) and focus on animals. Decide whether to have students work individually or in groups. For older students, share with them *The Visual Display of Quantitative Information* (2001) by Edward Tufte. Tufte, a statistician and artist, is known for his creative visual representation of numerical data. Refer to the Specific Grade-Level Ideas for additional suggestions. This lesson is based on a research project about honeybees.

> "At the intersection of art and algorithm, data visualization schematically abstracts information to bring about a deeper understanding of the data wrapping it in an element of awe."
>
> —Maria Popova (2009, para. 1)

Procedure

1. Explain to students that one thing that mathematicians do is collect and share information, and artists help us to "see" the data in meaningful ways. Discuss how images help us understand relationships among data that are less obvious when only numbers are shown.

2. Introduce students to the idea of infographics as a strategy to take complex data and information and translate it into easy-to-understand visuals. Tell them they will take on the role of a graphic designer challenged to present the data in a simple, understandable, and also engaging way.

3. Show students the visual representations of data you have chosen and have pairs talk about what they see and how the visualizations capture the main ideas of the data.

4. Share with students the art terms from *Elements of Visual Art* and *Principles of Design* and have them identify the elements within one of the infographics you shared. Ask, "How do elements of art and principles of design help communicate the data?"

5. Share the following information about bees from *Honeybee: The Busy Life of Apis Mellifera* by Candace Fleming (or a similar fact from your chosen topic): One hard-working honeybee produces 1/12 teaspoon of honey in its entire lifetime, which can last from 36 days in peak summer to 3 to 4 months in winter.

6. Have students discuss how the specific numbers help them understand the life of a bee and ask, "How could a visual representation help communicate those ideas?" Have them brainstorm follow-up questions to these data such as: "How many bees does it take to make a jar of honey? How does the longevity of a bee compare with that of other insects?"

7. Explain to students that they are going to be mathematicians who collect data from a variety of sources and then designers who represent that data in captivating ways.

8. Divide the class into pairs and provide time for partners to talk about the data they want to collect and the references they will use. Students may wish to collect several examples of numerical data related to their topic. For example, if they chose bees as their topic, students could consider the average number of times their wings beat per minute, the number of different species of

Representation *(cont.)*

bees, the average number of eggs the queen bee lays in a day, or the dilemma of hive collapse. Students also could compare some of these data with those of other insects, representing related ratios and percentages. Have students record their planning on the *Data Collection Planner*. Use the Planning Questions to support students' thinking. Once they have checked their plans with you, their research can begin.

9. Once students have completed their research, have them work together to complete the *Data Collection Planner* and *Data Collection Summary*.

10. Tell students they will now create infographics of the data they collected. Encourage them to consider the *Elements of Visual Art* as they plan. Have them complete the *Infographic Planner*. Once you approve their plans, offer students a choice of art materials with which to create their infographics. Encourage students to think critically about which materials they will use to create their visual representation. As they complete the *Infographic Planner*, encourage students to think about what they want people to see in their data and how they can represent that visually. Ask, "How might you use visual symbols to represent your data in interesting ways?"

11. Invite students to think about the role of composition in an infographic. The goal of an infographic is to make data attractive and easy-to-read, create a sense of flow, and give data a feeling (Workerbee 2014). See the *Infographic Sample*.

12. Give students time to create their infographics.

13. Have students share their renderings and use the Discussion Questions to discuss their findings. Encourage them to compare the different methods of representation.

Planning Questions

▸ What information about your topic interests you?

▸ What research will be helpful?

▸ How will you collect and keep track of the data?

▸ How will design principles help you communicate the data?

▸ What images will you include?

▸ How will you organize the composition of the infographic to guide the viewer's eye?

▸ How will you integrate processes that highlight mathematical thinking? For example how will you:

- organize information?
- document mathematical thinking?
- connect to the real world?

Discussion Questions

▸ What artistic choices did you make to create your infographic?

▸ What struck you about the infographics of your peers?

▸ How did working with visual-arts materials help you think of ideas for your visual representation?

▸ How does the creation of an artistic work move beyond simple reporting of numerical data? What did you learn from looking at the visual representation of data?

▸ What data might you collect next that might lead to interesting infographics?

Representation *(cont.)*

Specific Grade-Level Ideas

Grades K–2

Help students choose a topic they can focus on as a class. They can then work in pairs to collect data from picture books. Once they have found information, have each student work individually to create an illustration of one numerical fact that interests them. Students can then each add their illustration to create a collaborative infographic. Some students may be able to combine some of the data and include it in a bar graph. The visual representation of ideas is essential in all areas of mathematics. Students who develop strong visual images of numbers, for example, are able to see that 6 is one more than 5 or that 8 is less than 10. Students also can use visual representations to show information in a story problem or what they did to solve a problem.

Grades 3–5

If focused on animals, students can consider data related to the lengths, weights, average speeds, and average lifespans of animals. Encourage students to make such data more meaningful by adding comparative information. For example, a representation might show that a northern giraffe could be 20 feet tall alongside a picture of five children standing on top of one another. Visual representations can be more complex as students compare and contrast and work with more nuanced ways to tell the story the data reveals. For example, have students create pictorial representations of an animals' height over its lifetime along with more traditional representations such as bar graphs and line plots. Encourage students to share their infographics and explore artistic choices as well as how the data have been presented.

Visual models permeate mathematics. Students can use visual representations to show relationships among numbers. They can draw bars to organize information in a word problem or number lines to organize their thinking about the four operations. Consider expanding the visual language students can use to express their understanding.

Representation *(cont.)*

Specific Grade-Level Ideas *(cont.)*

Grades 6–8

Students can work with data from any area of interest and collect data outside the classroom or online. Invite students to design their infographics for printing and create a classroom gallery.

Encourage students to depict data in nontraditional ways as well as in traditional formats (graphs and plots). Ask them to comment on how the different visual representations affect the communication of the mathematical ideas.

Representation of relationships is key to algebraic thinking, as students are expected to make links among tables, graphs, and equations. Representation also helps students model operations with integers, discover proportional relationships, experiment with functions, and have facility with other mathematical processes.

Grades 9–12

Have students collect data related to real-world issues with the goal of persuasion (for example, climate change, income inequalities, peer pressure). Students can integrate data shown in histograms and box plots within their nontraditional, more artistic representations of the data. Display the representations randomly and have students try to match the traditional mathematical representations to their nontraditional representations. Have students discuss visual choices made to support their persuasive arguments and consider options for publishing in the student or local newspaper.

Infographic Sample

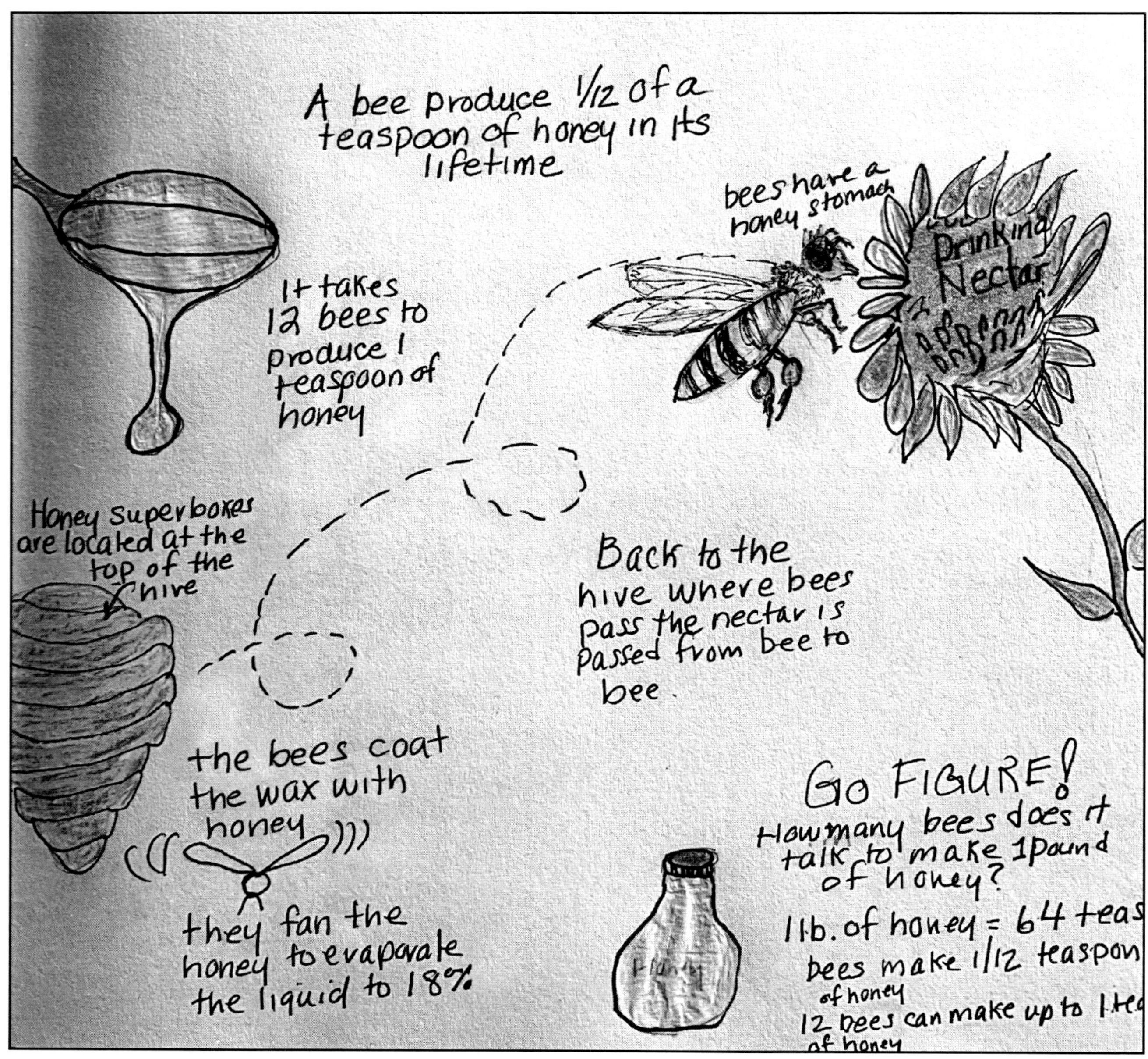

Name: _______________________________________ Date: _________________

Data Collection Planner

Directions: Answer the questions to help you plan for your data collection.

1. What topic interests you?

   ____

   ____

2. How will your group make decisions about what data to collect?

   ____

   ____

   ____

3. What will you research? What sources will you use?

   ____

   ____

   ____

4. What questions might you ask to discover the big ideas in your data?

   ____

   ____

   ____

5. What images might you include?

   ____

   ____

   ____

   ____

Data Collection Summary

Directions: Organize and think about the data you collected. Answer these questions to help you plan for your data infographic.

The data I found:

____

____

____

____

The data makes me wonder:

____

____

____

____

The most interesting piece of data to me is . . . because . . .

____

____

____

____

Name: ____ Date:_______________________

Infographic Planner

Directions: Complete these sections to plan your composition.

What big ideas do I want to communicate?

____

____

____

What visuals do I want to use to show math ideas? (Examples: sketches, arrows, symbols, pictures, numbers, words)

____

____

____

How will I place images on the page?

____

____

What materials will I use?

____

____

My thumbnail sketch to plan the composition of my infographic:

Visual Observation

Model Lesson: Masterpiece Math

Overview

When focusing on the work of well-known artists or art movements, students gain an appreciation for art and its history. They can draw mathematical concepts from visual representation. This activity focuses on the work of Solomon (Sol) LeWitt, who worked with a variety of media and whose work is connected to conceptual art and minimalism. For his wall art, he created guidelines or simple diagrams of what others were to draw or paint directly on walls. Students follow and create directions for similar works using ideas involving geometry and measurement. Ways to connect the work of other visual artists to mathematics are provided in the Specific Grade Level Ideas. All works referenced can be found on the internet.

Materials

▸ file folders (*optional*)

▸ *Solomon LeWitt Sample* (page 209)

▸ *Solomon LeWitt Planner* (page 210)

▸ *Elements of Visual Art* and *Principles of Design* (pages 179–180)

▸ mural paper (*optional*)

▸ paint, colored pencils, or crayons (*optional*)

▸ rulers

Standards

Grades K–2

▸ Compares and analyzes simple geometric shapes by basic properties, similarities, and differences between simple geometric shapes

▸ Uses observation and investigation in preparation for making a work of art

▸ Interprets art by identifying subject matter and describing relevant details

Grades 3–5

▸ Classifies and describes shapes using geometric language

▸ Understands basic properties of figures

▸ Identifies and demonstrates diverse methods of artistic investigation

▸ Interprets art by analyzing characteristics of form and structure and visual elements

Grades 6–8

▸ Understands the defining properties of triangles

▸ Develops criteria to guide making a work of art that meets an identified goal

▸ Interprets art by analyzing subject matter and characteristics of form and structure

Grades 9–12

▸ Translates between the geometric description and the equation

▸ Applies media, techniques, and processes with sufficient skill, confidence, and sensitivity that one's intentions are carried out in artworks

Visual Observation *(cont.)*

Preparation

Become familiar with the work of Solomon (Sol) LeWitt by searching the internet or visiting the website of the Massachusetts Museum of Contemporary Art (**www.massmoca.org/lewitt/**). Select a few wall murals to share with students and choose one on which to focus their attention. At the end of the activity, students will create their own LeWitt-style drawings with instructions. The scope of the work is up to you. Depending on what you decide, you will provide mural paper and tempera paints, colored pencils or crayons, and regular plain paper, or have students complete their final drawings outside of class. Read the Specific Grade-Level Ideas for other ways to connect to the work of visual artists. These activities could be explored over time or combined at a learning station.

> "Inserting fine art into mathematics classes makes the learning experience more inwardly active and the subject matter more comprehensible. This connection enables different views and approaches to knowledge, deepening and personalizing the learning experience. Such a perspective in mathematics opens opportunities for exciting discussions in which students enthusiastically report the different methods they have found leading to the same solution."
>
> —Anja Brezovnik (2015, 16)

Procedure

1. Write the following LeWitt-type directions on the board. Read the directions to students and have them make a sketch based on them. Encourage students to work independently, perhaps creating a private office space by placing file folders upright around their papers. (Adapt the directions to better meet the readiness of students.)

   Divide your paper into halves.
   In one half draw two rectangles and one triangle.
   The lengths of the sides of the triangle should all be different.
   Add color or pattern in the triangle and one of the rectangles.
   There should be four thick lines, each one-inch long, drawn in the other rectangle. Each of the lines should be a different color.
   In the other half, draw two lines that are perpendicular.
   Add color or pattern to the regions the lines formed.

2. Have students share their sketches and identify how they are different and alike.

3. Tell students that an artist named Solomon LeWitt, known as Sol, wrote directions for wall drawings that others then followed to create murals. Share some images of LeWitt's work with students, asking them to note common colors and shapes. Draw their attention to the expansiveness of these wall drawings. Point out when and where these murals were created.

4. Show a single image of a LeWitt mural. Ask students to talk with a partner about the directions LeWitt may have written so that others could create this work. Have partners take notes about their ideas and provide time for several pairs to present their thinking. Discuss the variety of directions. Ask, "Which directions would be best if the goal was to create an exact copy?" Tell students that LeWitt was open to the interpretation of his directions. Ask, "Which directions would be best if this was his intention?"

Visual Observation *(cont.)*

5. Share the *Elements of Visual Art* and *Principles of Design*. Discuss how these ideas can inform artistic choices. Ask students what elements and principles of design were used in the example.

6. Tell students that they will now create their own LeWitt drawings by first writing the directions and then drawing an image based on those directions. Distribute and have students complete the *Solomon LeWitt Planner*. As students work, use the Planning Questions to guide their thinking.

7. Once you approve their plans, provide the materials and time for students to either create the drawings in class or as homework. Create a display of the completed projects, along with their directions.

8. Use the Discussion Questions to debrief the completed projects.

Planning Questions

▸ What shapes, colors, and lines do you want to use? Why?

▸ How will you use measurements and geometric terms to describe your picture?

▸ Do you want your directions to be exact or open to interpretation?

▸ Are there other ways to describe this?

▸ How might you use a code or diagram to represent this information?

Discussion Questions

▸ What does your artwork communicate about math?

▸ What choices did you make?

▸ What colors, shapes, lines, or patterns did you use, and why?

Visual Observation *(cont.)*

Specific Grade-Level Ideas

Grades K–2

Students can explore the style of Sol LeWitt by using directions with references to color, number, length, position, and basic two-dimensional shapes. They also can include references to terms that describe spatial relations such as *above*, *below*, and *between*. Measurement directions should be in whole units, and the units may be informal or standard. You may want to display a few of their representations, read the directions for one of them, and have students identify the matching drawing.

Try experimenting with creating artwork as a class. Go around the room to have each student add another element of the artwork, like a line, shape, or color. Record the instructions together and trade them with another class. Invite the other class to replicate the artwork. Compare and contrast the two artworks.

Other masterpieces to observe to stimulate mathematical ideas include the still-life paintings of Robert Seldon Duncanson such as "Still Life with Fruits and Nuts." Ask questions such as, "Why do you think the artist organized the shapes in this way? How does the number of each food item compare? How might you estimate the number of each food item?" Allow time for students to sketch their own still-life pictures and talk about their sketches in artistic and mathematical terms.

Grades 3–5

Students can focus on directions with references to color, number, length, and two-dimensional shapes. Directions involving measurements can include fractions of a unit as well as references to area and perimeter. Types of angles also may be included. Students can exchange directions and create their artwork based on someone else's description.

Other masterpieces to observe to stimulate mathematical ideas include the vivid quilts of Gee's Bend in Southern Alabama. Show pictures of the quilts and ask students how the quilts compare to others they have seen. Have students take turns describing the geometric figures in one of the quilts as listeners try to identify the quilt that is depicted. Students can create their own similar geometric designs with construction paper.

Visual Observation *(cont.)*

Specific Grade-Level Ideas *(cont.)*

Grades 6–8

Students can focus on directions with reference to proportional relationships, special properties of triangles, and transformations. Additionally, students can observe the proportional relationships within a person's face. Ask, "How widely set are the eyes? What is the variation among people's face lengths? Does it relate to the widths of faces?" Have students conduct research online, in art books, or experimentally by measuring the faces of people they know and combining their data. Next, have them explore the proportional relationships within the faces in famous masterpieces. For example, students can compare the face drawn by Mary Stevenson Cassatt in *Young Woman in Green* with Pablo Picasso's cubist painting *Woman in a Blue Hat*. Students also can explore the caricature-like ways Kabuki actors are portrayed in the woodblock prints of Toshusai Sharaku. Have students consider how the proportions in these faces suggest that they are caricatures. Students who wish to explore such relationships further may research the *Vitruvian Man* drawn by Leonardo da Vinci and the notion of the golden rectangle.

Grades 9–12

Look at geometric artworks by Op artist Bridget Riley. Challenge students to write an algorithm to replicate one of Riley's artworks, using mathematical terminology. Or challenge them to make their own artwork by graphing a series of ellipses and applying color (with colored pencils, for example). Have each student write the mathematical expressions/equations to replicate the ellipses and trade the equations with a partner. Have partners see if they can use the equations to graph the ellipses and reproduce the original artwork.

Students also can research other conceptual artists and learn the controversy related to this field. For example, they can give directions for three-dimensional creations and examine the sculptures of Charles O. Perry. One of Perry's sculptures, *Continuum*, is located in front of the National Air and Space Museum in Washington, DC, and is based on explorations of the Möbius strip. Students also can explore the tessellations and paradoxes in the etchings of M. C. Escher.

Solomon LeWitt Sample

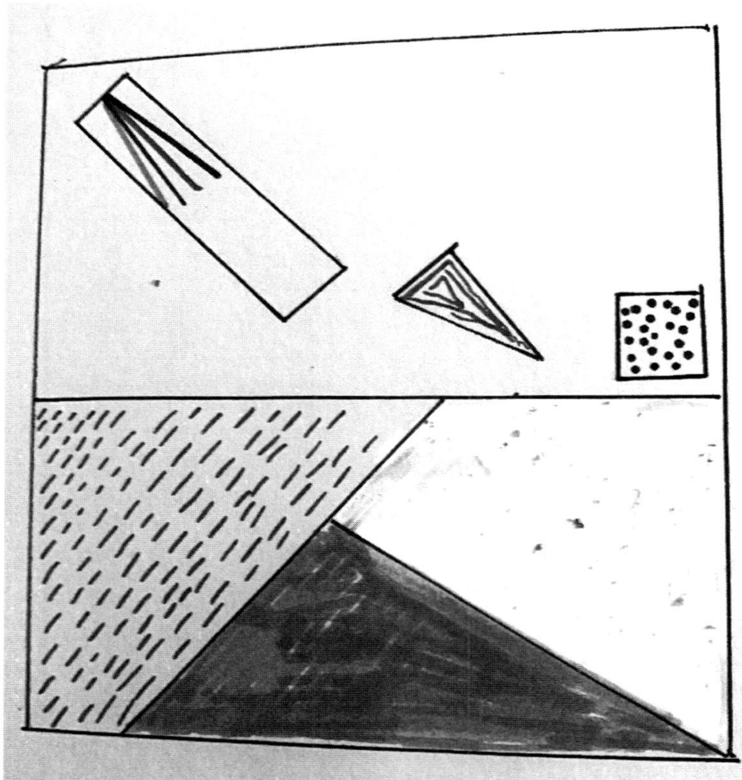

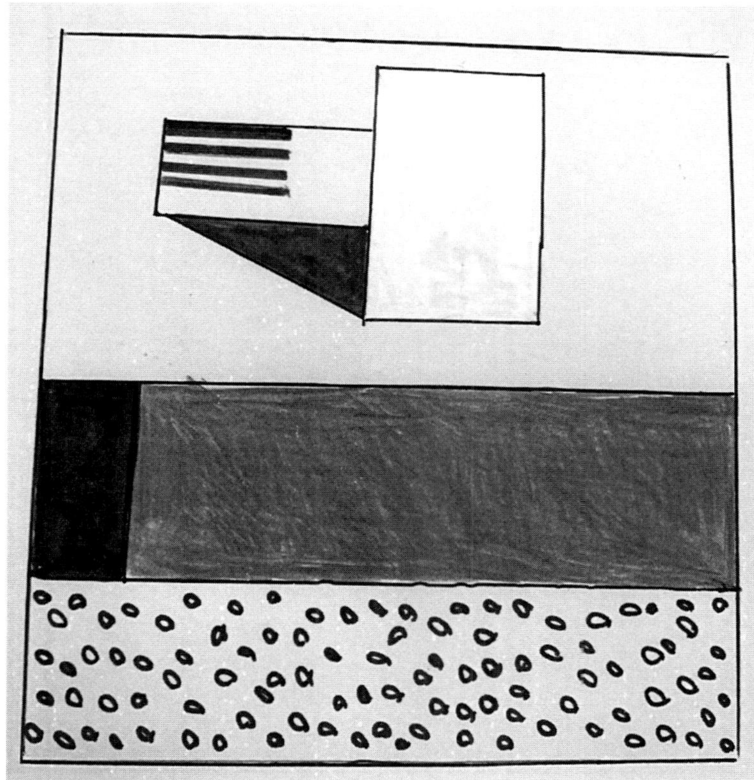

Name: ____ Date: ___________________

Solomon LeWitt Planner

Directions: Use this planning sheet to record the directions for your drawing, the materials you will use, and a sketch of how the drawing will look.

My directions:

____

____

____

____

The materials I will use:

____

____

____

My sketch:

© Shell Education

Mixed Media

Model Lesson: Collage

Overview

In this strategy, students complete a collage inspired by the geometric shapes they see around them. Each shape they include in their collage will represent an object, such as a piece of furniture, in a designated interior space. Students will explore how items in their surroundings can be described through geometric terminology and represented visually, with careful attention to spatial relationships.

Materials

▸ examples of artworks by well-known collage artists (see Preparation for ideas)

▸ *Collage Composition Planner* (page 216)

▸ heavy paper to serve as a backing for the collage

▸ a variety of colorful papers, such as tissue paper, construction paper, parchment, sand paper, rice paper, newsprint, or magazine clippings

▸ *Elements of Visual Art* and *Principles of Design* (pages 179-180)

▸ other flat materials that can be glued down, such as fabric scraps, ribbon, or clear acetate sheets

▸ glue sticks and/or liquid glue

▸ rulers, compasses, scissors

Standards

Grades K–2

▸ Reasons with shapes and their attributes

▸ Creates art that tells a story about a life experience

▸ Makes art with various materials and tools to explore personal interests, questions, and curiosity

Grades 3–5

▸ Reasons with shapes and their attributes

▸ Applies knowledge of available resources, tools, and technologies to investigate personal ideas through the art-making process

▸ Identifies and analyzes cultural associations suggested by visual imagery

Grades 6–8

▸ Draws construct, describes geometrical figures, and describes the relationships between them

▸ Formulates an artistic investigation of personally relevant content for creating art

▸ Analyzes ways that visual components and cultural associations suggested by images influence ideas and emotions

Grades 9–12

▸ Understands and applies theorems about circles

▸ Applies media, techniques, and processes with sufficient skill, confidence, and sensitivity that one's intentions are carried out in artworks

Mixed Media *(cont.)*

Preparation

View examples of artworks by well-known collage artists, such as Hannah Höch, Kurt Schwitters, Romare Bearden, Kike Congrains, and Lance Letscher. Select at least one example to discuss with the class. Choose a designated interior space for students to explore, such as the classroom, school library, or school cafeteria. If you select a space other than the classroom, consider taking photographs of the space so that students can refer to them later.

> "When we think about the fact that students are more often than not (about sixty five percent) visual learners, it stands to reason that connecting difficult math concepts with visual images would help kids make connections."
>
> —Pat Klos (2013, para. 1)

Procedure

1. Review geometric shapes as needed. Discuss defining attributes of specific shapes versus nondefining attributes.

2. Go to the interior space you've chosen, such as the classroom, the school library, or the school cafeteria. Provide each student with a copy of the *Collage Composition Planner* and a clipboard and ask them to go on an observation walk to list all the objects they see that can be simplified as a geometric shape or that are made up of geometric shapes. For example, the desktop might be a square, the clock on the wall might be a circle, the rug on the floor might be a rectangle, and a box fan might be a square and a circle.

3. Discuss what students have recorded on their *Collage Composition Planner*, paying close attention to objects that many students noticed and documented, as well more obscure, complex objects that might

spark debate. Note that many objects in our surroundings are three-dimensional, such as a chair, but when simplifying an object we may notice that the back of the chair can be distilled into a rectangular shape.

4. Gather students to view the preselected examples of collages by well-known artists. Define *collage* as a type of artwork made by gluing different materials, such as papers or fabric, onto a backing. Encourage students to pay close attention to the elements of art seen in the examples, such as color, line, texture, and shape. See if they can identify geometric shapes within the collage.

5. Explain that students will each make their own 2-D collage that represents a portion of the designated space they explored. The collage will feature geometric shapes to represent the various objects and furniture in the room. Explain to students that the final artwork will have an *abstract* look. Explain that abstract art may or may not represent visual reality. Instead of a realistic representation, it relies on shape, color, form, and texture to impact the viewer. This means that students are not aiming to make their collages look like a realistic representation of the space; rather, the space will be simplified into colors and shapes that represent the real objects in the room.

6. Demonstrate how to begin the collage by starting with the backing on which all other objects will be glued down. Display the variety of papers and flat materials that are available for the class to use.

7. Share with students the *Elements of Art Terms* and *Principles of Design*. Invite students to be intentional about the juxtaposition of color, shape, line, and texture and to experiment with the visual effects of overlapping and use of texture.

    117847—Integrating the Arts in Mathematics   © Shell Education

Mixed Media *(cont.)*

8. Have students decide which section of the designated space will be represented in their collages. Stress that the whole room will not be depicted in the collage; it will just show a portion of the space, and this is up to the artist to decide. Show students how to refer to the *Collage Composition Planner* to remember what could be included in the artwork. If the designated space was not the classroom, display the photographs of the space if you have them. Use the Planning Questions to support students' thinking.

9. Demonstrate how to choose a paper/material from which a geometric shape can be cut. Encourage students to make connections to the paper's color and texture and the color and texture of the actual object. For example, if the rectangular table is worn away and bumpy, then a crumpled piece of brown craft paper may be a meaningful choice. Show how to use a ruler and/or compass and a pencil to measure out a geometric shape that approximates the real object. Use scissors to cut out the shape from the paper/material.

10. Introduce the term *composition*. In visual art, composition refers to the way that elements are arranged in the artwork. Encourage students to be aware of the relationships between the geometric shapes on their pages. For younger students, use positional words such as *next to, under, on top of,* and so on. Remind students that while the collage will not be realistic, they should still pay attention to how the shapes interact spatially. For example, on top of the oval rug may be a rectangular table. Show students how to overlap the two shapes and glue them down. Continue with the demonstration as long as necessary. Remind students that not every single object needs to be depicted in the collage; each artist must make choices about what to include and what to omit.

11. Distribute the heavy backing paper, rulers, scissors, glue, and other papers/materials.

12. Provide students with ample time to create their collages.

13. Have students share and discuss their complete collages using the Discussion Questions.

Planning Questions

▸ How will you decide which portion of the interior space to show in your collage?

▸ How can you communicate which objects the geometric shapes represent through the use of color, texture, orientation, and size?

▸ How will you decide which objects to include in your artwork and which objects to omit?

▸ How can you ensure that you're cutting out an accurate geometric shape?

Discussion Questions

▸ What did you learn about the shapes in your designated place by making an abstract collage of it?

▸ What can a person who has never seen the space before learn from your collage?

▸ How did color and texture play a part in your collage?

▸ Can you point out defining attributes of one of the shapes? How about nondefining attributes?

▸ Compare and contrast your collage to a classmate's collage. How are they the same? How are they different?

Mixed Media *(cont.)*

Specific Grade-Level Ideas

Grades K–2

In addition to rulers for making shapes, you could provide young students with premade shape stencils.

Ask students to go on a shape hunt around the classroom and gather hand-held items that are composed of geometric shapes. Gather all the items and select some of them to make a unique tabletop arrangement. As a class, create a geometric shape *still life* collage based on the arranged items.

Grades 3–5

Challenge students to work with just one type of geometric shape, such as a triangle. Encourage students to figure out creative ways to use the shape to represent all the items in collage. For example, two triangles might be placed together to make a rectangle. Students might cluster shapes according to common attributes such as *has a right angle*. They also could make collages to depict examples of fractions in their surroundings.

Grades 6–8

Have students exchange their artworks with classmates and then challenge them to calculate the area of as many of the shapes as possible. You also can invite students to create a collage depicting a visual equation that shows how the same quantity can be added to both sides of an equation.

Grades 9–12

Students at this level could focus on curves in their surroundings. They could artistically highlight the curves in their collages as well as include accompanying mathematical descriptions and possible equations.

Sample Mixed Media Collage

Name: _______________________________________ Date:_________________

Collage Composition Planner

Directions: Complete this chart to support the design of your collage.

Object	Shape	Sketch

 117847—Integrating the Arts in Mathematics

© Shell Education

Creative Movement

Creative Movement

Understanding Creative Movement

Integrating creative movement across the curriculum is an engaging approach to learning that allows students to experience, translate, and communicate mathematics ideas kinesthetically. Howard Gardner identified bodily kinesthetic intelligence within his theory of multiple intelligences (2011) as one way that students learn. Neuroscientists are finding that memory and recall are improved when the body is engaged in the learning process (Zull 2002) and that the mind uses the body to make sense of ideas (Carpenter 2011).

Opportunities to express themselves nonverbally can be powerful for students. Such opportunities can provide students with access to mathematics content that would not be possible otherwise. Stacey Skoning (2008) states that creative movement, or dance, "is important to incorporate into our inclusive classrooms if we want to meet the needs of more diverse groups of students" (9).

Creative movement allows students to be physically active, which often increases students' attention span, but it is much more than just the incorporation of movement into classroom activities. When students are involved in creative movement, they become more mindful of their bodies' ability to communicate, explore what happens when they move with intention, engage in problem solving through movement, and develop awareness of their creative choices. It is important to keep the possibilities for this work in mind as students explore these lessons.

As students deconstruct and reconstruct concepts, they take ownership of the ideas through kinesthetic means and creative choices. Writer and choreographer Susan Griss (1994) makes the point that creative movement is "expressive, informative, and analytical." It can heighten learning in the mathematics classroom by supporting the understanding of numerical and spatial relations, as well as creating meaning for abstract ideas, and helping students develop a more positive attitude toward mathematics (Werner, 2001).

> "Creative movement embraces an *every body* spirit. All the activities can be done seated or standing, stationary or ambulatory."
>
> —Celeste Miller, Choreographer and Educator (personal communication, May 4, 2021)

Elements of Creative Movement

These elements are drawn from the Kennedy Center (Bodensteiner 2019), PBS Learning Media (KQED 2015), the Institute for Arts Integration and STEAM (Riley 2017), the National Core Arts Standards, and the Perpich Center for Arts Education (2009).

- **Body:** Creative movement works with the parts of the body to move, isolate, manipulate to create shape and movement through space.

- **Space:** Creative movement interacts with and occupies space on different levels, in different pathways, in different size and scope of movement.

- **Action:** *Non-locomotor*, which is axial-movement around the body's axis and *locomotor*, movement that travels through space

- **Time:** Movement happens over time and can communicate through tempo and rhythm.

- **Energy:** The qualities (sustained, percussive, suspended, etc.), weight (heavy, light, etc.), and flow (continuous, controlled, etc.) of how movement occurs

Creative Movement *(cont.)*

Strategies for Creative Movement

Each creative movement strategy results in a short piece of choreography: repeatable dances made up of original movements created by students. The final strategy, Choreographic Structure, is an advanced step in this process that introduces students to several tools of choreography and the suite form.

Answer Me in Movement

Students respond to a question from the teacher, and, instead of answering with words, they "answer" by creating their own movement to express their response. This could be as simple as an arm gesture such as circling the arms over the head to represent the sun. Answer Me in Movement invites students to develop the skill of translating ideas into new forms, exploring the meaning of concepts in new ways.

Movement Strings

Students invent a series of movements that can be strung together, similar to beads on a string. This strategy works well with lists of ideas that can be organized sequentially.

Progressions

Students focus on the transitions between their movements. It is a further development of Movement Strings. This strategy provides an opportunity to connect concepts, processes, and events into a movement phrase that links ideas together in meaningful ways.

Interpretation

This strategy invites students to make sense of a story, idea, or visual representation through creative movement. Students dig deeper into content, teasing out information that may not be immediately apparent. Through movement students make inferences, analyze data, and apply their own ideas about the meaning of what is presented.

This strategy is particularly helpful when students map change over time, recognize cause-and-effect relationships, and express their internal thought processes.

Choreographic Structure

In each creative movement strategy students are creating dances. This is choreography. Choreography begins with improvisation to create original movements and experiment with different ways to do them: fast or slow, big or little, and so on. From this experimentation the choreographer (or collaborative choreographers) selects the movements they want to use and orders them into sequences and patterns. This is called a *dance suite*. These now predetermined movements are repeatable. Students then rehearse the movements to prepare for their presentation. In this strategy, students are introduced to five choreographic structures to create a dance suite.

> "A dance suite can be thought of as a set of 'mini-dances' about the same topic or theme."
>
> —Celeste Miller, Choreographer and Educator (personal communication, May 4, 2021)

Creative Movement *(cont.)*

Choreography in the Classroom

Each of the creative movement strategies has been used successfully in classrooms by choreographer and educator Celeste Miller. The strategies are organized to build on each other, increasing in depth and complexity. Thus, it is highly recommended that you introduce the strategies to students in the order presented in this section:

1. Answer Me in Movement

2. Movement Strings

3. Progressions

4. Interpretation

5. Choreographic Structure

Students can move through the strategies sequentially, culminating in a short choreographed piece, or the strategies can be completed individually as one-time lessons.

All activities can be done in the classroom by moving tables/desks and seats to the outskirts of the room in an organized fashion. You also may take this process outside, use an open meeting area, or plan to use another open space such as the gym or cafeteria. A large space is not necessary for this process, but rather just another possibility. Students should stand in a circle formation with the teacher when given instructions and when sharing their creative products. Student breakout groups can be scattered throughout the room.

In the creative movement lesson plans, the word *dance* is used as a noun—"what is created"—and also as a verb—"to dance." We often think of dance as steps done to music, with a beat. In creative movement, dance encompasses unique motions created by the individual to express ideas. Creative movement dances can be done to silence or to words, in addition to music. Creative movement is unique and does not have to mimic the steps or a particular dance genre (though it can). In the lesson plans, students are

often referred to as "dancers." This is to empower students to own their agency as creative makers using dance. Teachers should make the decision to use the word based on the climate of their classroom; sometimes the word *dance* carries cultural or gendered overtones that inhibit student participation. Good substitute words for *dance* are *movement* (verb) or *movers* (noun). Teachers can refer to what their students are making as "creative movement explorations," instead of "dances." This is at your discretion.

Teaching the Strategies

Because these strategies build on each other, the first set of how-to lessons (pages 223–234) models how to introduce each strategy to students. The second set of lessons (pages 235–274) models one way to use the strategies with graphs. Each strategy allows students to use movement to further investigate the graphs in terms of the collection, representation, and interpretation of data, culminating in a combination of all the movements (strategies) into one choreographed piece. Should you choose to use a different graph, the lessons can serve as a guide to your thinking. Look for these characteristics in identifying graphs that work well with movement such as those that:

- show multiple changes

- focus on data that students will find relevant or interesting

- draw attention to the best types of graphs to summarize specific types of data

- stimulate investigations into related data

Creative Movement *(cont.)*

Helpful Terms

- **Dance**: Movement aware of itself done with purpose. These movements may be unique to each person who creates them.

- **Movement**: Individual movements, often gestures. These are discrete units that can be organized in any order. Movements or gestures are the equivalent of a "word" in a sentence.

- **Movement sequence**: The stringing together of several discrete movements. Movement sequences can be thought of as "sentences."

- **Choreography**: Purposeful movements arranged for effect to communicate ideas.

- **Choreography tools**: Forms that can be used to create movement patterns.

- **Shape**: A frozen pose that you hold. A shape is not limited to circle, square, triangle, and so on. Rather it is the design of the body, similar to a sculpture, that can be held in stillness. Shapes are done with the whole body. For example: Stand on one foot, with the free leg bent and the toe touching the standing leg knee. Arms are straight out to the side.

- **Level**: Levels are where the body is on a vertical plane: low, middle, or high. You could be close to the ground (low), or as high as you can reach (high), or in between high and low (middle).

Music is a helpful tool to use with students in creative movement. Check out this creative movement Spotify playlist by choreographer and educator Celeste Miller: (**open.spotify. com/playlist/7bvVFJ1Zj0gJgC1wv1Bwsz**). You can use this playlist with any of the lessons in this section.

- **Neutral stance**: This is a resting stance, whether seated or standing. A student once defined a neutral stance as: "It's like when a car is in neutral. It's not moving yet, but it is ready to go."

- **Call and response**: The leader does a movement, then the group responds by repeating the same movement back to the leader.

- **Copying**: The leader's back is to the group, and the group copies the leader. Thus the leader's right arm is the copier's right arm. If the leader moves to their right, everyone moves to their right.

- **Mirroring**: The leader faces the group. The group sees the leader as a mirror image. Thus the leader's right arm is the group's left arm. If the leader moves to their right, the group moves to their left.

- **Unison**: Everyone is doing the same thing at the same time in sync with one another.

- **Counter unison**: Endless versions and configurations of how different people are doing different things.

- **Transition**: The ability to connect movement ideas (for example, a person can go from skipping to walking or from reaching upward to twisting around themselves).

- **Fan**: One person does a movement while everyone else is still, then the second person does a movement while everyone else is still, and so on. Every student gets a turn, then the movements are completed in reverse order.

- **Rondo**: Dancers perform their individual movements in unique sequences, so everyone in the group must learn everyone else's movement. Each dancer completes each movement but in a different order from the rest.

- **Recurrence**: The repetition of something that has been done in a dance before, but usually with a slight twist.

Introducing the Strategies

Answer Me in Movement Introduction

1. Explain to students that in the Answer Me in Movement strategy, we use our bodies instead of words to communicate an idea. We do this by creating a single-movement response based on a prompt. Tell students to think of the movement as a gesture, similar to the common gestures of using a wave to say "hello" or your pinky and thumb to say "call me."

   One way to help students understand Answer Me in Movement is to reference the "live" function on a smartphone camera, where there is a slight bit of movement before the photo still is captured.

2. Share with students that you are going to give them a prompt, and you want them to show their movements en masse, which means "all together." Explain to students that they stay frozen at the end of their movement, thus creating a "snapshot" moment that nonverbally expresses their response to the prompt. Then, on your instruction to release, students should return to a neutral position. Say: "When I clap, I want you to answer me in movement, what is . . . ? When I clap again, go back to a neutral position."

   Example:

   Teacher: Answer me in movement, what is the weather today? *(Clap)*

   Students respond in movement with a unique original gesture that indicates today's weather; for example, on a sunny day one student may make a circle with her arms to indicate the sun and another student may turn his face upward and smile to indicate sunshine falling welcomingly on his face.

   After a short pause in which all students are frozen in their "answer," clap and have students relax into a neutral position.

3. Give each student a chance to show their movement and then share verbally what the movement represented and why it was their movement choice. **Note:** We never try and guess what a movement means; rather, this final step in the process gives students an opportunity to verbally share their movement-choice reasoning.

Introducing the Strategies *(cont.)*

Movement Strings Introduction

1. Explain to students that the Movement Strings strategy builds on the Answer Me in Movement strategy. Remind them that in that strategy they created gestures in single, original, and unique movements.

2. Share with students that in Movement Strings, their movements will last longer and contain more action before they freeze in their final pose. **Optional**: Consult the *Helpful Terms* (page 222) for movement types, sequences, or ideas to support students' creation of actions. Make sure you introduce the vocabulary as well as model the movements.

3. Read a sequential text with students (or refer to a previously read text), then have them brainstorm a list of the sequence of information or events that occurred in the text.

4. Help students create a movement for each item on the list. Then have them link those series of individual movements together so that they can perform the movements in sequence, similar to beads on a string, one after the other. Remind students, however, that each movement idea is discrete, so the order of the sequence could be rearranged. This will give students the opportunity to learn how altering how information is distributed can alter a narrative's message.

Example:

A student creates a movement for the idea "Connections are built." The student begins crouched down low to the ground with both hands on the ground, then slowly rises while keeping one hand to the floor, as she makes a staircase-like sequence of movements with her other hand getting higher and higher. Her movement concludes with a long stretch connecting the hand on the floor to the hand up in the air, and she looks first down to the hand on the floor and then up to the hand overhead. She decides to do her movement sequence slowly, gradually increasing in speed, while turning in place.

5. Provide each student the opportunity to show their movement to the class, share what the movement represented, and why they made that movement choice.

Introducing the Strategies (cont.)

Progressions Introduction

1. Display the word problem shown below or choose a problem to show students.

   Javier and Adina organized a collection of canned foods. On Saturday, they collected 48 cans. On Sunday, they were excited to realize that they collected 15 more cans than they had on Saturday. How many cans did they collect during these 2 days?

2. Instruct students to create a list of the sequence of events and factual information that is shared as well as the question asked. Explain that their focus should indicate the sequence of ideas, as well as the transitions between the ideas. Use chart paper to record their ideas.

3. Explain that inference is a tool that we use in Progressions, which means there is room for interpretation of emotional states when using this strategy.

4. Organize the sequence of events in a two-column chart, as shown in the Sample Progression chart (page 226). Explain to students that the left side of the chart details the sequence of events/information from the word problem. The right side of the chart details the movements that students choose to represent each part of the text. In this strategy, students focus on developing the ideas in column 2 so that the movements flow from one to the next. We avoid static positions, keeping the action going throughout.

5. Have students generate movement ideas for column 2, always linking their movements from what came before to what comes next. Students make their own interpretation about to how to end their progression.

Introducing the Strategies *(cont.)*

Sample Progression

The example of the canned foods problem is provided here.

Canned Foods Problem	Movement Ideas: For Four Students
Javier, Ella, Sean, and Adina organized a collection of canned foods.	Four students swirling around from place to place.
On Saturday they collected 48 cans.	Two students move arms in a welcoming motion, gathering everything in. They walk in a circle enclosing their collection.
On Sunday they were excited to realize that they collected 15 more cans than they had on Saturday.	Two different students standing apart from the other two students, move arms in a welcoming motion, gathering everything in. They walk in a circle enclosing their collection. They expand the circle to let more in while jumping up and down gleefully.
How many cans did they collect during these 2 days?	Each pair of students skips around their enclosed space, one space larger than the other. The two groups take long slow steps as they merge together, reaching their hands out to form a border for the one, large group. The four students put hands on thighs and take two labored breaths. Hands are joined in a circle. This final pose is held to complete the movement progression.

Introducing the Strategies *(cont.)*

Interpretation Introduction

1. Explain to students that the Interpretation strategy uses movement to communicate their interpretation of something.

2. Explain that you can interpret many different kinds of things, such as something you see (a graph or a picture), something you read (a story or an equation), or even something you feel (emotions). Also explain that in Interpretation we use our bodies to express ideas.

3. Tell students they are going to practice with concepts and tools related to measurement. Work through an example together such as "How can you show the concept of speed through movement? How would you describe the quality of the movement that depicts speed?"

4. Discuss with students different qualities of movement. For example, students can stay in one place and swing their arms (axial movement) or move through space. They can vary the speed and timing of their movements as well as the sharpness or fluidity. They can use their bodies to make shapes at different levels (low, medium, high) and/or make pathways.

5. Display the following ideas and tools related to measurement:
   - heavy
   - capacity
   - measuring tape
   - area
   - increasing height

6. As a class, practice creating interpretive movements for each of the concepts or tools. Have students play with movement ideas and describe what kinds of movement capture their essence. Encourage students to work with the concept or special use of the concepts or tools as opposed to an actual dramatization. For example, instead of showing someone using a measuring tape, one might move in circles to capture its special ability to measure curved lengths.

Introducing the Strategies *(cont.)*

Choreographic Structure Introduction

1. Explain to students that a dance suite is a choreographic structure for making longer and more complicated dances than they have made previously. An example of a dance suite is Carol Burch Brown's *Salt Marsh Suite*, which has six sections: tides, water, mud, birds, crabs, and grasses. Each section is its own topic, but all topics fit in the overall concept of the salt marsh.

2. Explain to students that they are going to practice creating a dance suite. They will use five choreographic tools for each of five sections of their dances. Choreographic tools are specific ways that movements can be arranged with one another.

3. Provide students with a theme around which to anchor their movements, such as the ocean, playground games, or animal habitats. If desired, select music to play in the background that matches the theme you select. This also may help students think about different movements they can use.

4. Place students into groups of five. (Groups of four or six also work, depending on the number of students in your class.) Distribute a copy of the *Choreography Planning Guide* (page 231–234) to each student. Introduce students to each of the five choreographic tools.

5. Explain that the first choreographic tool is called Call and Response. This is when one person (the soloist) performs a movement or movement sequence and then the rest of the group performs that movement or sequence as a response back to the soloist.

If you use verbal Call and Response in your classroom, make a connection to that.
For example:
Teacher: One, two, three, eyes on me . . .
Students: Four, three, two, looking at you!

6. To practice Call and Response, have one student in each group make some kind of motion and the rest of the group "answer back" with that same motion. If desired, play music while groups practice this choreographic tool. Have students record their movement in the Call and Response section of their planning guide.

7. Explain that the next choreographic tool is called Unison. This is where everyone does the same thing at the same time. Provide groups time to create an action or short movement sequence that they want to do in unison and briefly practice it. Have students record their movement in the Unison section of their planning guide.

8. Have groups put the movements they selected for the first two tools together. First they do their Call and Response movement(s) and then they do the Unison movement(s). Play music during this portion, as desired.

9. Explain that the third choreographic tool that they will learn is called the Fan. This is a sequence of movements where one student does a movement while everyone else is still, then the second person does a movement while everyone else is still, and so on. Have students think of this like a waterfall. In sports arenas, this is similar to the crowd doing the wave. However, in Fan, everyone does their own unique movement.

10. Provide groups time for each student to decide on their Fan movement as well as the order in which they want to do their movements. Have students record their movement in the Fan section of their planning guide.

Introducing the Strategies *(cont.)*

Choreographic Structure Introduction *(cont.)*

11. Select one group to help model this strategy. To do this, Student A does movement 1, Student B does movement 2, Student C does movement 3, Student D does movement 4, Student E does movement 5. Then Student E does movement 5 again, then Student D does movement 4, Student C does movement 3, Student B does movement 2, and Student A does movement 1. They arrive back where they started to complete the Fan.

12. Have students practice completing the Fan movement sequence.

13. Have groups put the movements they selected for all three tools together in sequence: Call and Response, Unison, Fan. Play music during this portion, as desired.

14. Explain that the next choreographic tool they will learn is called Rondo. This is when students perform their individual movements in unique sequences, so everyone in the group must learn everyone else's movement. For this practice, have students use the same movements they did in Fan, but have them teach them all to each other.

15. Display the Movement Sequence Guide shown on the next page to show how each student performs the movement sequence in a different order, but everyone is moving at the same time. Whereas in Unison everyone is doing the same thing at the same time, in Rondo it is similar to a round.

16. Have students record their movements in the Rondo section of their planning guide. Provide students time to practice.

17. Have groups put the movements they selected for all four tools together in sequence: Call and Response, Unison, Fan, Rondo. Play music during this portion, as desired.

18. Explain that the last choreographic tool students will learn is called Recurrence. This is the repetition of something that has been done before, but usually with a slight twist.

19. Have groups select a movement or movement sequence they have already done and then put a creative twist on it. For example, if students swayed their hands in the air earlier, this time they could sway their hands in the air while turning in a circle. Provide students time to practice their selected movement. Have them record their movement in the Recurrence section of their planning guide.

20. Have groups put all the movements for all five tools together in sequence: Call and Response, Unison, Fan, Rondo, Recurrence. Play music during this portion, as desired.

21. If desired, give each group time to share their dance suite with the rest of the class. This could be further developed into a school assembly.

Consider breaking up the introduction to the strategies over three to four days so that students feel comfortable with each choreographic tool before moving on.

Introducing the Strategies *(cont.)*

Movement Sequence Guide

Student A Sequence	Student B Sequence	Student C Sequence	Student D Sequence	Student E Sequence
1	2	3	4	5
2	3	4	5	1
3	4	5	1	2
4	5	1	2	3
5	1	2	3	4

Name: _________________________________ Date:_________________

Choreography Planning Guide

Directions: Work with your group to select a movement or movement sequence for each choreographic tool. Draw or describe the movements, and think about and respond to the questions provided.

Call and Response: One student performs a movement or movement sequence, and then the group performs that movement or sequence as a response back to the student.

Draw a diagram that describes how you will use Call and Response.

Who will be the "caller"? Will the caller always be the same?

What is the formation (circles, lines, or random)? Will the formation always be the same?

Name: _________________________________ Date:_________________

Choreography Planning Guide *(cont.)*

Unison: Everyone is doing the same thing at the same time.

Draw or describe the movement that everyone will learn.

Fan: One person does a movement while everyone else is still, then the second person does a movement while everyone else is still, and so on. Each student gets a turn, then the movements are completed in reverse order.

Draw a diagram that shows the order of everyone in the Fan. Describe each person's movement(s).

Name: _______________________________________ Date:__________________

Choreography Planning Guide *(cont.)*

Rondo: This is when you will perform your individual movements in unique sequences, so everyone in the group must learn everyone else's movement(s).

Draw or describe each person's movement(s).

Name: _______________________________________ Date:__________________________

Choreography Planning Guide (cont.)

Use the chart to record the order in which each person will perform the movements.

Student A Sequence	Student B Sequence	Student C Sequence	Student D Sequence	Student E Sequence

Recurrence: This is the repetition of something that has been done before, but usually with a slight twist.

Select one of the choreographic tools and plan to repeat it, but with a twist! What will that twist be?

© Shell Education

Answer Me in Movement

Model Lesson: What Do You Notice in This Graph?

Overview

In this lesson, students look at a graph without a title and with only one axis labeled to spark curiosity and to encourage them to think about the reasonableness of data in real-world situations. Students will use movement to communicate their initial thoughts and reactions. You begin with an introductory question for students to discuss: "What do you notice in this graph?" Then you ask students to respond to this question as well as to those about information missing from the graph. The sample graph and teacher–student dialogue are not intended to be prescriptive; rather, they are meant to guide your thinking and model how the strategy may play out. This activity is best done in a circle so that it is easy to move the turn from one person to the next without having to call on anyone or prioritizing order. The circle is a democratizing practice that gives everyone a turn.

Materials

- *Answer Me in Movement Graph* (page 238)
- *Elements of Creative Movement* (page 219)
- *Helpful Terms* (page 222)

Standards

Grades K–2

- Represents and interprets data
- Explores movement inspired by a variety of stimuli and identifies the source

Grades 3–5

- Solves problems using information presented in a graph
- Experiments with a variety of self-identified stimuli for movement

Grades 6–8

- Summarizes and describes distributions
- Relates similar or contrasting ideas to develop choreography using a variety of stimuli

Grades 9–12

- Summarizes, represents, and interprets data on a single count or measurement variable
- Explores a variety of stimuli for sourcing movement to develop an improvisational or choreographed dance study
- Analyzes the process and relationship between the stimuli and the movement

Answer Me in Movement *(cont.)*

Preparation

Have students practice using the Answer Me in Movement strategy (page 223) before beginning this lesson. Find a graph appropriate for students or use the *Answer Me in Movement Graph* provided. If you choose your own graph, make a copy of it and eliminate the title and label for the *y*-axis. Make copies or prepare for the projection of the graph. Additional suggestions are provided in the Specific Grade-Level Ideas.

Procedure

1. Arrange students in a circle and remind them to respond after a clap for the Answer Me in Movement strategy.

2. Show students the graph and invite them to silently consider what they notice. Then say, "When I clap, answer me in movement, or show me with movement, not with words, one thing you notice about the graph that you think is important."

3. Suggest that students think of their movement in three parts. "What is your beginning pose? What is the motion that happens? What is your ending pose? We will all begin together, but some people's movement might last a little longer than someone else's, so when you finish, end by staying frozen in your final pose. Wait until everyone is done, then I will clap and we can all relax our final positions."

4. To help you understand how students might respond in movement, here are some examples:

   ‣ Students who notice that the *x*-axis lists the months of the year could begin with their arms waist high and their palms face up to represent that they are holding a calendar, then they could make a flipping motion, flipping all pages of the calendar at once, to show the change from January to December.

They could then freeze to show that December is the last month in the year.

   ‣ If students associate the winter months with being cold and notice the higher measures in the first quadrant of the year, they could begin suggesting they are cold by folding their arms around themselves and scrunching up their shoulders. Then while shivering, they could stand on their tiptoes, stretching to be tall, to suggest the greater amounts shown during those months. They could then freeze in that position.

   ‣ If students noted the significant change between November and December, they could begin crouched down low to the floor. Then they could pop up quickly to their full height to show the rapid change. Then they could freeze in that position, as it is the end of the year.

5. Go around the circle and have students take turns showing their movement. When a student has finished, the student next to them takes a turn.

6. Go around the circle a second time. With this round, have students one at a time show their movement again and then tell the class what they were thinking and why they chose their movement to express their ideas about what they noticed in the graph.

7. Repeat the procedure, asking, "Answer me in movement: What do you think could be the label for the *y*-axis? What might be the title of the graph?"

8. As a class, discuss how labels are essential to communicating data.

9. Debrief this lesson, using the Discussion Questions.

Answer Me in Movement (cont.)

Option: Add music (without lyrics) and let students do the movement sequence to music.

Planning Questions

▸ What did you notice about the graph?

▸ How could you use movement to show what you think the graph was about?

▸ How would you like your movement to begin and end?

Discussion Questions

▸ How did movement help you better understand the information in the graph?

▸ How did movement get your message across in a way different from how words communicate an idea?

▸ How can movement be an effective communicative tool?

Specific Grade-Level Ideas

Grades K–2

Have students describe the attributes of a shape, one shape at a time. Students also could explore the time blocks on a schedule, for example: "Show me what we do at 8:30 in the morning." Answer Me in Movement also could be used to explore comparative terms (for example, *more, fewer*) and words associated with addition and subtraction.

Grades 3–5

Have students explore the definitions related to the concept of fractions: *denominator, numerator, parts of a whole, equal parts*. Students can explore a variety of geometric terms such as those used to classify angles and lines and those associated with the coordinate plane. They can also explore terms related to multiplication and division.

Grades 6–8

Have students explore the definition of *square root*. Geometric terms include *prism, vertex, net, surface area*, and *volume*. Additionally, terms related to proportional reasoning, types of numbers, and statistics and probability are appropriate for this strategy. Discuss how certain elements of movement such as alignment, balance, and weight shift are used to explore these terms.

Grades 9–12

Students can consider three-dimensional figures. Examples of geometric terms include *arc, chord*, and *tangent*. In addition to geometric terms and those related to statistics and probability, students can use terms related to functions or the lower bound of a parabola. Discuss how strength, flexibility, agility, and coordination are used in these movements.

Answer Me in Movement Graph

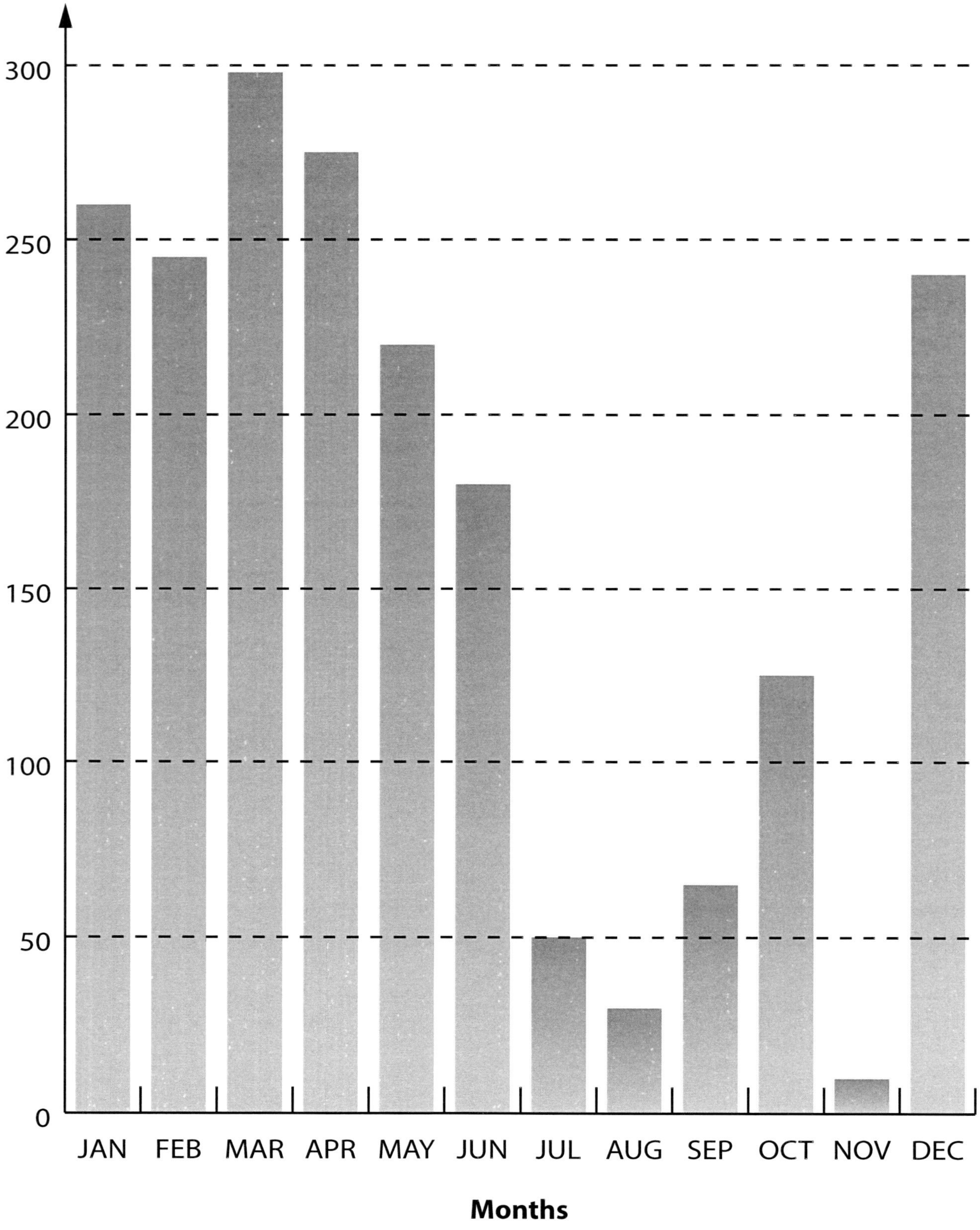

117847—Integrating the Arts in Mathematics

Movement Strings

Model Lesson: What Do We Know about This Kind of Graph?

Overview

In the Movement Strings strategy students explore ideas by creating individual movements and then linking them to form a sequence, like beads strung on a necklace. Whereas in the Answer Me in Movement strategy there is a single response, in Movement Strings students collect several ideas to create a "list" of movement ideas. In this example, students make observations about the different types of graphs and their purposes.

Materials

- chart paper or whiteboard
- *Elements of Creative Movement* (page 219)
- *Helpful Terms* (page 222)

Standards

Grades K–2

- Represents and interprets data
- Chooses movements that express a main idea or emotion or follow a musical phrase

Grades 3–5

- Solves problems using information presented in a graph
- Develops a dance phrase that expresses and communicates an idea or feeling

Grades 6–8

- Summarizes and describes distributions
- Implements movement from a variety of stimuli to develop dance content for an original dance study or dance

Grades 9–12

- Summarizes, represents, and interprets data on a single count or measurement variable
- Explores a variety of stimuli for sourcing movement to develop an improvisational or choreographed dance study

Movement Strings *(cont.)*

Preparation

Have students practice using the Movement Strings strategy (page 224) before beginning this lesson. Additionally, this strategy builds on what was learned from the Answer Me in Movement strategy. If students are not familiar with that strategy, practice it with them first before beginning Movement Strings. You may wish to gather reference books for students to consider, such as math textbooks or books with many graphs in them. Additional suggestions are provided in the Specific Grade-Level Ideas.

Procedure

1. Ask students to name the types of graphs with which they are familiar. List them on the board, leaving room to add additional comments near each type identified.

2. Name one of the graphs listed and ask, "What do you know about this kind of graph?" Record students' responses. Note that students are likely to identify obvious characteristics about the graphs initially, such as it has bars, it's a line, it's a circle, and there are a bunch of separate dots. Encourage students to note the more pertinent attributes, such as it shows categorical data and makes comparisons easy; it shows relationships between the variables; the data are continuous, and the graph often shows change over time; the percentages add to 100, as the graph about the portions within one whole and makes comparisons easy; it shows relationships; and it's used when there are many different data points and will show patterns within the data, such as clustering.

3. Decide whether you would like students to work individually, in pairs, or in triads. If working individually, have students select one important idea from the brainstormed list for each graph to represent in a movement string. If working in a group of two or three, have students represent two important ideas for each graph in a movement string.

4. Have students think of a movement idea for each graph that your class brainstorms. Explain that the movement ideas must allow everyone in the group to participate. You may wish to organize the order in which students consider the graphs. Use the Planning Questions to support students' thinking.

Example

Note that students can brainstorm movements to represent the mathematical ideas. These can be abstract; they do not need to have literal connections. The idea is that students have a rationale for how the movement depicts some aspect of the graph characteristics that will be meaningful and memorable to them. Creative movement captures the qualities of an idea. Possible choices include the following:

▸ For bar graphs students could represent categorical data by standing in a line, separated from one another. To show the ease with which bar graphs allow comparisons to be made, students could stand in a line, separated, and bend their knees to form different heights.

▸ For line graphs, students could represent continuous data by standing together with arms outstretched. To depict change over time, students could together wave their arms up and down like waves in the ocean.

▸ For circle graphs, students could represent the one whole, by standing together and moving as one; for the portions within the whole that account for 100 percent, students could nestle together in a circle on the floor with their backs touching and their legs outstretched and then open their legs to form different angles or portions of the whole.

Movement Strings *(cont.)*

- For scatter plots, students could move to different locations, each moving in unique ways and coming to a frozen position, placing their bodies in low, medium, or high levels. To show clustering, a few of the students could choose to be near each other.

5. Once groups have decided on their movements, have them practice "stringing" them together to create the movement string. Groups should practice their movement strings until they have memorized them and feel comfortable with the sequence of motions.

6. Have groups perform their movement strings for the rest of the class. If desired, play music without lyrics during each performance. When each group performs, let the music play as atmosphere. When groups present their movement strings, have students wait in stillness until they hear the music. When they are done, students come to stillness and wait for you to fade the music before they relax. This heightens the awareness of the movement.

7. Have the class observe the movement string presentations closely and identify the ideas the groups portray, as well as the movement choices they found most compelling. Use the Discussion Questions to further debrief each movement string presentation.

Planning Questions

- For each graph, what is a characteristic that you think is important?

- How might you use movement to represent that idea?

- In what order do you want to present the graphs?

Discussion Questions

- How did creating movement ideas, or watching the ideas of others, challenge you to think differently about the different graphs?

- Do you have any new questions about the different types of graphs? For instance, do you know how a histogram is different from a bar graph?

- What connections did you notice between your artistic choices and the math content you explored?

- What did you notice in the movement strings created by others that illuminated your thinking about this math topic or about the power of dance to communicate ideas?

Movement Strings *(cont.)*

Specific Grade-Level Ideas

Grades K–2

You might explore the following content ideas through movement strings: double facts, counting, combinations that make the number 10, or 2-D and 3-D shapes in the world.

Grades 3–5

Additional content at this level includes listing place value positions in order, objects that show lines of symmetry, different types and degrees of angles, and steps to solve a word problem.

Grades 6–8

Additional content at this level includes listing place value positions in order, objects that show lines of symmetry, different types and degrees of angles, and steps to solve a word problem.

Grades 9–12

At this level you could also explore parts of an algebraic equation, order of operations, the Pythagorean theorem, or parts of a budget.

Progressions

Model Lesson: How Can We Create a Circle Graph?

Overview

Progressions are like Movement Strings, in that movements are put together in a sequential sequence; but in Progressions, students focus on the emotional development and transitions of how one thing evolves into the next. The Progressions strategy is particularly useful in mathematics to understand the steps of a process. In this lesson, students focus on the process of creating a circle graph from a table.

Materials

▸ *Sample Progressions Movement Chart* (page 248)

▸ *Progressions Circle Graph* (page 249)

▸ chart paper

▸ *Progressions Movement Chart* (page 250)

▸ *Elements of Creative Movement* (page 219)

▸ *Helpful Terms* (page 222)

Standards

Grades K–2

▸ Represents and interprets data

▸ Chooses movements that express a main idea or emotion or follow a musical phrase

Grades 3–5

▸ Represents and interprets data

▸ Develops a dance phrase that expresses and communicates an idea or feeling

Grades 6–8

▸ Summarizes and describes distributions

▸ Implements movement from a variety of stimuli to develop dance content for an original dance study or dance

Grades 9–12

▸ Summarizes, represents, and interprets data on a single count or measurement variable

▸ Explores a variety of stimuli for sourcing movement to develop an improvisational or choreographed dance study

Progressions *(cont.)*

Preparation

Have students practice using the Progressions strategy (page 225) before beginning this lesson. Additionally, this strategy builds on what was learned from the Answer Me in Movement and Movement Strings strategies. If students are not familiar with those strategies, practice them first before beginning the Progressions strategy. In this lesson, students develop an understanding of the steps involved in making a circle graph. Use the *Progressions Circle Graph* or a different circle graph of your choice. Additional suggestions are provided in the Specific Grade-Level Ideas.

Procedure

1. Display the *Progressions Circle Graph* or the circle graph you selected. Activate students' prior knowledge about circle graphs by asking questions such as "What do you notice about the data? What conclusions might you draw from this graph? Why do you think the percentages do not add to 100?" (Rounding errors in real data often make the sum close to, but not exactly, 100, although it still represents 100 percent of the people surveyed.)

2. As a class, consider what you would need to know to create this kind of graph. Encourage students to brainstorm ideas and then order their ideas in a list. Looking at the given circle graph may help them think about what is needed. Record their thinking on a sheet of chart paper. A possible list might include the following:

   ▸ Collect the data.

   ▸ Define the categories.

   ▸ Determine the number in each category.

   ▸ Find the total number.

   ▸ Find the percentage for each category.

   ▸ Use a protractor to measure the angles.

   ▸ Add labels and the key.

3. Divide the class into small groups. Have groups create a movement idea for each step on the list. Remind students to think about not only a movement for each step, but also how they want to transition from one movement to the next. Use the Planning Questions to support students as they work.

4. If needed, support students by creating a table or prompt list to help them organize their thoughts such as the one shown. (See the *Sample Progressions Movement Chart.*) Have students use the *Progressions Movement Chart* to organize their thinking.

5. Once groups have decided on their movements that carry them through the progression of steps and transitions, have groups rehearse and memorize their movements so they can perform their completed progressions for the rest of the class.

   Example Progression Description: Students begin scattered throughout the space in frozen positions. They begin to move through space making scooping motions as if they are collecting things (imagined data) from the ground and air. They come together to place the imagined data into several pre-identified places around the room. Students break up and cluster in small groups around one of the assigned areas where imagined data have been placed and use gestures to pat and shape the imagined material. Positioning themselves in different levels (low, medium, high), students point to imagined piles of data in their area and point fingers as if they are counting.

   Students in each area come together around imagined data, crouch at a lower level, and move as if lifting the data (showing the weight of the data through movement). Students place their

Progressions *(cont.)*

imaginary data down, form a circle, and with their arms make divisions in the circle so that each category has a "slice" of the data. Each group of students creates a signature group movement for their slice of the circle and performs it group by group and then as a whole. The groups come to a frozen position to end.

The group takes a collective deep breath together.

6. Allow groups time to share their progression with the rest of the class.

7. Debrief, using the Discussion Questions.

Planning Questions

▸ How will you show the first step with your body?

▸ How will you best communicate the call to action by making a thoughtful transition that engages the viewer to get ready for the next step?

▸ When you get to the end of that movement idea, what will the transition to the next step?

▸ Is the transition a quick shift? Does it happen gradually? Does everyone change at the same time, or does the transition move through the group?

▸ Does the transition move to another part of the room/performance area?

Discussion Questions

▸ How did movement help you to understand the steps?

▸ Why do you think this graph is in the shape of a circle and not a square or trapezoid?

▸ How does a creative mover keep our interest through the use of transitions?

▸ What did you learn from observing your classmates' performances?

Progressions *(cont.)*

Specific Grade-Level Ideas

Grades K–2

Some students can work on combining numbers with sums to 10. Other students will be able to work with symbolic representations of the commutative property. First- and second-grade students also can explore the inverse relationship between addition and subtraction by creating a series of movements that suggest a doing and undoing. For example, show students the equation $7 + 3 = 10$ and ask them to use movement to show what else they know ($3 + 7 = 10$, $10 - 3 = 7$, and $10 - 7 = 3$).

Have students look at different ways to creatively combine two numbers of movements for a given total number. Such an experiment could facilitate students' discovery of all the possible combinations of 10.

Work with students to count forward 10 numbers on a hundred board. Give students the opportunity to discover that moving across 10 numbers, one step at a time, gives the same result as moving directly down to the next 10 in one movement. Note they should move creatively within these movements, perhaps choosing slow movement when making a set of 10 consecutive one-step movements and a high-intensity movement, such as leaping when moving down 10 in one movement.

Grades 3–5

Have students create and perform a numeric pattern that is similar to this: 8 jumps, 4 jumps, 2 jumps, 1 jump. Example: 10 hops, 5 hops, 1 hop.

Other potential experiments include exploring the associative property of addition: $(x + y) + z = x + (y + z)$. The parameter is that students experiment with the order in which they combine three groups to find their total.

Additionally, help students explore patterns among multiples. Have small groups of students choose a number and move in creative ways to show that number's multiples on the hundreds board. One member of the group must be left on each multiple as it is found. Other students from the audience could then continue the pattern. So if the number 5 is chosen, the first student would move creatively to 5 and stand there, the second to 10, the third to 15, and so on. After six students are standing on the board, ask questions to stimulate thinking, such as "What do you think the board will look like if we continue? Why do you think there are two people standing in each row of the chart? How many spaces are there between each person? What connections can we make between how we are standing and the remainders we get when we divide by five?" Students can explore common multiples by moving according to different numbers and discovering where more than one student lands. So if the students standing on the multiples of 5 remained while the activity is repeated for the multiples of 6, two students will be standing on 30, the first common multiple of 5 and 6.

Progressions *(cont.)*

Specific Grade-Level Ideas *(cont.)*

Grades 6–8

Students at this level might explore slope. Or have students explore the addition and subtraction of negative and positive numbers. Too often, these processes are taught as a set of rules such as "Two negatives make a positive." Have students create a model by moving on a large number line. For example, how might they model 7 − 2? How would this be different from 7 − (−2)? Will they move forward or backward? Will they face the positive or negative end of the line? The goal is for students to create movement explorations, using their growing knowledge of shape, level, and tempo that expands their understanding of how to add and subtract positive and negative numbers.

Students can look at the generalization of the properties of arithmetic. As properties are introduced in the earlier grades with whole numbers, not all students will recognize that they apply to all rational numbers. Furthermore, at this grade level, properties are often listed as abstract rules that have not been developed through concrete models. Have students explore an expression such as −2(4 − 6) and have them physically confirm the distributive property.

Grades 9–12

Students can use progressions to help solve multistep algebraic problems. They also might explore the work of building functions through movement or the shape of trigonometric functions. They also could represent the process of finding the components of a vector.

Sample Progressions Movement Chart

Step 1: Collect the data	**Transition:** How do we move from individual responses to identifying categories?	**Movements:** Students move through space, making scooping motions, and come together to place the imagined data into identified places around the room.
Step 2: Define the categories	**Transition:** Turning from the categories to find the number in each identified.	**Movements:** Students cluster around one of the assigned areas where imagined data have been placed and use gestures to pat and shape the imagined material.
Step 3: Determine the number in each category	**Transition:** Knowing how many in each category, move to find the total.	**Movements:** Positioning themselves in different levels (low, medium, high), students point to imagined piles of data in their area and point fingers as if they are counting.
Step 4: Find the total number	**Transition:** When you know the number in the parts and the number in the whole, how do you find the percentages?	**Movements:** Students in each area come together around imagined data, crouch at a lower level, and move as if lifting the data (showing the weight of the data through movement).
Step 5: Find the percentage for each category	**Transition:** How do the percentages lead you to show them within the circle?	**Movements:** Students cluster in a circle, holding their category of data in small groups.
Step 6: Use a protractor to measure the angles	**Transition:** With the graph drawn, what do you need to add to make the data clear?	**Movements:** Students place their imaginary data down, form a circle, and with their arms make divisions in the circle so that each category has a "slice" of the data.
Step 7: Add labels and the key	**Transition:** N/A	**Movements:** Each group of students creates a signature movement for their slice of the circle and performs it group by group and then as a whole.

Progressions Circle Graph

Proportions of Teens Who Spend Time with Screen Media

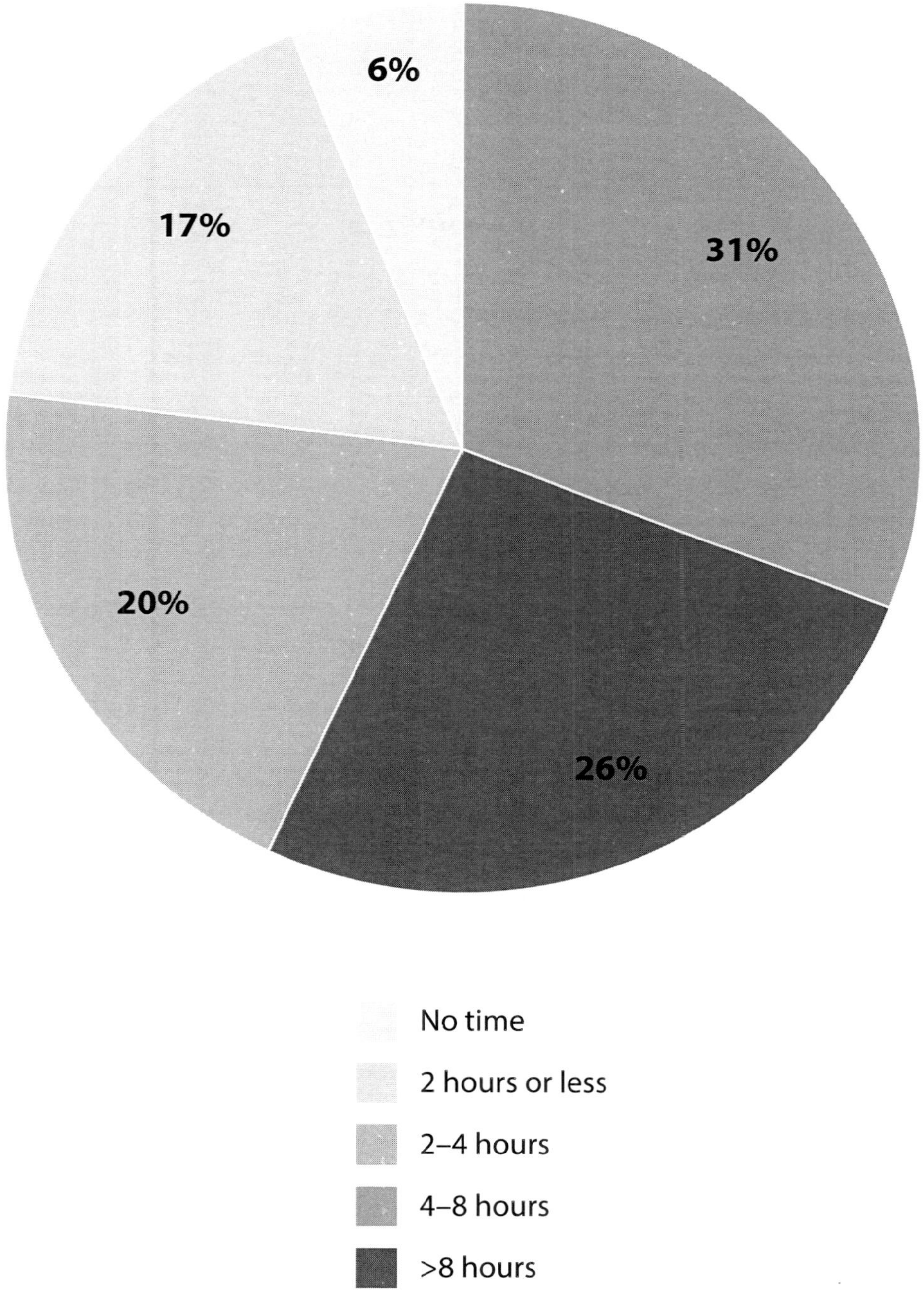

Source: Common Sense Media. 2015. "The Common Sense Census: Media Use by Tweens and Teens." www.commonsensemedia.org/sites/defaults/files/uploads/research/census_researchreport.pdf.

Progressions Movement Chart

Directions: Record your ideas to organize your thinking about the steps to make a circle graph.

Step 1:	Transition:	Movements:
Step 2:	Transition:	Movements:
Step 3:	Transition:	Movements:
Step 4:	Transition:	Movements:
Step 5:	Transition:	Movements:
Step 6:	Transition:	Movements:
Step 7:	Transition:	Movements:

Interpretation

Model Lesson: What Do Line Segments Indicate in a Graph?

Overview

In this strategy, students decide how to represent the changes in a given line graph in movement. As students consider line segments within a graph, they explore the relationships between the variables as they embody what the graph communicates. Qualities of slope are unveiled as students consider how things change over time and how changes in rate may affect the movement experience.

Materials

- *Temperature Line Graph* (page 254)
- *Distance over Time Graph* (page 255)
- *Sample Graph Story Planner* (page 256)
- *Graph Story Planner* (page 257)
- *Elements of Creative Movement* (page 219)
- *Helpful Terms* (page 222)

Standards

Grades K–2

- Represents and interprets data
- Explores movement inspired by a variety of stimuli and suggests additional sources for movement ideas

Grades 3–5

- Represents and interprets data
- Solves problems using information provided in a graph
- Builds content for choreography using several stimuli

Grades 6–8

- Summarizes and describes distributions
- Relates the choice of measures of center and variability to the shape of the data distribution and the context in which the data were gathered
- Relates similar or contrasting ideas to develop choreography using a variety of stimuli

Grades 9–12

- Summarizes, represents, and interprets data on a single count or measurement variable
- Interprets differences in shape, center, and spread in the context of the data sets, accounting for possible effects of extreme data points (outliers)
- Explores a variety of stimuli for sourcing movement to develop an improvisational or choreographed dance study
- Analyzes the process and the relationship between the stimuli and the movement

Interpretation (cont.)

Preparation

Have students practice using the Interpretation strategy (page 227) before beginning this lesson. Additionally, this strategy builds on what was learned from the Answer Me in Movement, Movement Strings, and Progressions strategies. If students are not familiar with those strategies, practice them first before beginning the Interpretation strategy. Select other line graphs to use if you prefer something different from what is provided in the lesson. Additional suggestions are provided in the Specific Grade-Level Ideas.

Procedure

1. Display the *Temperature Line Graph* or an alternate line graph of your choice. Activate students' prior knowledge about line graphs by asking questions such as the following:

   ▸ What is the general trend in the change of temperature?

   ▸ What does the horizontal line tell you?

   ▸ What do the broken lines indicate? (This is a good opportunity to review the term *range*, as it is the wide range of data that makes these breaks necessary.)

   ▸ How would the graph look different if the units for temperature were degrees Fahrenheit?

   ▸ What story does this graph tell you?

2. Display the *Distance over Time Line Graph* and ask students what they notice about the labels. (*The label is missing on the x-axis; the title doesn't tell us what is moving.*)

3. Divide the class into small groups and explain that they are going to create movements to interpret the graph—that is, to tell the story of the graph. Distribute copies of the *Graph Story Planner* to help students interpret the graph and plan appropriate movements for each portion of the graph. A possible scenario is provided

in the *Sample Graph Story Planner* to help you better understand this task and support students' thinking.

4. Use the Planning Questions to help students further define their story of the graph.

5. Once groups have completed their charts, explain to them that they must order the movements together so that they can perform them one after another. Tell students to rehearse and memorize their movements so that they can perform them for the class without pause or break, moving continuously from one idea to the next. While always relevant to dance, this is particularly important here, as the line graph represents continuous data.

6. After each group has created and practiced their dance, provide time for each group to show it to the rest of the class.

7. Use the first three Discussion Questions to debrief with students after each group presents. You can offer the other questions for students to consider after viewing all the performances.

Planning Questions

▸ When do you want to be moving at different speeds over time?

▸ What units would make sense based on your choice of what is moving?

▸ Look at each part of the graph. What does that line segment tell you about how fast the movement is in comparison to the other line segments?

▸ What might have caused the change in speed?

▸ If your mover is alive, what emotions might it have felt at the different speeds?

Interpretation *(cont.)*

Discussion Questions

- What did you appreciate about what you saw? Why?

- What did you notice about the relationships between what was making the trip and the units identified?

- Was there anything that this group did that gave you an idea of something you would like to use in your next dance?

- If you were to keep working on this dance, what would you add, take away, or change?

- How would your dance change if the graph represented this same trip, but the y-axis represented distance traveled rather than speed?

Specific Grade-Level Ideas

Grades K–2

Students at this level might consider graphs about time spent outside, time spent helping others, or time reading at home. You also could facilitate making a graph from questions related to students' favorite genre to read, favorite color, and other everyday topics that are important to them in their lives.

Grades 3–5

Students can examine graphs related to their local community, including the number of restaurants, public bathrooms, parks, community spaces, museums, and more. Through reading the completed graph, they might consider this question: What are the needs of our community?

Grades 6–8

Students at this level might investigate data related to topics about which they are passionate. Once they have interpreted the data, they can think about which graphs are most persuasive and how they might present them to the school as a whole. Topics might be related to quality of lunches, study hall options, and the addition of a gaming room.

Grades 9–12

Students at this level can also investigate data related to topics about which they are passionate. They can think about which graphs are most persuasive, and how they might present them in a presentation to stakeholders in their community. Topics might be related to conservation efforts, fundraisers, food insecurity, and green space.

Temperature Line Graph

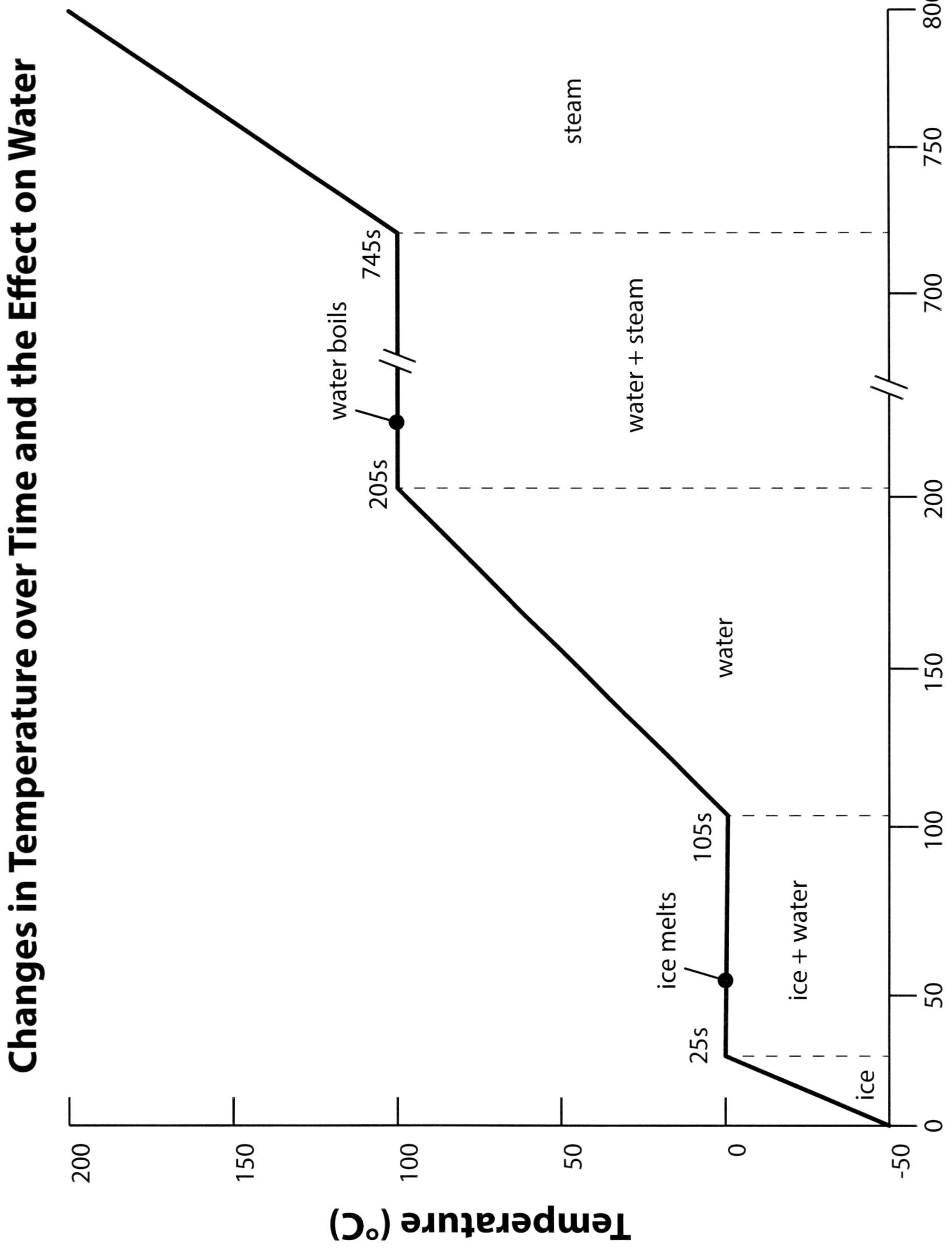

Changes in Temperature over Time and the Effect on Water

Temperature (°C)

200 — 150 — 100 — 50 — 0 — -50

0 — 50 — 100 — 150 — 200 — 700 — 750 — 800

25s — ice melts
105s
205s — water boils
745s

ice
ice + water
water
water + steam
steam

Distance over Time Graph

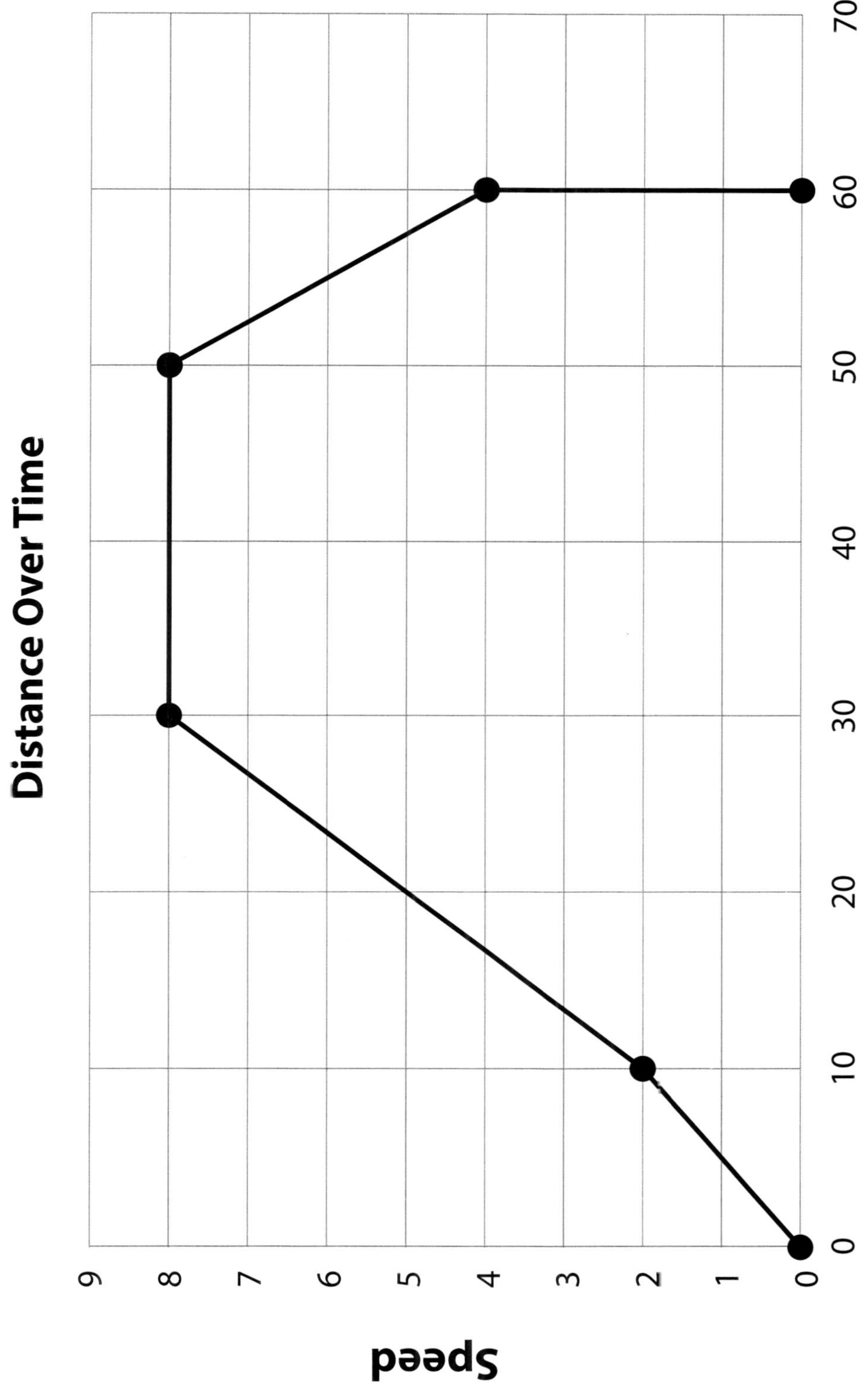

Sample Graph Story Planner

Directions: Answer the questions and complete the chart for each segment of the graph.

What will move? _Me on my skateboard_

The unit for the *x*-axis will be _seconds_

The unit for the *y*-axis will be _miles per hour_

Portion of the Graph	What's Happening	Movement Idea
Describe the first line segment: In the first 10 seconds I go from 0 to 2 miles per hour.	I hop on my skateboard and push off with my foot to get going. I'm happy to be on my skateboard.	I step forward and make a pushing motion with one foot then balance with my arms out. (10 seconds)
Describe the second line segment: At 10 seconds, I start to gain steady speed from 2 mph to 8 mph.	I start going down a short hill. I ride the hill, increasing as I go, making turns to keep me at an even increase, without gaining too much speed.	I continue to balance, moving up and down and pivoting, showing turns to the left then to the right, my arms moving up and down to hold balance. (20 seconds)
Describe the third line segment: At 30 seconds my speed is steady at 8 mph.	I make turns gently when I need to so I can keep my speed steady.	I stand up straight with my arms down, moving my hips to show gentle turns. (20 seconds)
Describe the fourth line segment: At 50 seconds, my speed begins to decrease at a steady pace.	I still have some speed left from going downhill, but I am steadily slowing down.	I continue to balance carefully while keeping my body low so I can maintain some of my speed. (10 seconds)
Describe the fifth line segment: At 60 seconds I am no longer moving.	My wheel falls off, and I come to a grinding stop. I fall, and I'm scared!	My body moves forward quickly and awkwardly spirals down, arms circling back and clutching at the air. I freeze in a heap on the ground.

Name: _________________________________ Date: _______________

Graph Story Planner

Directions: Answer the questions and complete the chart for each segment of the graph.

What will move? ____

The unit for the *x*-axis will be ____.

The unit for the *y*-axis will be ____.

Portion of the Graph	What's Happening	Movement Idea
Describe the first line segment:		
Describe the second line segment:		
Describe the third line segment:		
Describe the fourth line segment:		
Describe the fifth line segment:		

Choreographic Structure

Model Lesson: Collecting and Graphing Data Choreography

Overview

For each previous creative movement strategy (Answer Me in Movement, Movement Strings, Progressions, and Interpretation), students have essentially choreographed short creative movement dances. In this culminating lesson, students collect data, choose a graph to represent it, and interpret the graph made by a classmate. Their thinking develops by using choreographic tools and placing them in the choreographic structure known as a suite. Students are introduced to choreographic tools and how to create overall more complex choreography.

Materials

- *Graph Choreography Sample* (pages 264–265)
- *Collecting Data and Making a Graph Planner* (pages 266–267)
- *Graph Choreography Planning Guide* (pages 268–274)
- *Elements of Creative Movement* (page 219)
- *Helpful Terms* (page 222)

Standards

Grades K–2

- Generates data, draws a graph to represent the data set, and interprets data
- Demonstrates a range of locomotor and nonlocomotor movements, body patterning, and dance sequences that require moving through space using a variety of pathways

Grades 3–5

- Generates data and draws a graph to represent the data set
- Solves problems using information provided in a graph
- Recalls and executes a series of dance phrases using fundamental dance skills

Grades 6–8

- Constructs and interprets graphs to investigate patterns of association within the data
- Relates the choice of measures of center and variability to the shape of the data distribution and the context in which the data were gathered
- Embodies technical dance skills to replicate, recall, and execute spatial designs and musical or rhythmical dance phrases

Grades 9–12

- Gathers, summarizes, represents, and interprets data on two categorical and quantitative variables
- Interprets differences in shape, center, and spread in the context of the data sets, accounting for possible effects of extreme data points (outliers)
- Embodies technical dance skills to retain and execute dance choreography

Choreographic Structure *(cont.)*

Preparation

Have students practice using the Choreographic Structure strategy (page 228) before beginning this lesson. Additionally, this strategy builds on what was learned from the Answer Me in Movement, Movement Strings, Progressions, and Interpretation strategies. If students are not familiar with those strategies, practice them first before beginning the Choreographic Structure strategy. Review the Planning Questions ahead of time to support students/groups as needed throughout the entire lesson. Additional suggestions are provided in the Specific Grade-Level Ideas.

Procedure

1. Explain to students that they are going to collect and graph data and then make sense of the graph through a series of choreographic structures.

2. Divide the class into groups of four to five students. Distribute copies of *Collecting Data and Making a Graph Planner* to help students work together to design their survey, collect the data, and identify the type of graph they will use to represent their results. Have groups check with you before collecting their data.

3. Provide time for students to collect their data and make their graphs.

> Alternatively, you could provide students with a graph and modify the questions to best meet their needs.

4. Once students have created their graph, have them complete the *Graph Choreography Planning Guide*, which poses the following questions and has students choose movements to share their response:

1. What topic did you choose for your graph?

2. Why does this topic interest you?

3. What type of graph did you choose to make?

4. Why is this type of graph a good fit for your data?

5. What is the shape of your data?

6. What is the mode of your data?

7. Is there much variation in your data?

8. What is something important that you learned from your data?

9. What do you wonder now?

5. Remind students that they should choose clear movement(s) to depict their response to each question, as these will be repeated in the dance suites. If needed, let students use words and drawings to help them remember each movement. See the *Graph Choreography Sample*.

6. Provide students time to make decisions about the axes, units, and mover, and to interpret the graph. Have them complete the "Movement Description" column of the *Graph Choreography Planning Guide* and check their responses with you. After you approve, they can plan and practice the movement they will make to represent their responses.

7. Explain to students that they are going to use five different choreographic tools—Call-and-Response, Unison, Fan, Rondo, and Unison with Recurrence—to create a dance suite to celebrate the story in the graph.

Choreographic Structure *(cont.)*

Call and Response

1. Remind students that Call-and-Response is when one person (the soloist) performs a movement or movement sequence and then the rest of the group performs that movement or sequence as a response back to the soloist.

2. Explain to students that they will use all nine movements they selected for the graphing questions to create their Call-and-Response.

3. Prompt students to consider formation for the Call-and-Response. Is the caller in the center of a circle, with the responders around them? Or does the caller stand in front of the responders in a row? Will just one person be the caller, or will different students have a turn? Have students record information about their formation in their *Graph Choreography Planning Guide.*

4. Provide students with time to practice this until they can perform it with confidence.

Unison

1. Remind students that the choreographic tool Unison is used when all members of the group are doing the same thing at the same time in a continual flow from start to end.

2. Explain to students that they will use all nine movements they selected for the graphing questions, but they need to decide in what order they want to perform the movements and in what formation.

3. Have students record information about their sequence and formation in their planning guide.

4. Provide students time to practice this until they can perform it with confidence.

Fan

1. Remind students that a Fan is a sequence of movements where one person does a movement while everyone else is still, then the second person does a movement while everyone else is still, and so on, like the wave at a sports arena, except everyone is doing their own unique movement.

2. Explain to students that they will use all nine movements they selected for the graphing questions, but they need to decide in what order they want to perform the movements and in what formation. For example:

   Formation: Students make a single line facing the audience, one behind the other from shortest to tallest.

   Action
   Student A does movement 1, then freezes.
   Student B does movement 2, then freezes.
   Student C does movement 3, then freezes.
   Student D does movement 4, then freezes.
   Student E does movement 5, then freezes.
   Student D does movement 6, then freezes.
   Student C does movement 7, then freezes.
   Student B does movement 8, then freezes.
   Student A does movement 9, then freezes.

3. Explain to students that the Fan should happen as smoothly as possible so that when one movement ends, the next student's movement comes fairly quickly afterward.

4. Have students record information about their sequence and formation in their planning guide.

5. Provide students time to practice this until they can perform it with confidence.

Choreographic Structure *(cont.)*

Rondo

1. Remind students that in Rondo, each student performs the sequence in a different order, but all at the same time.

2. Explain to students that they will use all nine movements they selected for the graphing questions, but they need to decide in what order they want to perform the movements and in what formation. Have students use the table on their planning guide to create the movement sequence for each person in their group.

   Example
   Student A: 1, 2, 3, 4, 5, 6, 7, 8, 9
   Student B: 2, 3, 4, 5, 6, 7, 8, 9, 1
   Student C: 3, 4, 5, 6, 7, 8, 9, 1, 2
   Student D: 4, 5, 6, 7, 8, 9, 1, 2, 3
   Student E: 5, 6, 7, 8, 9, 1, 2, 3, 4

3. As students decide how they want to perform the sequences, explain that their goal is to work on timing so that even though each person's sequence is different, everyone begins and ends the Rondo at the same time.

4. Provide students time to practice until they can perform these movements with confidence.

Unison with Recurrence

1. Explain to students that they will use the choreographic tools of Unison and Recurrence for the last section of their dance suite. Remind them that Recurrence is the repetition of something that has been done before, but usually with a slight twist.

2. Explain that students will use the same Unison technique and movements from earlier. Have groups work together to decide what kinds of twists they want to put on the original movements.

3. Once groups have decided on their movements, have them record the information in their planning guides.

4. Provide students time to practice until they can perform these movements with confidence.

Putting It Together

1. Explain to students that now it is time to put everything together into one full performance.

2. Allow groups time to review all the movements and practice them in sequence.

Planning Questions

▸ What formation will the five students in the group take in relationship to one another? You could all be in a circle, in two rows facing the audience, in a single line facing the audience, in a random pattern, and so on. Have students draw various formations that dancers could make. Use a dot to represent each dancer. This could be done on individual paper or have students come to the board and share an idea.

   Example: Dancers could all be in a circle.
   Example: Dancers could be in two rows.
   Example: Dancers could be lined up behind one another.
   Example: Dancers could be scattered randomly.

▸ Will the movements all be done in one place, or will the movements cause the dancer to move from one location to another? In dance, we call this "traveling" or "locomotion." You could walk, skip, run, crawl, leap, and so on to get from one place to another.

▸ The suite form is in distinct sections, but what kinds of transitions will link all the sections together? How will the dancers get from one formation to another?

Choreographic Structure (cont.)

Specific Grade-Level Ideas

Grades K–2

Create a suite on the topic of geometric shapes. For example, students might classify polygons and nonpolygons. You also might use this strategy to facilitate students' understanding of the teen numbers as 1 ten plus some ones. First- and second-grade students can explore making two-digit numbers as well as a group of 10 tens to form 1 hundred. To begin, ask students representing tens to each raise 10 fingers one by one while moving to a new location and then clasp their hands together to show that there is a complete group of ten. To show a hundred, the 10 students showing tens can come together to make a huddle, perhaps stamping their feet once as they do so. Ask students if they have other ideas for showing the creation of a unit of ten. Try out a range of ideas and discuss them.

Ask students how they might use creative movement ideas to show groupings of ten, linking intentional movement, counts, and creative choices to a compelling representation of grouping. Students can draw simple choreography plans on large blank paper by making Xs to represent the movers and drawing simple pathways.

Pay attention to how students recognize the numbers modeled. For example, if 6 students have raised their 10 fingers, do the observing students count by tens from 10 to 60 or count the tens by ones and recognize the 6 groups of 10 as 60 when asked to identify the number? Are they comfortable counting either way?

Grades 3–5

Create a suite on different fraction relationships. Students at this level also can demonstrate grouping; for example, the thousands can be grouped as 10 hundreds or tenths as ones. Three- or four-digit numbers might be indicated by using different body levels that correspond to the place values (highest thousands, high hundreds, middle tens, low ones). Students can choreograph a sequence of movements in which 10 hundredths become tenths, tenths become ones, ones become tens, tens become hundreds, and so forth. Students could hold a stack of cards that show the different place values (0.01, 0.1, 1, 10 . . .). As the next grouping process begins, movers could identify their new values by putting that number at the front of their stack.

Students also can choreograph fractions forming wholes. Have students cut a large rectangle into parts, label each part, and place the parts around the room to be gathered to form a whole. Additional sheets of paper can represent wholes as needed. Or, to emphasize that fractions are numbers, have students collect strips of paper of equal size and two labels, one for zero and one to represent fractions represented on a number line. Simple groupings of fractions with the same denominators can be presented, or unlike denominators and mixed numbers also can be included.

Students' choreography plans can indicate a variety of pathways as well as locations. They also can indicate the order in which the movers (or objects) are joined or removed from a group.

Choreographic Structure *(cont.)*

Specific Grade-Level Ideas *(cont.)*

Grades 6–8

Students also can explore the ideas provided for grades 3–5. Grouping parts as wholes should focus on mixed numbers, unlike denominators, or combinations of fractions and decimals.

If your classroom has a tile floor, identify an intersecting point of the tiles as the origin (0, 0). Choreographers then can designate locations on their plans by identifying the coordinate points. Each mover can work with multiple pathways in the development of their movement sequence. For example, each mover could combine straight, zigzag, and curved pathways as they move from one location to another. This requires more detailed notation.

Grades 9–12

Students could create a suite focusing on a mathematical theorem such as the Pythagorean theorem or the Prime Number theorem. Encourage students to do some research to learn more about the theorem they choose. For example, students could depict the time period in which Pythagoras lived, the links he found between mathematics and music, and the apparent use of a rope with 12 knots to make a 3, 4, 5 triangle to form a right angle when resurveying land after the Nile flooded.

This collection of dance suites could be performed for a whole school assembly. To do this, assign a student, or teacher, to read the text aloud to the audience. After the audience has listened to the text, each group performs. It may be helpful to use music as background as well.

Graph Choreography Sample

How Many Stress-Reducing Strategies Do You Use?

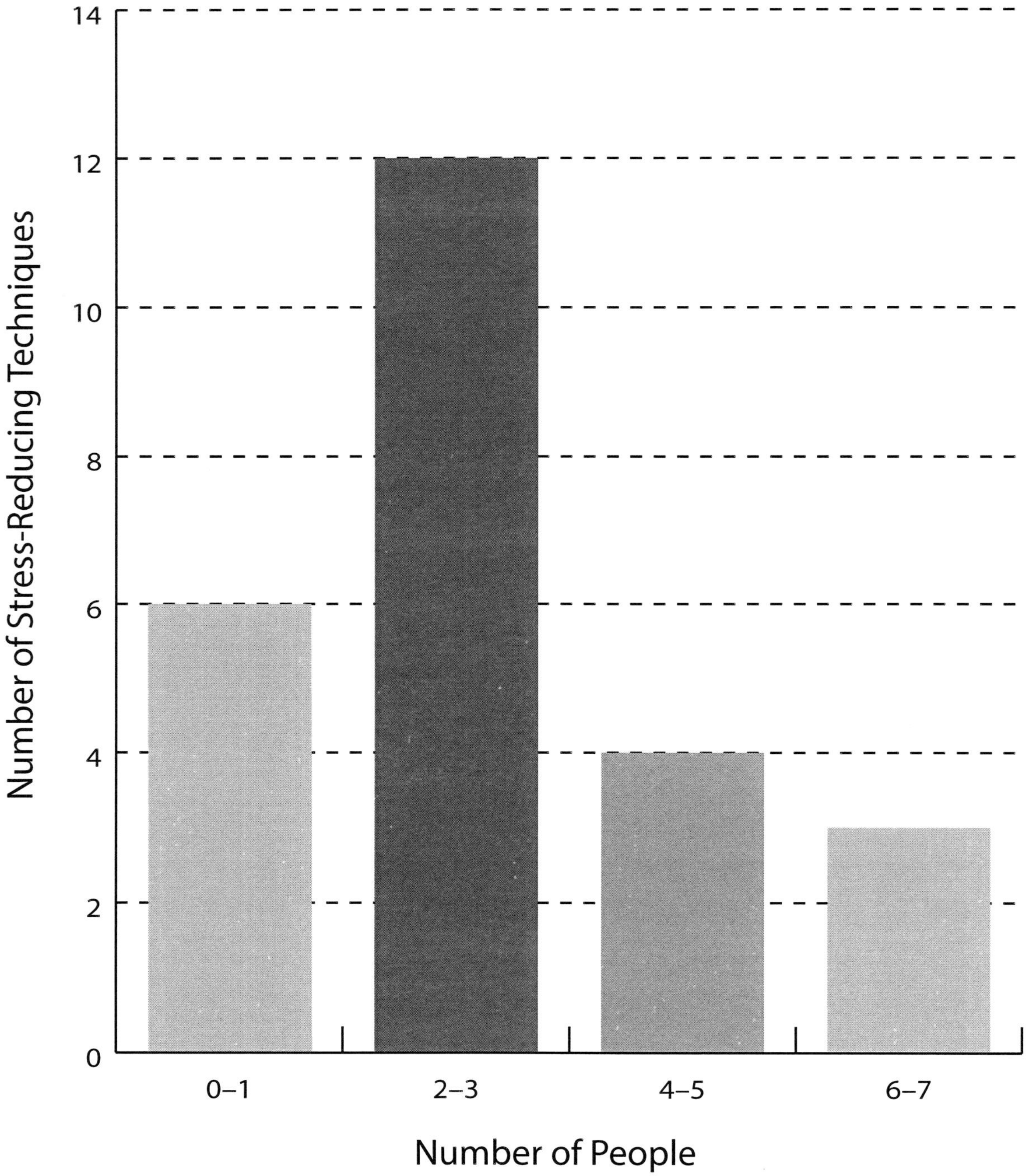

Number of Stress-Reducing Techniques (vertical axis)
Number of People (horizontal axis): 0–1, 2–3, 4–5, 6–7

117847—Integrating the Arts in Mathematics

© Shell Education

Graph Choreography Sample *(cont.)*

Question	Response	Movement Description
What topic did you choose for your graph?	Strategies for reducing stress	Start huddled in position bending over; dancers pull at hair, grimace, and then slowly unfurl upward, taking a deep breath while the body relaxes.
Why does this topic interest you?	We are concerned about the amount of stress in people's life.	Move arms overhead frenetically leaning left then right and pulsing legs, moving up and down.
What type of graph did you choose to make?	Bar graph: We want to show how many techniques people use.	Walk quickly in a small circle, reaching out in a gathering motion (as if to grab something from the air) and pulling hands in close to the abdomen.
What is the shape of your data?	It starts low, moves up to a peak, and goes down low again.	Begin in crouched position and in slow motion move to a high level, reaching arms overhead then down again.
What is the mode of your data?	Between 2 and 3	Reach to the left (signifying 1), to the middle (signifying 2), to the right (signifying 3), swaying back and forth between 2 and 3.
Is there much variation in your data?	Yes	Stand close together in a line and bend knees, up and down at different rates to show a lot of variation.
What is something important that you learned from your data?	Some people don't have very many different ways to reduce stress, and some have a lot.	Raise hands overhead rotating hands in a spinning motion (showing many ideas), then lower them, leaning over and releasing them toward the ground (suggesting fewer ideas).
What do you wonder now?	How to help more people have more ways to de-stress	Point fingers toward the head, moving in a circular motion (suggesting thinking), then gradually move them in increasingly larger circles to show action.

Name: ____ Date:_________________

Collecting Data and Making a Graph Planner

Directions: Work with your group. Discuss the data you want to collect, the way you will organize yourselves to collect the data, and how you will represent the data in a graph.

What data would you like to collect from your classmates? Brainstorm some ideas and then circle the one you choose.

Answer the survey yourselves to test it out and get a sense of the type of responses you might receive. Revise your survey question as necessary.

Make a plan as to how you will collect your data efficiently while being sure to include all your classmates.

Discuss the types of graphs you could use to represent your data and identify which one you will use.

  117847—Integrating the Arts in Mathematics   © Shell Education

Name: _________________________________ Date: _______________

Collecting Data and Making a Graph Planner *(cont.)*

Explain what you need to do with your raw data to make your graph; for example, do the data need to be counted, categorized, or plotted?

Make your graph in the space below.

Name: ____ Date:____________________

Graph Choreography Planning Guide

Directions: Work with your group. Answer each question in the space provided. Draw or describe the movements you and your group select for each question.

Question	Response	Movement Description
1. What topic did you choose for your graph?		
2. Why does this topic interest you?		
3. What type of graph did you choose to make?		
4. Why is this type of graph a good fit for your data?		

Name: _________________________________ Date: _______________

Graph Choreography Planning Guide *(cont.)*

Question	Response	Movement Description
5. What is the shape of your data?		
6. What is the mode of your data?		
7. Is there much variation in your data?		
8. What is something important that you learned from your data?		
9. What do you wonder now?		

   117847—Integrating the Arts in Mathematics   

Name: _______________________________________ Date:_________________

Graph Choreography Planning Guide *(cont.)*

Directions: Draw or describe the movements you and your group select for each question.

Call-and-Response

Draw a diagram that describes how you will use Call-and-Response. Use the movements from the planning questions.

Who will be the "caller"? Will the caller always be the same?

What is the formation (circles, lines, random, and so on)? Will the formation always be the same?

117847—Integrating the Arts in Mathematics

© Shell Education

Name: _______________________________________ Date:___________________

Graph Choreography Planning Guide *(cont.)*

Unison

Use all nine movements from the graphing questions. Draw or describe the formation you will use.

Record the order you will perform the movements.

Graph Prompt	Movement Description
1	
2	
3	
4	
5	
6	
7	
8	
9	

Name: ____ Date:_____________________

Graph Choreography Planning Guide *(cont.)*

Fan

Draw or describe the formation you will use for the Fan. Use all nine movements from the graphing questions.

Record the order that each person will perform the movement.

Order of Movement	Student Name
1	
2	
3	
4	
5	
6	
7	
8	
9	

Name: ____ Date: _______________

Graph Choreography Planning Guide *(cont.)*

Rondo

Use the movements from the graphing questions. Record the order that each person will perform the movements.

Student A Sequence	Student B Sequence	Student C Sequence	Student D Sequence	Student E Sequence

Draw or describe the formation you will use to perform the movement sequence.

Name: ____ Date:_____________________

Graph Choreography Planning Guide *(cont.)*

Unison with Recurrence

Rewrite the movements from the graphing questions. Make sure to include a "twist" with at least two of the movements.

Draw a diagram that describes the sequence of the movements and how you will use Unison. What is the formation (circles, lines, random, and so on)? Will the formation always be the same?

References Cited

Academy of American Poets. n.d. "Glossary of Poetic Terms." Accessed October 1, 2021. poets.org/glossary.

Alexander, Kwame. 2019. *The Write Thing*. Huntington Beach, CA: Shell Education.

American Mathematical Society. n.d.-a. "Mathematics and Music," Accessed October 12, 2021. www.ams.org/publicoutreach/math-and-music.

American Mathematical Society. n.d.-b. "Math Poetry," Accessed October 12, 2021. www.ams.org/programs/students/math-poetry.

Andersen, Christopher. 2004. "Learning in 'As-If' Worlds: Cognition in Drama in Education." *Theory into Practice* 43 (4): 281–286.

Anderson, Lorin W., David R. Krathwohl, Peter W. Airasian, Kathleen A. Cruikshank, Richard E. Mayer, Paul R. Pintrich, James Raths, and Merlin C. Wittrock. 2000. *A Taxonomy for Learning, Teaching, and Assessing: A Revision of Bloom's Taxonomy of Educational Objectives*. Boston: Allyn & Bacon.

Barack, Lauren. 2019. "Integrating Storytelling into Math Classes Builds Critical, Creative Thought." *K12 Dive*, April 3, 2019. www.k12dive.com/news/integrating-storytelling-into-math-classes-builds-critical-creative-though/551712/.

Bellisario, Kerrie, and Lisa Donovan with Monica Prendergast. 2012. "Voices from the Field: Teachers' Views on the Relevance of Arts Integration." Unpublished manuscript. Cambridge, MA: Lesley University.

Bodensteiner, Kirsten. 2019. "Do You Wanna Dance? Understanding the Five Elements of Dance." The Kennedy Center. www.kennedy-center.org/education/resources-for-educators/classroom-resources/media-and-interactives/media/dance/do-you-wanna-dance/.

Bogard, Jennifer M., and Mary C. McMackin. 2015. *Writing Is Magic, or Is It? Using Mentor Texts to Develop the Writer's Craft*. Huntington Beach, CA: Shell.

Borris, Chris. 2016. "The Power of Poetry." *Scholastic Teacher* 25 (5): 44–45. www.scholastic.com/teachers/articles/teaching-content/power-poetry/.

Brezovnik, Anja. 2015. "The Benefits of Fine Art Integration into Mathematics in Primary School." *C.E.P.S. Journal* 5 (3): 11–32. files.eric.ed.gov/fulltext/EJ1128967.pdf.

Bruce, Eloise, Maureen Heffernan, Sanaz Hojreh, Wendy Liscow, Shawna Longo, Michelle L. Marigliano, Erica Nagel, et al. 2020. *New Jersey's Arts Integration Think and Do Workbook: A Practical Guide to Think about and Implement Arts Integration*. Morristown, NJ: Geraldine R. Dodge Foundation. njpsa.org/documents/ArtsIntLdshpInst2020/artsintegrationWorkbook2020.pdf.

Cahill, Bryon. 2006. "Ready, Set, Write!" *Writing* 29 (1): 12.

References Cited *(cont.)*

Calkins, Lucy, and Kathleen Tolan. 2015. "Research Clubs: Elephants, Penguins, and Frogs, Oh My!" In *Units of Study for Teaching Reading, Grade 3*, edited by Lucy Calkins, Kathleen Tolan, Julia Mooney, Kristin Smith, and Alexandra Marron. Portsmouth, NH: Heinemann.

Carpenter, Siri. 2011. "Body of Thought: How Trivial Sensations Can Influence Reasoning, Social Judgment, and Perception." *Scientific American Mind*, January 2011, 38–45.

Cash, Justin. n.d. "The 12 Dramatic Elements." *The Drama Teacher* (blog). Accessed October 1, 2021. thedramateacher.com/wp-content/uploads/2008/02/The-12-Dramatic-Elements.pdf.

Center for Applied Special Technology. n.d. "About CAST." Accessed October 10, 2012. www.cast.org/about/index.html.

Clark, Deborah Haar Clark. n.d. "1, 1, 2, 3, 5, 8, Fun..." *Poetry Foundation*. Accessed October 1, 2021. www.poetryfoundation.org/articles/68971/1-1-2-3-5-8-fun/.

Cole, Laura. 2013. "Teaching Mathematics in the Classroom through Theatre." *Broadway Educators*, May 27, 2013. broadwayeducators.com/teaching-mathematics-in-the-classroom-through-theatre/.

Collins, Polly. 2008. "Using Poetry throughout the Curriculum." *Kappa Delta Pi Record* 44(2): 81–84.

Collins, Rita. 2009. "Using Story Boxes in Language Learning." *English Teaching Forum* 47 (1): 18–21. eric.ed.gov/?id=EJ923444.

Collom, Jack, and Sheryl Noethe. 2005. *Poetry Everywhere: Teaching Poetry Writing in School and in the Community*. New York: Teachers and Writers Collaborative.

Cornett, Claudia E. 2007. *Creating Meaning through Literature and the Arts: An Integration Resource for Classroom Teachers*. Upper Saddle River, NJ: Pearson/Merrill/Prentice Hall.

Dacey, Linda, Kathleen O'Connell Hopping, and Rebeka Eston Salemi. 2018. *Why Write in Math Class? K-5*. Portsmouth, NH: Stenhouse.

Dacey, Linda, and Rebeka Eston. 2002. *Show and Tell: Representing and Communicating Mathematical Ideas in K–2 Classrooms*. Sausalito, CA: Math Solutions.

Deasy, Richard J. 2002. *Critical Links: Learning in the Arts and Student Academic and Social Development*. Washington, DC: Arts Education Partnership.

Diaz, Gene, Lisa Donovan, and Louise Pascale. 2006. "Integrated Teaching through the Arts." Presentation given at the UNESCO World Conference on Arts Education, Lisbon, Portugal, March 8, 2006.

Donovan, Lisa, and Louise Pascale. 2022. *Integrating the Arts Across the Curriculum, Second Edition*. Huntington Beach, CA: Shell Education.

Dunn, Sonja. 1999. "Just What Is a Chant?" www.songsforteaching.com/sonjadunn/whatisachant.htm.

References Cited (cont.)

Elliott-Johns, Susan E., David Booth, Jennifer Rowsell, Enrique Puig, and Jane Paterson. 2012. "Using Student Voices to Guide Instruction." *Voices from the Middle* 19 (3): 25–31.

Emmanuel, Adeshina. 2012. "Those 857 Desks? A Message for the Candidates." *New York Times*, June 20, 2012. www.nytimes.com/2012/06/21/education/857-desks-call-attention-to-dropout-problem.html?_r=1&smid=tw-share.

Erdoğan, Serap, and Gülen Baran. 2009. "A Study on the Effect of Mathematics Teaching Provided Through Drama on the Mathematics Ability of Six-Year-Old Children." *Eurasia Journal of Mathematics, Science and Technology Education* 5 (1): 79–85.

Estrella, Espie. 2019. "An Introduction to the Elements of Music." *LiveAbout*. November 4, 2019. www.liveabout.com/the-elements-of-music-2455913.

Flynn, Rosalind. 2019. "Process Drama." *ThoughtCo*, February 5, 2019. www.thoughtco.com/process-drama-strategy-teacher-in-role-2713006.

Gardner, Howard. 2011. *Frames of Mind: The Theory of Multiple Intelligences*. 3rd ed. New York: Basic Books.

Garland, Trudi Hammel, and Charity Vaughan Kahn. 1995. *Math and Music: Harmonious Connections*. Palo Alto, CA: Dale Seymour Publications.

Geist, Kamile, and Eugene Geist. 2008. "Do Re Mi, 1-2-3: That's How Easy Math Can Be—Using Music to Support Emergent Mathematics." *Young Children* 63 (2): 20–25.

Glatstein, Jeremy. 2019. "Formal Visual Analysis: The Elements and Principles of Composition." The Kennedy Center. www.kennedy-center.org/education/resources-for-educators/classroom-resources/articles-and-how-tos/articles/educators/formal-visual-analysis-the-elements-and-principles-of-compositon/.

Goalbook Toolkit. n.d. "Act Out a Problem." Accessed October 12, 2021. goalbookapp.com/toolkit/v/strategy/act-out-a-problem.

Goral, Mary B., and Cindy Gnadinger. 2006. "Using Storytelling to Teach Mathematics Concepts." *Australian Primary Mathematics* 11 (1): 4–8. files.eric.ed.gov/fulltext/EJ793906.pdf.

Griss, Susan. 1994. "Creative Movement: A Language for Learning." *Educational Leadership* 51 (5): 78–80.

Growney, JoAnne. 2009. "What Poetry Is Found in Mathematics? What Possibilities Exist for Its Translation?" *Mathematical Intelligencer* 31 (4): 12–14.

Hamilton, Martha, and Mitch Weiss. 2005. *Children Tell Stories: Teaching and Using Storytelling in the Classroom*. Katonah, NY: Richard C. Owen Publishers.

Heagle, Amie I., and Ruth Anne Rehfeldt. 2006. "Teaching Perspective-Taking Skills to Typically Developing Children through Derived Relational Responding." *Journal of Early and Intensive Behavior Intervention* 3 (1): 1–34.

References Cited *(cont.)*

Heard, Georgia. 1999. *Awakening the Heart: Exploring Poetry in Elementary and Middle School.* Portsmouth, NH: Heinemann.

Heathcote, Dorothy, and Gavin Bolton. 1995. *Drama for Learning: Dorothy Heathcote's Mantle of the Expert Approach to Education.* Portsmouth, NH: Heinemann.

Herman, Corie. 2003. "Teaching the Cinquain: The Quintet Recipe." *Teachers & Writers* 34 (5): 19–21.

Hetland, Lois. 2009. "Nilaja Sun's 'No Child' Revealing Teaching and Learning through Theater." *Teaching Artist Journal* 7 (1): 34–39.

Hetland, Lois, Ellen Winner, Shirley Veenema, and Kimberly Sheridan. 2007. *Studio Thinking: The Real Benefits of Visual Arts Education.* New York: Teachers College Press.

Hipp, Jamie, and Margaret-Mary Sulentic Dowell. 2021. "Arts Integrated Teacher Education Benefits Elementary Students and Teachers Alike." *EdNote* (blog), February 1, 2021. ednote.ecs org/arts-integrated-teacher-education-benefits-elementary-students-and-teachers-alike/.

International School of Athens. n.d. "Drama Handbook." Accessed May 4, 2021. isa.edu.gr/files/319/Drama_Handbook.pdf.

Irvine, Veronika. 2012. "Curve Stitching." *A Visual Quest*, November 7, 2012. visquest.blogspot.com/2012/11/curved-stitches.html.

Jacobsen, Daniel Christopher. 1992. *A Listener's Introduction to Music.* Dubuque, Iowa: Wm. C. Brown Publishers.

J. Paul Getty Museum. n.d.-a. "Elements of Art." Accessed October 1, 2021. www.getty.edu/education/teachers/building_lessons/formal_analysis.html/.

———. n.d.-b. "Principles of Design." Accessed October 1, 2021. www.getty.edu/education/teachers/building_lessons/formal_analysis2.html

Jensen, Eric. 2001. *Arts with the Brain in Mind.* Alexandria, VA: Association for Supervision and Curriculum Development.

Johnson, Amanda. 2017. "How I Combined Music and Mathematics in My Elementary Classroom." study.com/blog/how-i-combined-music-and-mathematics-in-my-elementary-classroom.html.

Kennedy, Randy. 2006. "Guggenheim Study Suggests Arts Education Benefits Literacy Skills." *New York Times*, July 27, 2006.

KET. 2014. "Principles of Design." PBS Learning Media. pbslearningmedia.org/resource/459077ac-6d7d-4eef-bd7e-e38d12e7ce97/principals-of-design/

Klos, Pat. 2013. "Math + Visual Arts = Connection." Institute for Arts Integration and STEAM. artsintegration.com/2013/08/19/math-visual-arts-connection/.

References Cited *(cont.)*

KQED Art School. 2015. "The Five Elements of Dance." PBS Learning Media. pbslearningmedia.org/resource/d7fcd19b-ee9b-4d90-a550-833fbe22865c/the-five-elements-of-dance/.

Kuta, Katherine. 2003. "And Who Are You?" *Writing* 25 (5): 30–31.

LaBonty, Jan, and Kathy Everts Danielson. 2004. "Reading and Writing Poetry in Math." *Reading Horizons* 45 (1): 39–54.

Lamb, Evelyn. 2018. "How Poetry and Math Intersect." *Smithsonian Magazine*, April 24, 2018. www.smithsonianmag.com/science-nature/how-poetry-and-math-intersect-180968869/.

Landorf, Hilary. 2006. "What's Going on in This Picture? Visual Thinking Strategies and Adult Learning." *New Horizons in Education & Human Resource Development* 20: 28–32.

Lane, Barry. 1992. *After THE END: Teaching and Learning Creative Revision*. Portsmouth, NH: Heinemann.

Light, Bria. 2021. "Moving Mountains with Imagination: Local Theater Camp Presents Original Show 'Wizard Tricks and Full Eclipse.'" *Telluride Daily Planet, The Norwood Post*, June 29, 2021. www.telluridenews.com/news/article_b6be4fbe-d924-11eb-bc95-63896e12e95f.html.

Literary Devices. n.d. "Anthropomorphism." Accessed October 21, 2021. literarydevices.net/anthropomorphism.

Lyon, George Ella. 2010. "Where I'm From." www.georgeellalyon.com/where.html.

MacDonald, William. 2020. "Writing a Scene: What Are the 10 Key Steps to Dramatic Excellence?" *Industrial Scripts* (blog), April 28, 2020. industrialscripts.com/writing-a-scene/.

Mantle of the Expert. n.d. "Introduction to Mantle of the Expert." Accessed October 19, 2021. www.mantleoftheexpert.com/what-is-moe/introduction-to-moe/.

Marzano, Robert J. 2007. *The Art and Science of Teaching: A Comprehensive Framework for Effective Instruction*. Alexandria, VA: Association for Supervision and Curriculum Development.

Masoum, Elahe, Mohsen Rostamy-Malkhalifeh, and Zahra Kalantarnia. 2013. "A Study on the Role of Drama in Learning Mathematics." *Mathematics Education Trends* 2013: 1–7 www.researchgate.net/publication/274582627_A_Study_on_the_Role_of_Drama_in_Learning_Mathematics.

McKim, Elizabeth, and Judith W. Steinbergh. 1992. *Beyond Words: Writing Poems with Children: A Guide for Parents and Teachers*. Brookline, MA: Talking Stone Press.

Modi, Kalpana. 2012. "Story Telling in Mathematics," *Voice of Research* 1 (2): 31–33. www.voiceofresearch.org/Doc/Sep-2012/Sep-2012_9.pdf.

National Coalition for Core Arts Standards. 2014. "Glossary of Terms: Theatre." docplayer.net/29830664-Glossary-for-national-core-arts-theatre-standards.html.

National Storytelling Network. n.d. "What Is Storytelling?" Accessed April 30, 2021. storynet.org/what-is-storytelling/.

Norfolk, Sherry, Jane Stenson, and Diane Williams. 2006. The Storytelling Classroom. Westport, CT: Libraries Unlimited.

O'Neill, Cecily. 1995. *Drama Worlds: A Framework for Process Drama*. Portsmouth, NH: Heinemann.

Oliver, Mary, 1994. *A Poetry Handbook: A Prose Guide to Understanding and Writing Poetry*. Orlando, FL: Mariner Books.

Partnership for 21st Century Learning. 2019. "Framework for 21st Century Learning." static. battelleforkids.org/documents/p21/P21_Framework_Brief.pdf.

Perpich Center for Arts Education. 2009. "The Elements of Dance." www.nationalartsstandards.org/sites/default/files/Dance_resources/ElementsOfDance_organizer.pdf.

Perret, Peter, and Janet Fox. 2006. *A Well-Tempered Mind: Using Music to Help Children Listen and Learn*. New York: Dana Press.

Plessinger, Kristin. 2012. "Engaging Learners: Call and Response." *The Marquette Educator* (blog), April 16, 2012. marquetteeducator.wordpress.com/tag/call-and-response/.

Popova, Maria. 2009. "Data Visualization: Stories for the Information Age." *Bloomberg Business*, August 12, 2009. www.bloomberg.com/news/articles/2009-08-12/data-visualization-stories-for-the-information-age.

President's Committee on the Arts and the Humanities. 2011. "Reinvesting in Arts Education: Winning America's Future Through Creative Schools." www.pcah.gov/sites/default/files/PCAH_Reinvesting_4web_0.pdf.

Reed, Bracken, and Jennifer Railsback. 2003. *Strategies and Resources for Mainstream Teachers of English Language Learners*. Portland, OR: Northwest Regional Educational Laboratory. educationnorthwest.org/sites/default/files/ell.pdf.

Reed, Stephen K. 2010. *Cognition: Theories and Application*. 8th ed. Belmont, CA: Wadsworth Cengage Learning.

Reeves, Douglas. 2007. "Academics and the Arts." *Educational Leadership* 64 (5): 80–81.

Reif, Nancy, and Leslie Grant. 2010. "Culturally Responsive Classrooms through Art Integration." *Journal of Praxis in Multicultural Education* 5 (1). digitalscholarship.unlv.edu/jpme/vol5/iss1/11.

Riley, Susan. 2017. "The Elements of Art Anchor Charts." Institute for Arts Integration and STEAM. July 1, 2017. artsintegration.com/2017/07/01/elements-art-anchor-charts/.

Rinne, Luke, Emma Gregory, Julia Yarmolinskyay, and Mariale Hardiman. 2011. "Why Arts Integration Improves Long-Term Retention of Content." *Mind, Brain, and Education* 5 (2): 89–96.

References Cited *(cont.)*

Rose, Todd. 2012. "Learner Variability and Universal Design for Learning." *Universal Design for Learning Series*. udlseries.udlcenter.org/presentations/learner_variability.html.

School Curriculum and Standards Authority. 2014. "Drama Elements." k10outline.scsa.wa.edu.au/home/teaching/curriculum-browser/the-arts/visual-arts2/arts-overview/glossary/elements-of-drama#.

Schoolyard. 2019. "Benefits of Incorporating Art Concepts in Elementary Math." *21st Century Learning* (blog), October 29, 2019. blog.schoolspecialty.com/benefits-of-incorporating-art-concepts-in-elementary-math/.

Science Education Resource Center (SERC) at Carleton College. 2018. "Why Teach with Classroom Experiments?" *Pedagogy in Action*, September 13, 2018. serc.carleton.edu/sp/library/experiments/why.html.

Segaren, Sharuna. 2019. "Is Arts Integration in Schools All It's Cracked Up To Be?" *Study International*, January 14, 2019. www.studyinternational.com/news/is-arts-integration-in-schools-all-its-cracked-up-to-be/.

Skoning, Stacey. 2008. "Movement in Dance in the Inclusive Classroom." *TEACHING Exceptional Children Plus 4* (6). files.eric.ed.gov/fulltext/EJ967723.pdf.

Steen, Lynn Arthur, ed. 1990. *On the Shoulders of Giants: New Approaches to Numeracy*. Washington, DC: National Academies Press.

Strauch-Nelson, Wendy J. 2011. "Book Learning: The Cognitive Potential of Bookmaking." *Teaching Artist Journal* 9 (1): 5–15.

The Teacher Toolkit. n.d. "Tableau." Accessed October 12, 2021. www.theteachertoolkit.com/index.php/tool/tableau.

Tomecek, Steve. n.d. "Good Vibrations (Simple Physics/Sound)." *Dirtmeister's Science Lab*. teacher.scholastic.com/dirt/vibes.htm/.

Toor, Amanjot, and Joyce Mgombelo. 2015. "Teaching Mathematics through Storytelling: Engaging the 'Being' of a Student in Mathematics." CERME 9—Ninth Congress of the European Society for Research in Mathematics Education, Charles University in Prague, Faculty of Education, ERME, Prague, Czech Republic, February 2015: 3276–3282. hal.archives-ouvertes.fr/hal-01289881/document.

Werner, Linnette Robin. 2001. "Using Dance to Teach Math: The Effects of a Co-Teaching Arts Integration Model on Teacher Practice and Student Learning." Phd diss., University of Minnesota. World Cat (OCLC 50764621).

Windmill Theatre Company. n.d. "Elements of Drama." Accessed October 1, 2021. windmill.org.au/wp-content/uploads/2018/09/Elements-of-Drama.pdf.

Workerbee. 2014. "The Art of Infographics (and How to Make Your Own)." *99designs* (blog). 99designs.com/blog/design-tutorials/infographics-how-to-make-your-own/.

References Cited *(cont.)*

Yellin, David, Mary Blake Jones, and Beverly A. DeVries. 2007. *Integrating the Language Arts.* Scottsdale, AZ: Holcomb Hathaway Publishers.

Yeltekin, Emel, and Sonay Ay Zeynep. 2019. "The Effects of Storytelling in Mathematics Education on Students' Problem Solving Skills and Problem Posing Skills." Paper presented at Emerging Researchers' Conference, September 2, 2019. eera-ecer.de/ecer-programmes/conference/24/contribution/48554/.

youcubed. n.d. "Maths and Art." Accessed October 12, 2021. www.youcubed.org/maths-and-art/.

Zazkis, Rina, and Peter Liljedahl. 2009. *Teaching Mathematics as Storytelling.* Rotterdam, the Netherlands: Sense Publishers.

Zull, James E. 2002. *The Art of Changing the Brain: Enriching Teaching by Exploring the Biology of Learning.* Sterling, VA: Stylus.

Digital Resources

Accessing the Digital Resources

The digital resources can be downloaded by following these steps:

1. Go to **www.tcmpub.com/digital**

2. Use the ISBN to redeem the digital resources.

   ISBN 978-0-7439-7025-9

3. Respond to the question using the book.

4. Follow the prompts on the Content Cloud website to sign in or create a new account.

5. Choose the digital resources you would like to download. You can download all the files at once, or a specific group of files.

Please note: Some files provided for download have large file sizes. Download times for these larger files vary based on your internet speed.